Careers in Financial Services

Careers in Financial Services

SALEM PRESS
A Division of EBSCO Information Services, Inc.
Ipswich, Massachusetts

GREY HOUSE PUBLISHING

∞ The paper used in these volumes conforms to the American National Standard for Permanence of Paper for Printed Library Materials, Z39.48 1992 (R2009).

Publisher's Cataloging-In-Publication Data
(Prepared by The Donohue Group, Inc.)

Title: Careers in financial services.
Other Titles: Careers in--
Description: [First edition]. | Ipswich, Massachusetts : Salem Press, a division of EBSCO Information Services, Inc. ; [Amenia, New York] : Grey House Publishing, [2017] | Includes bibliographical references and index. |
Identifiers: ISBN 978-1-68217-595-8 (hardcover)
Subjects: LCSH: Financial services industry--Vocational guidance--United States. | Finance--Vocational guidance--United States.
Classification: LCC HG181 .C37 2017 | DDC 332.02373--dc23

First Printing

PRINTED IN THE UNITED STATES OF AMERICA

CONTENTS

PUBLISHER'S NOTE

Careers in Financial Services contains 25 alphabetically arranged chapters describing specific fields of interest in this industry. Merging scholarship with occupational development, this single comprehensive guidebook provides students planning to pursue a career in financial services with the necessary insight into potential opportunities, and provides instruction on what job seekers can expect in terms of training, advancement, earnings, job prospects, working conditions, relevant associations, and more. *Careers in Financial Services* is specifically designed for a high school and undergraduate audience and is edited to align with secondary or high school curriculum standards.

Scope of Coverage

Understanding the wide net of jobs in the financial services industry is important for anyone preparing for a career within it. *Careers in Financial Services* comprises twenty-five lengthy chapters on a broad range of occupations including traditional and long-established jobs such as Bank Teller, Budget Analyst, and Tax Examiner, as well as in-demand jobs: Financial Analyst, Portfolio Manager, and Venture Capital Professionals. This excellent reference also presents possible career paths and occupations within high-growth and emerging fields in this industry.

Careers in Financial Services is enhanced with numerous charts and tables, including projections from the US Bureau of Labor Statistics, and median annual salaries or wages for those occupations profiled. Each chapter also notes those skills that can be applied across broad occupation categories. Interesting enhancements, like **Fun Facts**, **Famous Firsts**, and dozens of photos, add depth to the discussion. A highlight of each chapter is **Conversation With**—a two-page interview with a professional working in a related job. The respondents share their personal career paths, detail potential for career advancement, offer advice for students, and include a "try this" for those interested in embarking on a career in their profession.

Essay Length and Format

Each chapter ranges in length from 3,500 to 4,500 words and begins with a Snapshot of the occupation that includes career clusters, interests, earnings and employment outlook. This is followed by these major categories:

- **Overview** includes detailed discussions on: Sphere of Work; Work Environment; Occupation Interest; A Day in the Life. Also included here is a Profile that outlines working conditions, educational needs, and physical abilities. You will also find the occupation's Holland Interest Score, which matches up character and personality traits with specific jobs.

- **Occupational Specialties** lists specific jobs that are related in some way, like Set Designer, Animators, and Photographer. Duties and Responsibilities are also included.
- **Work Environment** details the physical, human, and technological environment of the occupation profiled.
- **Education, Training, and Advancement** outlines how to prepare for this field while in high school, and what college courses to take, including licenses and certifications needed. A section is devoted to the Adult Job Seeker, and there is a list of skills and abilities needed to succeed in the job profiled.
- **Earnings and Advancements** offers specific salary ranges, and includes a chart of metropolitan areas that have the highest concentration of the profession.
- **Employment and Outlook** discusses employment trends, and projects growth to 2020. This section also lists related occupations.
- **Selected Schools** list those prominent learning institutions that offer specific courses in the profiles occupations.
- **More Information** includes associations that the reader can contact for more information.

Special Features

Several features continue to distinguish this reference series from other career-oriented reference works. The back matter includes:

- Appendix A: Guide to Holland Code. This discusses John Holland's theory that people and work environments can be classified into six different groups: Realistic; Investigative; Artistic; Social; Enterprising; and Conventional. See if the job you want is right for you!
- Appendix B: General Bibliography. This is a collection of suggested readings, organized into major categories.
- Subject Index: Includes people, concepts, technologies, terms, principles, and all specific occupations discussed in the occupational profile chapters.

Acknowledgments

Thanks are due to Micah Issitt, the volume editor, Allison Blake, who took the lead in developing "Conversations With" and to the professionals who communicated their work experience through interview questionnaires. Their frank and honest responses provide immeasurable value to *Careers in Financial Services*. The contributions of all are gratefully acknowledged.

EDITOR'S INTRODUCTION

Financial Careers: An Introduction

Financial experts help individuals and institutions to manage their money and increase their wealth in a variety of different ways. Some finance experts offer services aimed solely at wealthy individuals and corporations, while other finance experts work with the general public. Finance careers range from customer service positions with financial institutions to highly specialize analytical roles that require extensive training and expertise in mathematics and finance. Finance is classified as a service industry, which is a business in which professionals provide services for customers, rather than producing a product. Service industry professionals typically work collaboratively, either directly their clients or with a team of other finance professionals. In general, finance is a conventional career path suitable for those with skill in practical skills rather than creativity and is an enterprising field in which success depends on a professional's drive and ability to compete.

Nature of the Field

There are dozens of different finance careers, each of which may have different requirements in terms of education and experience. In general, when choosing a career in finance, an individual should consider their level of skill in subjects like mathematics, customer service, marketing and sales, and must also decide what broad sector of society he or she wishes to work in, i.e. institutional, governmental, corporate, or public. Finally, salaries for financial professionals range across a wide spectrum depending on an individual's experience, level of education, and specific field of finance.

Many careers in finance require skill with mathematics and at least an introductory knowledge of accounting and basic bookkeeping. The educational requirements for careers in the field depend on the specific field, with analytical careers requiring high levels of mathematics expertise, while sales and entry level positions are suitable for professionals with interpersonal and marketing skills. Students preparing for a career in finance should aim for obtaining a higher education degree in accounting, mathematics, finance, economics, or business, and should also take classes in computer science, composition, public speaking, and critical thinking.

Branches of Finance

Corporate finance is one of the largest and most lucrative financial fields, and involves working with companies to manage corporate assets. Corporations utilize a wide variety of specialists, from accountants to quantitative analysts, investment experts, and regulatory officers. Some positions, like mergers and acquisitions specialists, occur only within the world of corporate finance, while corporations also hire a variety of general financial experts whose skills may translate to other branches of finance as well.

Commercial finance involves working with financial organizations and institutions that offer services to the public and/or to corporations. There are many job opportunities in commercial finance, from entry level bank teller positions, to advanced economic forecasting. Commercial banking institutions also offer loans and financing and so employ many professionals to help manage these practices, such as loan officers, IRA officers, and investment specialists.

For those interested in investment, the practice of buying and selling interest in other institutions, companies, or services, investment banking can be a lucrative career path. Professionals in this field buy and sell securities, including stocks and bonds, provide financial guidance and advice to companies and individual investors, and help manage assets for their clients or employers. Other investment experts work in hedge funds, which are largely unregulated private investment funds that managers use to build wealth for clients. Hedge fund companies hire financial analysts, quantitative analysts, marketing professionals, and portfolio managers, as well as accountants and regulatory officers.

Another field within the broader investment industry involves providing private equity and venture capital investments. Private equity investors and firms help companies to finance various projects, including mergers and acquisitions and expansion projects. Venture capital professionals work in high-risk investments, investing in start-ups or businesses unable to obtain financing through banks or traditional lenders. Though venture capitalists specialize in high risk investments, and therefore there is a high rate of failed investments in the industry, investing in start-ups and innovative, if unproven ventures, can also translate to some of the highest potential earnings in the entire financial field.

Those interested in working with the public might consider a position in financial planning or private accounting, in which professionals help individuals to manage their finances and assets and to navigate taxes, loans, and other debts and financial obligations. Careers in personal or public finance vary widely in terms of Work Environment and potential compensation, and jobs in the field may appeal primarily to those with an interest in public service, customer service, or interacting with others. Other careers in the field involve selling assets or financial services to consumers, which may include property, insurance or banking services, or a variety of other financial products.

Insurance is another major subfield within finance that involves developing, marketing, and selling insurance protection to companies and individuals. Insurance companies help protect companies and individuals from losses and there are many potential positions in the field, from sales representatives responsible for selling insurance policies directly to consumers or companies, to economic experts who analyze financial markets and help insurance companies determine how to manage their policies and other services. Actuaries, for instance, compute risks based on quantitative financial data, while underwriters evaluate potential clients to determine whether or not providing a policy poses a risk to the company.

Another broad branch of finance involves regulation and compliance. Individuals in these positions are concerned with enforcing laws and regulations that apply to companies, individuals, and governmental agencies. Tax agents, for instance, are responsible for ensuring that individuals and corporations pay their required taxes to local, state, and federal governments. Regulatory compliance officers work in many different types of companies and fields as are responsible for ensuring that companies, and their employees, adhere to regulations, thus protecting the company from potential legal issues that may occur when an individual or company is found to have violated financial laws.

A Changing Field

Digital technology, the Web and the Internet, and mobile digital devices, have greatly changed the financial field. Financial analysts and investment professionals, for instance, now regularly use programs and algorithms that accurately track market changes in real time and can be used to make automatic investments. Web-based and software-based financial tools and planning resources have also transformed the field, making it possible for individuals to take a more active role in their own financial planning without the need for professional help. In general, technological advancement has resulted in a reduction in job growth in some branches of finance and has shifted the focus of financial professionals. Financial experts spend less time on helping make stock purchases or helping customers to make basic transactions, and more time on advanced prediction, risk management, and analysis. In addition, the advent and rapid evolution of accounting and financial software provides new tools for financial experts to conduct more detailed, accurate, analysis than in the past and this has led to increased specialization. Financial analysts, for instance, may now specialize in creating programs for financial service companies or consumers or in utilizing a specific algorithm or computer program to help their clients.

Another broad change in the field involves an increasing focus on oversight following the 2007-2009 financial crisis in the United States and subsequent exploration of how lax finance-industry controls, corrupt and exploitative banking practices, and insufficient centralized controls to force financial institutions to serve the public interest, contributed to the recession. While oversight has increased in the 2000s and 2010s, the future of finance oversight in uncertain. In general, conservative politicians oppose government regulation and believe that competition among corporations is sufficient to protect public interest. As a result, conservative administrations typically reduce oversight and promote legislation that provides greater freedom to large corporations, including those in the financial industry.

In the 2010s, finance is a global industry, and many financial companies operate on a national or international scale. This evolution is the result of ongoing economic globalization and the advent and spread of virtual markets that make it far easier for businesses and individuals to conduct business internationally. The globalization of the U.S. finance industry has created new opportunities and growth in many financial fields, and also creates a new impetus for companies and institutions that conduct business across national lines, to add multicultural expertise to their institutions. As this trend continues, and finance becomes increasingly global in scope, professionals with experience in multiple languages, global customs and cultures, and multinational finance will likely have an advantage in the field.

—Micah Issitt

Works Used

"Business and Financial Occupations." *Bureau of Labor Statistics*. Office of Occupational Statistics and Employment Projections. Dec 17, 2015. Web. 7 Jun 2017.

Fisher, Ronald C. *State and Local Public Finance*. New York: Routledge, 2015.

Jones, Charles P. and Gerald R. Jensen. *Investments: Analysis and Management*. Thirteenth Ed. Hoboken, NJ: Wiley Press, 2016.

Melicher, Ronald W. and Norton, Edgar A, eds. *Introduction to Finance: Markets, Investments, and Financial Management*. Sixteenth Edition. Hoboken, NJ: Wiley Publishers, 2016.

Ross, Stephen A., Westerfield, Randolph W., and Bradford D. Jordan. *Essentials of Corporate Finance*. Ninth Edition. New York: McGraw-Hill Education, 2017.

Singh, Nitish and Thomas J. Bussen. *Compliance Management*. Santa Barbara, CA: Praeger Press, 2015.

Accountant

Snapshot

Career Cluster(s): Business, Management & Administration Finance, Government & Public Administration
Interests: Keeping records, working with numbers, offering guidance, analyzing data
Earnings (Yearly Average): $68,150
Employment & Outlook: Faster Than Average Growth Expected

OVERVIEW

Sphere of Work

Accountants are responsible for the financial record keeping, financial efficiency, and fiduciary reporting of individuals, corporations, non-profit organizations, and government entities. Accountants offer diverse financial services, including financial document preparation and review, payroll, budget analysis, investment guidance, auditing, bankruptcy filing, and tax preparation. The main fields of accounting include internal accounting, public accounting, managerial accounting, and government accounting. Certified public accountants (CPAs) are the most common accounting position. CPAs may be independent contractors or employed by

public accounting firms providing financial services to businesses and individuals.

Work Environment

An accountant's Work Environment is generally office-based. Depending on the employer and particular job description, an accountant may telecommute from a home office, visit client offices as a contractor, or work on a full-time basis in an employer's office. Accountants may work as a full-time member of a team responsible for targeted financial responsibilities or may be hired as a project contractor. An accountant's Work Environment is dependent on technology (computers and accounting software programs), as well as having access to the most recent government regulations.

Profile

Working Conditions: Work Indoors
Physical Strength: Light Work
Education Needs: Bachelor's Degree
Licensure/Certification: Required
Opportunities For Experience: Part-time work, Military service, Internship
Holland Interest Score*: CRS

* See Appendix A

Occupation Interest

Individuals attracted to the accounting profession tend to be well-organized and detail-oriented people who find satisfaction in manipulating numbers and tracking financial trends. Accountants may also have an interest and affinity for technology and regulatory issues. For instance, those who excel in accounting tend to be adept at educating themselves about and responding to technological and regulatory change. Analytical people choosing to pursue the occupation of accountant may find satisfaction in implementing and auditing financial record keeping, as well as staying up to date on accounting best practices, ethical issues, and legal matters in accounting.

A Day in the Life—Duties and Responsibilities

Typical daily work tasks of a general accountant will include activities such as tax preparation, payroll, bookkeeping, and auditing. Organizations may also require accountants to select, implement, and troubleshoot accounting software systems, as well as stay up to date with regulatory and ethical issues and news in accounting by reading accounting industry journals and participating in industry associations. An accountant's daily occupational duties and responsibilities may also include meeting with clients, colleagues, supervisors, and employees as needed.

Clients, on a daily basis, may require accountants to provide financial counseling, tax preparation, payroll management, purchase order tracking, auditing, bankruptcy help, and contract preparation. Colleagues, on a daily basis, may require accountants to participate in discussions of work teams, workflows, dynamics, and best practices. Supervisors, on a daily basis, may require accountants to present their work and account for their work hours, take on extra work as needed, and strategize about organizational operations and best practices.

The duties of those accountants who have or supervise employees in their organizations will include managerial roles and responsibilities. Employees, on a daily basis, may need their supervising accountants to provide a review of the employee's financial document preparation or specific training related to accounting practices or technology. It is not unusual for accountants to advise or provide analysis to senior management on the financial implications of corporate performance, growth or acquisitions. Periodically, supervising accountants will also need to perform employee performance reviews.

External accountants who work for organizations with remote or multiple locations often travel to those locations to perform in-house auditing and bookkeeping work. Busy accountants will need to accommodate educational training, certification renewal, extended work travel, and commuting into their daily work schedules.

Duties and Responsibilities

- **Designing or modifying accounting systems, including computer systems**
- **Maintaining accounts or records**
- **Auditing contracts, purchase orders and vouchers and preparing related reports**
- **Preparing periodic financial statements and other management reports**
- **Directing and coordinating activities of workers engaged in keeping accounts and records**

OCCUPATION SPECIALTIES

Public Accountant

Public Accountants prepare federal, state and local tax returns of individuals, businesses or other organizations.

Budget Accountant

Budget Accountants apply principles of accounting to analyze past and present financial operations in order to prepare a budget.

Management Accountant

Management Accountants plan, set up and direct the operation of an accounting system to determine the cost of producing or selling an item or service.

Property Accountant

Property Accountants identify and keep records of company owned or leased equipment, buildings and other property.

Systems Accountant

Systems Accountants devise and install special accounting systems and related procedures in establishments which cannot use a standardized system.

Internal Auditor

Internal Auditors examine and analyze the accounting records of a business and prepare reports concerning its financial status and operating procedures.

WORK ENVIRONMENT

Physical Environment

Accountants generally work in office environments. The work of an accountant largely requires sitting at a desk and using computers for long periods of time each day. Accountants often meet with their immediate staff, and may be required to meet with corporate officers and outside auditing firms. Access to meeting spaces is often necessary.

Relevant Skills and Abilities

Communication Skills
- Speaking effectively
- Writing concisely

Interpersonal/Social Skills
- Being able to work independently
- Working as a member of a team

Organization & Management Skills
- Paying attention to an handling details

Research & Planning Skills
- Analyzing information

Technical Skills
- Working with data or numbers
- Working with machines, tools, or other objects

Human Environment

An accountant's human environment may be social or isolated depending on the assignment and organization. Accountants, depending on their work assignments and organization, may interact with clients, employees, supervisors, or colleagues.

Technological Environment

An accountant's technological environment will generally include computers, financial software packages for bookkeeping and auditing, telecommunication tools, and reference materials outlining legal and regulatory matters.

EDUCATION, TRAINING, AND ADVANCEMENT

High School/Secondary

High school students interested in someday pursuing a career in accounting should prepare themselves by building good study habits and exercising personal discipline. For those who feel at ease with numbers and mathematical functions, it is helpful to maximize the school's offering of mathematical and business courses, as well participate in any extracurricular activities relative to business and mathematics. Students should consider applying for internships or even volunteer work with local accountants or financial organizations to learn what it is accountants do on a daily basis.

Suggested High School Subjects

- Accounting
- Algebra
- Business
- Business & Computer Technology
- Business Data Processing
- Business Law
- College Preparatory
- Computer Science
- Economics
- English
- Mathematics
- Social Studies

Famous First

Mary T. Washington, of Chicago, became the first black woman to become a CPA in 1943, also becoming only the thirteenth African American CPA in history. Washington worked as a banking associate at Binga State Bank, one of the nation's largest black-owned banking institutions, before becoming a CPA. In 1968, Binga founded her own CPA firm, Washington, Pittman & McKeever, which became one of the largest black-owned accounting firms in the nation.

College/Postsecondary

Postsecondary (college and university) level students interested in pursuing a career in accounting should prepare themselves by building a foundation in mathematics, basic accounting, and business. Due to the importance of technology, law, and ethics in the practice of accounting, postsecondary students interested in pursuing a career in accounting will also benefit from studying computer science, political science, and possibly even philosophy (in order to explore the field of ethics). Postsecondary students committed to pursuing accounting may gain experience and build connections through accounting internships and entry-level employment with accounting businesses and firms. It's important to note that a college degree is a condition of CPA licensure in most states.

Related College Majors

- Accounting
- Business Accounting
- Finance, General
- Business, General
- Mathematics

Adult Job Seekers

Adults seeking accounting jobs have generally earned a bachelor's degree and, in some cases, an MBA. Adult job seekers will benefit from joining professional accounting associations as a means of professional networking. Professional accounting associations generally maintain job lists advertising open accounting positions. Adult job seekers who wish to join the accounting profession, but who lack a college degree, may gain access to the field by seeking out entry-level bookkeeping and clerk positions. Supervisors and mentors can help junior accountants to plan their career and educational choices.

Professional Certification and Licensure

Professional recognition through certification and licensure is extremely valuable in the job market. To become a CPA, it is also necessary to take a four-part two-day examination, mandated by the American Institute of Certified Public Accountants, that is the same for all states. Candidates are not required to pass all four parts at once, but most states require they pass all four parts within 18 months of passing the first part. Most states also require applicants for a CPA certificate to have some public accounting experience. Those interested in other types of accounting positions might also pursue certification in management or business accounting directly. Accountants can also train for positions as auditors through the Institute of Internal Auditors, which offers a Certified Internal Auditor (CIA) certification program.

Additional Requirements

Individuals dedicated to training and advancing in the accounting field generally work to develop their analytical, mathematical, and business abilities. Written and verbal communication skills are also important for accountants, as is proficiency with accounting software. High levels of integrity and ethics are required of accountants, as accountants often work with confidential documents. Membership in professional accounting societies is encouraged among junior and senior accountants as a means of building status within a professional community and networking.

EARNINGS AND ADVANCEMENT

Earnings depend upon the accountant's experience, level of education and certification as a public accountant. While larger firms usually pay higher starting salaries than small or medium-sized firms, the small and medium-sized firms usually offer the well-qualified employee an opportunity for more rapid advancement. Generally, certified public accountants (CPAs) and those with graduate degrees earn a higher beginning salary.

According to the Bureau of Labor Statistics (BLS), the average annual salary for accountants in the U.S. was $68,150 in 2016, with those at the lower end of the spectrum earning less than $42,140 and those at the higher side of the spectrum earning more than $120,000. The highest salaries for accountants can generally be found in the finance and insurance industries or working in management companies.

Metropolitan Areas with the Highest Employment Level in this Occupation

Metropolitan area	Employment	Employment per thousand jobs	Hourly mean wage
New York-Jersey City-White Plains, NY-NJ Metropolitan Division	90,790	13.78	$47.35
Los Angeles-Long Beach-Glendale, CA Metropolitan Division	45,240	10.72	$39.80
Houston-The Woodlands-Sugar Land, TX	37,990	12.94	$43.22
Chicago-Naperville-Arlington Heights, IL Metropolitan Division	37,170	10.22	$38.36
Washington-Arlington-Alexandria, DC-VA-MD-WV Metropolitan Division	33,500	13.45	$43.80
Dallas-Plano-Irving, TX Metropolitan Division	30,570	12.58	$39.09
Atlanta-Sandy Springs-Roswell, GA	27,500	10.77	$38.02
Boston-Cambridge-Newton, MA NECTA Division	24,450	13.56	$40.99
Denver-Aurora-Lakewood, CO	22,910	16.18	$38.63
Minneapolis-St. Paul-Bloomington, MN-WI	22,310	11.68	$34.88

Source: Bureau of Labor Statistics

EMPLOYMENT AND OUTLOOK

The Bureau of Labor Statistics estimated in 2014 that the accounting industry was growing at an annual rate of 11 percent, constituting much faster than average growth when compared to the 6-7 percent growth for all U.S. industries. The growth of the accounting market is closely linked with the overall health of the economy, with more jobs available in periods of financial growth. Globalization has created opportunities for accountants with overseas experience and expertise and the increasing tendency for businesses to conduct business internationally may increase opportunities in this sector of the industry. Though there are many accounting jobs available, competition for jobs at the upper end of the industry may be significant and those with advanced degrees and certification will therefore have an advantage.

Related Occupations

- Financial Analysts
- Management Analysts
- Personal Financial Advisors
- Tax Examiners and Collectors, and Revenue Agents
- Budget Specialists
- Financial Managers
- Appraisers, Examiners, and Investigators

Related Military Occupations

- Finance and Accounting Manager

Conversation With . . .
LYNN AMORE

Accountant
The Hanover Insurance Group
Accounting professional, 10 years

1. What was your individual career path in terms of education, entry-level job, or other significant opportunity?

When I got out of high school, I worked for Digital Equipment Corporation as a secretary. I took a lot of night classes. Then I got married and had a child. In 1996, I was laid off, so I went back to school full-time to finally get my degree. I was always good with numbers and got my degree in business administration. During that time, I took an internship at Hanover Insurance with no pay, but I got three credits. I was 36 years old! When my internship ended, they asked me to work through the summer as a temp. It was accounting work, reconciliations and so forth. At the end of the summer, they offered me a 30-hour permanent position as a reconciliation specialist, which is making sure that money that comes in the door is applied to a policy. I did that for a few years. During that time, I got a Series 6 license, which allows you to sell mutual funds and variable annuities. I always took advantage of the classes offered by Hanover. It's important to always keep improving. In my late 40s, I interviewed for a job that I didn't get. That motivated me to get my INS Certificate in General Insurance. You have to pass exams to get it. That made me more marketable, because I was 50 years old and I knew I was going to be up against younger people, competing for the same jobs. After that, I applied for an accountant's position that I wanted, and I got it.

2. What are the most important skills and/or qualities for someone in your profession?

It seems obvious, but you really need to understand basic accounting rules. You definitely need to know the Microsoft Office products: Excel, Access, Microsoft Word. You have to be a team player and be open to other people's ideas and new ideas. You must be organized and be thorough. You have to always double-check work. You have to deal with deadlines. In accounting, the end of the month can be a very busy time.

3. **What do you wish you had known going into this profession?**

   I wish I had known how to deal with different personalities and how to not take things personally. My first boss was a very critical person and I took it very personally. You have to know how to stand up for yourself.

4. **Are there many job opportunities in your profession? In what specific areas?**

   There are a lot of opportunities. Most businesses or organizations really want you to be a Certified Public Accountant (CPA). If you are a CPA or have your master's degree, or both, you're really golden. There are opportunities in finance, management, products.

5. **How do you see your profession changing in the next five years? What role will technology play in those changes, and what skills will be required?**

   You have to be proficient with Microsoft Access and Microsoft Excel and know the products inside and out, how to work with pivot tables that slice data and work with macros. You have to stay on top of the software because it's always changing. It's awesome. You have to like that stuff. One thing that they tell you at Hanover is you're in charge of your own career. We have to write development goals and progress reports. You can just sit back and do your job and do it every day, or you can learn and be ready as the profession changes. Always take advantage of training opportunities. You'll be lucky if you can work for a company that offers a lot of training.

6. **What do you enjoy most about your job? What do you enjoy least about your job?**

   It's close to home! But, seriously, I like working with the spreadsheets. I like getting creative with the databases and figuring out process improvements. I find that fun. And I like the people I work with. That said, though, what I like least is working alongside one of my coworkers who just talks so much about herself. She's a narcissist.

7. **Can you suggest a valuable "try this" for students considering a career in your profession?**

   Try to get an internship. That's such a great way to just sort of try it. But, short of that, create a spreadsheet or put a budget together. Create tabs and link all the data together. Kids—actually, everyone—should always do a budget.

SELECTED SCHOOLS

Many large universities, especially those with business schools, offer programs in accounting. The student can also gain initial training through enrollment at a liberal arts college or community college. Below are listed some of the more prominent institutions in this field.

Brigham Young University
Marriott School of Management
Campus Drive
Provo, UT 84602
801.422.4121
marriottschool.byu.edu

Indiana University, Bloomington
Kelley School of Business
1309 E. 10th Street
Bloomington, IN 47405
812.855.8100
kelley.iu.edu

New York University
Stern School of Business
665 Broadway, 11th Floor
New York, NY 10012
212.998.4500
www.stern.nyu.edu

Ohio State University
Fisher College of Business
120 Schoenbaum Hall
210 W. Woodruff Avenue
Columbus, OH 43210
614.292.2715
fisher.osu.edu

University of Illinois, Urbana-Champaign
College of Business
1515 East Gregory Drive
Champaign, IL 61820
217.333.2740
business.illinois.edu

University of Michigan, Ann Arbor
Ross School of Business
701 Tappan Avenue
Ann Arbor, MI 48109
734.763.5796
michiganross.umich.edu

University of Notre Dame
Mendoza College of Business
Notre Dame, IN 46566
574.631.7505
business.nd.edu

University of Pennsylvania
The Wharton School
1 College Hall
Philadelphia, PA 19104
215.898.6376
www.wharton.upenn.edu

University of Southern California
Marshall School of Business
3670 Trousdale Parkway
Los Angeles, CA 90089
213.740.8674
www.marshall.usc.edu

University of Texas, Austin
McCombs School of Business
1 University Station, B6000
Austin, TX 78712
512.471.5921
www.mccombs.utexas.edu

MORE INFORMATION

Accreditation Council for Accountancy and Taxation
1010 North Fairfax Street
Alexandria, VA 22314-1574
888.289.7763
info@acatcredentials.org
www.acatcredentials.org

American Accounting Association
5717 Bessie Drive
Sarasota, FL 34233-2399
941.921.7747
info@aaahq.org
aaahq.org/index.cfm

American Institute of Certified Public Accountants
1211 Avenue of the Americas
New York, NY 10036
212.596.6200
www.aicpa.org

The American Institute of CPA Student Scholarships
www.aicpa.org/BecomeACPA/Scholarships/Pages/default.aspx

Institute of Internal Auditors
247 Maitland Avenue
Altamonte Springs, FL 32701
407.937.1100
www.theiia.org

Institute of Management Accountants
10 Paragon Drive
Montvale, NJ 07645-1718
800.638.4427
ima@imanet.org
www.imanet.org

National Association of State Boards of Accountancy
150 4th Avenue North, Suite 700
Nashville, TN 37219
615.880.4200
www.nasba.org

Simone Isadora Flynn,
updated by Micah Issitt

Actuary

Snapshot

Career Cluster(s): Finance, Management & Administration Finance
Interests: Mathematics, statistics, finance, financial analysis, risk analysis
Earnings (Yearly Average): $100,610
Employment & Outlook: Much faster than average growth expected

OVERVIEW

Sphere of Work

Actuaries use statistics and data to assess the likelihoods of future risks such as death, sickness, injury, disability, environmental catastrophe, property loss, or investment loss. In some instances, the job of an actuary will include risk assessment and risk reduction through policy or business decisions. Actuaries design risk-based financial systems such as insurance and pension plans with specific premium costs, age and health requirements, and payout schedules in order to minimize an organization's potential financial losses and maximize organizational sustainability.

Work Environment

The majority of actuaries work in the insurance industry—in areas such as property insurance, life insurance, health insurance, and disability insurance. Other fields requiring actuarial skills include the financial industry, health care industry, and government programs such as Social Security and Medicare. Actuaries work as full-time salaried and contract employees in insurance companies, hospitals, investment firms, and social service government agencies. The actuarial profession, being in high demand and involving complex statistical analysis of data, tends to require long hours and great dedication.

Profile

Working Conditions: Work Indoors
Physical Strength: Light Work
Education Needs: Bachelor's Degree
Licensure/Certification: Nor Required
Opportunities For Experience: Part-time work, Apprenticeship
Holland Interest Score*: ISE

* See Appendix A

Occupation Interest

Individuals drawn to the actuarial profession have an interest in and an affinity for mathematics, analysis, statistics, and business processes. Actuaries are detail-oriented people who have the ability to analyze complex data. They use their findings to make big picture business and policy assessments and recommendations. Actuaries find satisfaction in solving complex problems and making informed predictions about future risk-based events.

A Day in the Life—Duties and Responsibilities

An actuary's occupational duties and responsibilities focus on gathering and analyzing statistical data to assess the probable risk of events such as accidents, sickness, disability, death, property loss, retirement, and natural or man-made disasters. Actuaries determine probable risk and then use this data to make decisions about insurance premiums, pension plan payouts, and tax rates. Actuaries are responsible for ensuring that an organization can make payments to beneficiaries without risk of present or future financial loss to the organization.

An actuary's daily tasks may include compiling economic and social data on organizational stakeholders, using a computer for data analysis and communication, and creating databases for statistical data. Actuaries may also assess financial risk of different business decisions and models; draft probability charts for events such as accidents, sickness, disability, death, property loss, retirement, and natural or man-made disasters; and calculate insurance and deductible rates. Actuaries may meet with stakeholders to explain the relationship between statistical data and company policies or with insurance carriers and management to discuss insurance rates.

Ultimately, an actuary's daily duties and responsibilities are diverse, challenging, and weighty. Actuaries have a central role in making decisions about insurance premiums, insurance payments, employee benefits, and pension amounts that affect daily life.

Duties and Responsibilities

- **Making sure that the price charged for the insurance will enable the company to pay all claims and expenses as they occur**
- **Calculating rates and determining policy contract provisions for each type of insurance offered**
- **Helping to determine company policy**
- **Being called upon to explain complex technical matters to company executives, government officials, policyholders, and the public.**
- **Helping companies develop plans to enter new lines of business**

WORK ENVIRONMENT

Physical Environment

Most actuaries work in office environments. The work of an actuary requires sitting at a desk and using computers for long periods each day. Actuaries who work on a contract basis may be required to travel to client offices to analyze data and attend meetings. Those working in manufacturing plants might be responsible for assessing risk to employees or measuring external risk for a company's products.

Relevant Skills and Abilities

Communication Skills

- Speaking effectively
- Writing concisely

Interpersonal/Social Skills

- Working with others
- Working in a team
- Working independently

Organization & Management Skills

- Making decisions
- Paying attention to and handling details
- Performing duties which change frequently

Research & Planning Skills

- Developing evaluation strategies
- Using logical reasoning

Technical Skills

- Performing scientific, mathematical, and technical work

Human Environment

An actuary's work involves interaction with clients, colleagues, supervisors, and employees. Actuaries use interpersonal skills to interact with fellow workers, communicate findings, and propose new ideas.

Technological Environment

Actuaries must have a strong familiarity with spreadsheets, databases, and statistical analysis software. Internet communication skills are usually required. Computer programming skills are generally not required for actuarial employment but are considered useful. Actuaries are usually required to keep their technology skills up to date as a condition of continued and successful employment.

EDUCATION, TRAINING, AND ADVANCEMENT

High School/Secondary

High school students who are interested in pursuing an actuarial career should prepare themselves by developing strong organizational skills, building good study habits, and exhibiting confidence in the study of mathematics, economics, and business. Students should consider applying for actuary-related internships to learn more about an actuary's daily work, skills sets, and challenges.

Suggested High School Subjects

- Accounting
- Calculus
- College Preparatory
- Computer Science
- Economics
- English
- Humanities
- Mathematics
- Statistics

Famous First

In 1693, British mathematician Edmund Halley was the first mathematician to correctly construct a "life table," demonstrating the correct premium that a person of a given age would pay to purchase life insurance, assuming a fixed interest. Until Halley and other pioneers began applying detailed statistical science to actuarial calculations, insurance rates varied widely and were not tied to legitimate statistical models. Halley is therefore often considered one of the pioneers of modern actuarial science.

College/Postsecondary

Actuaries generally earn a bachelor's degree prior to beginning professional actuarial work. College students interested in pursuing an actuarial career should study mathematics, computer science, and business. Particularly important areas of college study and coursework include finance, economics, calculus, algebra, probability and statistics, business, computer science, and technical writing. Due to the human impact of actuarial work, college students interested in actuarial careers will also benefit from studying sociology and political science, as well as keeping abreast of current events. Interested college students should consider pursuing actuarial internships and part-time actuarial related work, as well as educating themselves about the requirements of the actuarial exams.

Related College Majors

- Accounting
- Business Accounting
- Finance, General
- Business, General
- Mathematics

Adult Job Seekers

Adults seeking actuarial jobs have generally earned a bachelor's degree and passed a series of actuary exams. Adult job seekers will benefit from joining professional actuarial associations, including Casualty Actuarial Society (CAS) and the Society of Actuaries (SOA), as a means of professional networking. Professional actuarial associations often hold career-finding workshops and maintain job lists advertising open actuary positions. Actuarial recruiters and internships may also prove useful resources for adult job seekers. Supervisors and mentors can help junior actuaries to plan their career, exam schedule, and education choices.

Professional Certification and Licensure

The actuarial profession requires that individuals pass a series of examinations administered by the Casualty Actuarial Society (CAS) and the Society of Actuaries (SOA). Both societies sponsor the same entry-level exams, which include the Probability Exam, the Financial Mathematics Exam, Financial Economics Exam, Life

Contingencies Exam, and Construction and Evaluation of Actuarial Models Exam. A candidate seeking a career in life insurance, health benefits systems, retirement systems, or finance and investment would pursue the certification process developed by the SOA. A candidate seeking a career in property and casualty liability (auto, home, malpractice, workers compensation, and personal injury), would follow the requirements outlined by the CAS. Those involved in the federal pension field must follow requirements outlined by the federal government.

Professional actuaries usually take the series of required exams over the course of their careers. Mid-career actuaries who have passed the beginning exams may choose to pursue Actuarial Associateship or Fellowship status. These ranks are clearly defined by the CAS, SOA, and the federal government and require a combination of work experience and the satisfactory completion of professional workshops and exams.

Additional Requirements

Individuals who find satisfaction, success, and job security in the actuarial profession will be knowledgeable about the profession's requirements, responsibilities, and opportunities. Successful actuaries engage in ongoing development of their mathematical, financial, and business skills. Written and verbal communication skills are also important for actuaries, as is proficiency with computer spreadsheets and databases. High levels of integrity and ethics are required of actuaries, as actuaries often work with confidential and personal information. Membership in professional actuary associations is encouraged among junior and senior actuaries as a means of building status within a professional community and networking.

EARNINGS AND ADVANCEMENT

According to the Bureau of Labor Statistics (BLS), actuaries earned an average median wage of $104,500 a year, with salaries ranging from a low of $58,000 to close to $200,000 at the upper end of the spectrum. Actuaries who have passed specialized exams and pursued professional development are more likely to earn higher wages or to qualify for higher-paid positions. Some companies offer direct incentives to actuaries who pass additional certification exams. Advancing in the field might therefore involve gaining seniority in an institution or company or returning to education to obtain higher levels of certification and specialization.

Metropolitan Areas with the Highest Employment Level in this Occupation

Metropolitan area	Employment	Employment per thousand jobs	Hourly mean wage
New York-Jersey City-White Plains, NY-NJ Metropolitan Division	2,130	0.32	$68.74
Boston-Cambridge-Newton, MA NECTA Division	820	0.45	$51.35
Chicago-Naperville-Arlington Heights, IL Metropolitan Division	790	0.22	$46.78
Bloomington, IL	580	6.43	$52.08
Hartford-West Hartford-East Hartford, CT	540	0.93	$53.51
Des Moines-West Des Moines, IA	490	1.39	$46.77
Montgomery County-Bucks County-Chester County, PA Metropolitan Division	490	0.48	N/A
Los Angeles-Long Beach-Glendale, CA Metropolitan Division	480	0.11	$51.54
Kansas City, MO-KS	480	0.46	$60.23
Dallas-Plano-Irving, TX Metropolitan Division	460	0.19	N/A

Source: Bureau of Labor Statistics

EMPLOYMENT AND OUTLOOK

In 2014, there were 24,600 professional actuaries in the United States and the Bureau of Labor Statistics estimates that the field is growing at an average of 18 percent per year, which is far faster than the 6-7 percent growth estimated for all careers in the United States. Growth in the insurance industry leads to new opportunities for actuaries and the field also tends to grow in conjunction with the overall economy. Despite rapid growth, the field remains small and there is therefore significant competition for available positions, especially at the higher end of the pay spectrum. Those with specialization and certification will have an advantage when looking for jobs.

Related Occupations

- Accountants and Auditors
- Budged Analysts
- Cost Estimators
- Economists
- Financial Analysts
- Insurance Underwriters
- Mathematicians
- Personal Financial Advisors
- Statisticians

SELECTED SCHOOLS

Many colleges and universities, especially those with business schools, offer programs in accounting. The student can also gain initial training at a technical or community college. For some of the more prominent institutions in this field, see the list of selected schools in the "Accountant" chapter of this volume.

MORE INFORMATION

American Academy of Actuaries
1850 M Street NW, Suite 300
Washington, DC 20036
202.223.8196
www.actuary.org

American Society of Pension Professionals & Actuaries
4245 N. Fairfax Drive, Suite 750
Arlington, VA 22203
703.516.9300
asppa@asppa.org
www.asppa.org

Casualty Actuarial Society
4350 N. Fairfax Drive, Suite 250
Arlington, VA 22203
703.276.3100
www.casact.org

Society of Actuaries
475 N. Martingale Road, Suite 600
Schaumburg, IL 60173
847.706.3500
customerservice@soa.org
www.soa.org

Simone Isadora Flynn,
updated by Micah Issitt

Auditor

Snapshot

Career Cluster(s): Business, Management & Administration, Finance, Government & Public Administration
Interests: Analyzing data, accounting, finances, record-keeping, detail work
Earnings (Yearly Average): $68,150
Employment & Outlook: Faster than Average Growth Expected

OVERVIEW

Sphere of Work

Auditors use their training in accounting to review the accuracy of an organization's financial records. Auditors work for and verify the financial records of the public sector (including government agencies and departments) and the private sector (including large corporations, small businesses, and non-profit organizations). There are two main areas of auditing internal auditing and external auditing. Internal auditors review their organization's internal financial controls and record keeping for evidence of waste or fraud. External auditors are hired, often as a condition of regulatory and stakeholder compliance, from an outside organization to

review and verify the accuracy of an organization's financial controls and record keeping.

Work Environment

An auditor's Work Environment is generally desk-based. Depending on the employer and particular job description, an auditor may telecommute from a home office, visit client offices as a contractor, or work on a full-time basis in an employer's office. Auditors may work as a full-time member of a work team responsible for ongoing financial document review and documentation or may be hired as a contractor. An auditor's Work Environment is dependent on technology, including computers and financial software programs, as well as having access to the most recent government regulations.

Profile

Interest: Data
Working Conditions: Work Inside
Physical Strength: Light Work
Education Needs: Bachelor's Degree
Licensure/Certification: Required
Opportunities For Experience: Internship
Holland Interest Score*: REC

* See Appendix A

Occupation Interest

Individuals interested in the auditing profession tend to be well-organized and detail-oriented people who find satisfaction in reviewing and analyzing systems, processes, and large amounts of data. Auditors may also have an interest and affinity for technology and regulatory issues. For instance, those who excel in auditing tend to be adept at educating themselves about and responding to frequent technological and regulatory changes. Analytical people choosing to pursue the occupation of auditor may find satisfaction in staying up-to-date on auditing best practices.

A Day in the Life—Duties and Responsibilities

An auditor's daily occupational duties and responsibilities include reviewing, verifying, and certifying the accuracy and authenticity of financial records. Specific duties, schedules, and assignments vary between internal and external auditors. Further specialization can occur, as some choose to pursue interests in information technology (IT) auditing, environmental auditing, financial auditing, and compliance auditing.

Internal auditors will review their organization's financial records on an ongoing basis, looking for regulatory compliance or indications of employee mismanagement, waste, or fraud. Internal auditors review all financial records including ordering, payroll, inventory, expenses, work orders, equipment purchasing, profit/loss statements, and taxes. Internal auditors are also increasingly responsible for reviewing and overseeing financial software, as organizations move to automate financial transactions. Internal auditors report findings to management and often participate in developing the organization's financial policies and best practices.

External auditors, usually employed by public accounting firms, will be hired on a contract basis quarterly or annually to review the financial documents of businesses or government departments. Stakeholder and state and federal laws generally require businesses to seek an external independent audit of all financial records on a regular basis. External auditors most often report their findings to regulatory agencies such as the Securities and Exchange Commission (SEC) and the Internal Revenue Service (IRS).

Duties and Responsibilities

- **Auditing contracts, purchase orders and vouchers and preparing related reports**
- **Directing and coordinating activities of workers engaged in keeping accounts and records**
- **Writing opinion on financial statements**
- **Giving advice on profit planning, budgeting, and cost contro**

OCCUPATION SPECIALTIES

Internal Auditor

Internal Auditors examine and evaluate financial and information systems, management procedures, and internal controls. They check records to assure accuracy and to protect against fraud and waste.

County/City Auditor

County/City Auditors direct activities of personnel engaged in recording deeds and similar legal instruments, keep records of county or municipal accounts, compile and transmit fiscal records, prepare financial statements, and audit books of city or county offices.

Tax Auditor

Tax Auditors audit financial records to determine tax liability. They review information gathered from the taxpayer, such as material assets, income, surpluses, liabilities and expenditures to verify net worth or reported financial status.

WORK ENVIRONMENT

Physical Environment

Auditors generally work in office environments. The work of an auditor requires sitting at a desk and using computers for long periods of time each day. Auditors hired to perform external audits may be required to travel to client offices to review financial records and attend meetings.

Transferable Skills and Abilities

Interpersonal/Social Skills
- Being able to work independently
- Being honest
- Being patient
- Cooperating with others
- Working as a member of a team

Organization & Management Skills
- Paying attention to and handling details

Research & Planning Skills
- Analyzing information
- Solving problems Technical Skills
- Performing scientific, mathematical and technical work
- Using technology to process information
- Working with machines, tools or other objects

Human Environment

An auditor's human environment may be social or isolated depending on the assignment and the organization. These factors will influence interaction with clients, employees, supervisors, or colleagues. It must be noted that auditors—who are by their job definition responsible for finding problems, waste, and fraud—may be perceived in an adversarial or hostile way by some organizational employees.

Technological Environment

An auditor's technological environment will generally include computers, financial and auditing software, and telecommunication tools.

EDUCATION, TRAINING, AND ADVANCEMENT

High School/Secondary

High school students interested in pursuing an auditing career should prepare themselves by building good organizational skills and developing strong study habits. They should also develop strong mathematical skills. Students should consider applying for internships, part-time work if available, or even volunteer work with local financial organizations in order to learn what it is that auditors do on a daily basis.

Suggested High School Subjects
- Accounting
- Algebra

- Communications
- Business
- Business Law
- Calculus
- Computer Science
- English
- Geometry
- Mathematics
- Statistics
- Trigonometry

Famous First

The first known auditors described in history were essentially spies working for King Darius of Ancient Persia between 522 and 486 BCE. The term "auditor," developed during this time was taken from the work "to hear," as early auditors listened to oral reports from elite aristocrats and landowners and verified the authenticity of the information provided. Under Darius, auditors were responsible for ensuring that local leaders were giving accurate reports on the state of their territory to the king. Gradually, auditors became specialists in verifying written reports and later in verifying financial reports from companies and agencies. In the 1800s, modern auditing began in Britain where new laws forced companies to provide audited reports to shareholders.

College/Postsecondary

Postsecondary students interested in pursuing an auditing career should prepare themselves by building a foundation in mathematics, accounting, and business courses. Due to the importance of technology, law, and ethics in the practice of auditing, postsecondary students interested in pursuing a career in auditing will also benefit from studying both computer and political science. Postsecondary students committed to pursuing auditing will gain experience and build connections through auditing internships and part-time employment with financial businesses, such as accounting and auditing firms.

Related College Majors

- Accounting
- Business Administration & Management, General
- Economics, General
- Mathematics

Adult Job Seekers

Adults seeking auditing jobs have generally earned a bachelor's degree in accounting, business administration, or another closely related profession. Those individuals who intend to work toward managerial or supervisor roles in the auditing world may choose to earn a master's of business administration (MBA) or law degree. Adult job seekers will benefit from joining professional auditing associations as a means of professional networking. Professional auditing associations generally offer job-finding workshops and maintain job lists advertising open auditing positions. Adult job seekers who wish to join the auditing profession, but who lack a college degree, may be able to gain access to the field by seeking entry-level bookkeeping and clerk positions. Supervisors and mentors can help junior auditors plan their career and educational choices.

Professional Certification and Licensure

Auditors are required to have the same professional certification and licensure required of accountants. The most common professional license for auditors and accountants is the CPA certification issued by state boards of accountancy. Only licensed CPAs are legally allowed to submit financial reports to the SEC. CPA licensure is based on three elements: education, examination, and experience. CPAs are required to have at least 150 semester hours of college coursework, pass the CPA exam, and fulfill state experience requirements. The American Institute of Certified Public Accountants administers the universal CPA examination accepted by all states. The CPA examination includes four discrete parts that must be passed within an eighteen-month period. The CPA examination is computerized and offered multiple times a year at state testing centers.

In addition to the CPA certification, professional auditors may choose to pursue auditing-specific designations such as the Certified Internal Auditor license and the Certified Information Systems Auditor license. These two licenses, achieved through passing examinations, are the industry standard for demonstrating professional auditing competencies. As in any venture, a candidate should consult credible professional associations within their prospective field and follow professional debate as to the relevancy and value of any certification program.

Additional Requirements

Individuals who find satisfaction, success, and job security in the auditing profession will be knowledgeable about the profession's requirements, responsibilities, and opportunities.

Individuals dedicated to training and advancing in the auditing field generally work to develop their analytical, mathematical, and business abilities. Written and verbal communication skills are also important for auditors, as is proficiency with auditing software. High levels of integrity and ethics are required of auditors, as they often work with private and confidential documents. Additionally, external auditors often do their work within a corporation's offices—sometimes outside of the normal workday. Discretion and trust are essential to an effective working relationship between the outside auditor and his or her client.

Membership in professional auditing associations is encouraged among both junior and senior auditors as a means of building status within a professional community and networking.

EARNINGS AND ADVANCEMENT

According to the Bureau of Labor Statistics (BLS), median annual wage for accountants and auditors was $68,150 in 2016, with those at the lowest ten percent earning less than $42,140 and those at the upper end of the spectrum earning over $120,000. Advancing in a career as an auditor can involve accruing work experience and seniority within a firm or applying for higher level positions in other firms or organizations. Most auditors work full time, but overtime is common in the field, especially at certain times of the year, such as when reconciling end of year budgets. Auditors working in the finance field tend to earn higher wages, on average, than auditors in other fields.

Metropolitan Areas with the Highest Employment Level in this Occupation

Metropolitan area	Employment	Employment per thousand jobs	Hourly mean wage
New York-Jersey City-White Plains, NY-NJ Metropolitan Division	90,790	13.78	$47.35
Los Angeles-Long Beach-Glendale, CA Metropolitan Division	45,240	10.72	$39.80
Houston-The Woodlands-Sugar Land, TX	37,990	12.94	$43.22
Chicago-Naperville-Arlington Heights, IL Metropolitan Division	37,170	10.22	$38.36
Washington-Arlington-Alexandria, DC-VA-MD-WV Metropolitan Division	33,500	13.45	$43.80
Dallas-Plano-Irving, TX Metropolitan Division	30,570	12.58	$39.09
Atlanta-Sandy Springs-Roswell, GA	27,500	10.77	$38.02
Boston-Cambridge-Newton, MA NECTA Division	24,450	13.56	$40.99
Denver-Aurora-Lakewood, CO	22,910	16.18	$38.63
Minneapolis-St. Paul-Bloomington, MN-WI	22,310	11.68	$34.88

Source: Bureau of Labor Statistics

EMPLOYMENT AND OUTLOOK

As of 2014, auditors and accountants held more than 1.2 million jobs, with an average annual growth of 11 percent expected between 2014 and 2024, constituting faster than average growth when compared to the 6-7 percent estimated for all US occupations during the same period. Growth in the auditing and accounting fields is tied to overall economic growth, with an increasing number of jobs during periods of economic growth and reduced opportunities for employment during times of economic stress or instability. Another factor affecting growth in the industry involves financial regulation. When new legislation creates more stringent regulations, demand for qualified accountants and auditors increases as companies struggle to adjust to changing financial laws. While growth is strong, those who hold advanced degrees or professional certification, such as a CPA certificate, are likely to have an advantage on the job market.

Related Occupations

- Accountant
- Actuary
- Budget Analyst
- Credit Manager
- Energy Auditor
- Financial Analyst
- Financial Manager
- Insurance Underwriter
- Personal Financial Advisor
- Public Administrator

Conversation With . . .
LARRY HARRINGTON

Internal Auditor, Vice President, Raytheon Company
Waltham, Massachusetts
Auditor, 25 years

1. What was your individual career path in terms of education/training, entry-level job, or other significant opportunity?

I graduated from Bentley University in Waltham, Massachusetts, with a degree in accounting. I worked for a number of years before attending and graduating from the Advanced Management Program at Harvard Business School. My advice for people starting out in their careers is to gain valuable work experience for a few years before seeking an advanced degree; this will leverage your business experience with real-time learning. I strongly suggest a program with an international focus.

I started my career in public accounting before moving into the corporate world, as an internal auditor. The skills I gained as an internal auditor enabled me to be viewed as an agent of change. Companies could trust me to lead new functions even if I didn't have core skills in that discipline because of my leadership, creativity and ability to work with others who did have those core skills. Eventually, I held vice president roles in finance, human resources and operations before moving into my current role as the chief audit executive at Raytheon Company, creating positive change with a sense of urgency.

2. What are the most important skills and/or qualities for someone in your profession?

The most important skills and qualities for an internal auditor can, appropriately, be encapsulated with the acronym CHANGE:

Communicating with persuasion—both verbal and written.

Helping others succeed through critical thinking and change management skills.

Accounting, IT and other business skills help you to accomplish positive change.

Networking and building relationships within your business, industry, and profession; most jobs come through networking.

Growing: Invest in your own learning as employers seldom invest enough in you.

Enquiring mindset: Auditors are people who wonder about how businesses work.

3. **What do you wish you had known going into this profession?**

   The importance of leadership (even without the title), the power of networking, and the necessity to continually self-invest in my knowledge and skill, rather than relying solely on a company to provide training. I also would have sought an international assignment.

4. **Are there many job opportunities in your profession? In what specific areas?**

   Internal audit is a growth profession. All public companies have a requirement for internal auditors. There are also private companies that have an internal audit function to ensure they can get an internal objective view on their processes and any risks to the company. There are lots of early career positions as well as management positions.

5. **How do you see your profession changing in the next five years, what role will technology play in those changes, and what skills will be required?**

   The profession is forever morphing as businesses morph due to global competition, big data, and technology. Many internal audit groups are working to analyze data in real-time, using continuous monitoring so that we can spot problems sooner and fix them quicker.

6. **What do you like most about your job? What do you like least about your job?**

   The most enjoyable part is the development and coaching of people. I enjoy sharing my knowledge and mentoring people to create a career path and a plan to achieve that success. I learn from the people working for me as they help me continually learn and change, even at this point in my career.

   The least enjoyable part is people thinking that internal audit is here to make them look bad. We have to work hard to change our professional image, so that people know our role is to help them succeed by helping them improve processes, reduce costs, meet their business objectives, and help them avoid surprises.

7. **Can you suggest a valuable "try this" for students considering a career in your profession?**

   When you are out in your day-to-day life think critically about the processes you see, think about ways that you could improve those processes. An example may be the flow at a restaurant or the timing of the stoplights in a high traffic area. These are simple examples of logistical issues that may benefit from process improvement.

SELECTED SCHOOLS

Many large universities, especially those with business schools, offer programs in accounting. The student can also gain initial training through enrollment at a liberal arts college or community college. Below are listed some of the more prominent institutions in this field.

Brigham Young University
Marriott School of Management
Campus Drive
Provo, UT 84602
801.422.4121
marriottschool.byu.edu

Indiana University, Bloomington
Kelley School of Business
1309 E. 10th Street
Bloomington, IN 47405
812.855.8100
kelley.iu.edu

New York University
Stern School of Business
665 Broadway, 11th Floor
New York, NY 10012
212.998.4500
www.stern.nyu.edu

Ohio State University
Fisher College of Business
120 Schoenbaum Hall
210 W. Woodruff Avenue
Columbus, OH 43210
614.292.2715
fisher.osu.edu

University of Illinois, Urbana-Champaign
College of Business
1515 East Gregory Drive
Champaign, IL 61820
217.333.2740
business.illinois.edu

University of Michigan, Ann Arbor
Ross School of Business
701 Tappan Avenue
Ann Arbor, MI 48109
734.763.5796
michiganross.umich.edu

University of Notre Dame
Mendoza College of Business
Notre Dame, IN 46566
574.631.7505
business.nd.edu

University of Pennsylvania
The Wharton School
1 College Hall
Philadelphia, PA 19104
215.898.6376
www.wharton.upenn.edu

University of Southern California
Marshall School of Business
3670 Trousdale Parkway
Los Angeles, CA 90089
213.740.8674
www.marshall.usc.edu

University of Texas, Austin
McCombs School of Business
1 University Station, B6000
Austin, TX 78712
512.471.5921
www.mccombs.utexas.edu

MORE INFORMATION

Accreditation Council for Accountancy and Taxation
1010 North Fairfax Street
Alexandria, VA 22314-1574
888.289.7763
www.acatcredentials.org

American Institute of Certified Public Accountants
1211 Avenue of the Americas
New York, NY 10036
888.777.7077
www.aicpa.org

Information Systems Audit and Control Association
3701 Algonquin Road, Suite 1010
Rolling Meadows, IL 60008
847.253.1545
www.isaca.org

Institute of Internal Auditors
247 Maitland Avenue
Altamonte Springs, FL 32701-4201
407.937.1100
iia@theiia.org
www.theiia.org

Institute of Management Accountants
10 Paragon Drive
Montvale, NJ 07645-1718
800.638.4427
ima@imanet.org
www.imanet.org

National Association of State Auditors, Comptrollers and Treasurers
449 Lewis Hargett Circle, Suite 290
Lexington, KY 40503
859.276.1147
www.nasact.org

Simone Isadora Flynn & Micah Issitt/Editors

Bank Teller

Snapshot

Career Cluster(s): Finance
Interests: Handling money, helping people manage their money, communicating with others
Earnings (Yearly Average): $27,260
Employment & Outlook: Decline expected

OVERVIEW

Sphere of Work

Bank tellers are the first point of human contact at a bank and are responsible for processing routine financial transactions for customers. Customers usually interact with bank tellers to cash checks, make deposits and withdrawals, or discuss other banking services.

Work Environment

Bank tellers can work in large city banks or smaller branches in less central areas. They may also work for a savings and loan association or a similar financial institution.

Profile

Working Conditions: Work Indoors
Physical Strength: Light Work
Education Needs: High school diploma or equivalent
Licensure/Certification: Not Required
Opportunities For Experience: Internship, Part Time Work
Holland Interest Score*: CSE

* See Appendix A

Occupation Interest

Individuals interested in becoming bank tellers tend to have good cash-handling and customer service skills and find satisfaction in helping people manage their money. Bank tellers are able to count money quickly and accurately. They should be good salespeople—they are selling bank services at all times—and success in this area can lead to promotion to positions with more responsibility.

A Day in the Life—Duties and Responsibilities

Typical daily tasks of a bank teller are fairly similar across the banking field. At the beginning of each day, a teller may open the bank vault and remove the cash needed for that business day, usually in the company of another teller for security purposes. Each bank teller is responsible for his or her drawer, which means having sufficient deposit tickets and receipts and making sure that all money is accounted for at all times. Financial transactions throughout the day include cashing checks, depositing money, helping people with their bank accounts, and supplying information such as balances or holds with the goal of protecting their customers' interests.

At the end of each day, bank tellers must check their drawers against the official record for the day and account for any discrepancies due to questionable transactions or human error. Once this has been done, the money and other documents are returned to the vault.

Duties and Responsibilities

- **Operating a teller's machine**
- **Verifying deposit amounts and endorsements**
- **Cashing checks after verifying payee's signature and account balance**
- **Receiving mortgage and loan payments**
- **Selling cashier's checks, money orders, and traveler's checks**
- **Maintaining daily cash supply**
- **Receiving local utility payments**
- **Processing transactions from automatic teller machines**

OCCUPATION SPECIALTIES

Vault Teller

Vault Tellers fill orders for currency and coins and count and record cash deposits in the vaults of commercial banks. They also count out specific amounts of money to be shipped to branch banks and businesses, and prepare large denomination bills and food stamps for shipping to the Federal Reserve Bank.

Head Teller

Head Tellers supervise and coordinate the activities of workers who are engaged in receiving and paying out money and keeping records of transactions in banks and financial institutions. They train employees in banking procedures and adjust customer complaints.

WORK ENVIRONMENT

Relevant Skills and Abilities

Communication Skills
- Speaking effectively
- Interacting with customers
- Writing concisely

Interpersonal/Social Skills
- Cooperating with others
- Working as a member of a team

Organization & Management Skills
- Demonstrating leadership
- Following instructions
- Organizing information or materials
- Paying attention to and handling details

Research & Planning Skills
- Using logical reasoning

Technical Skills
- Working with data and/or finances

Physical Environment

Bank tellers work in air-conditioned banks, most often in a quiet, peaceful atmosphere. They are usually on their feet all day, which can cause discomfort; in some cases, a teller may be able to sit on a high stool instead, but this should not be relied upon. Full-time bank tellers work thirty-five to forty hours per week. Some work overtime once a week or more.

Human Environment

Bank tellers should be quick, courteous, and efficient. While bank tellers are not isolated at work, they operate at separate stations, mostly working directly with customers. There may be the opportunity for interaction between tellers depending on work assignments from supervisors.

Technological Environment

Bank tellers use computer programs such as accounting, document management, and office suite software. They may also be required to use teller terminals, check endorsing machines, alarm systems, or different types of printers throughout the day.

EDUCATION, TRAINING, AND ADVANCEMENT

High School/Secondary

A high school diploma is generally required for work as a bank teller. Students should take math classes such as algebra, geometry, calculus, statistics, and business math if available. Courses in the use of computers are helpful as well. Part-time jobs during the high school years can help students gain clerical experience and become familiar with providing good customer service.

Suggested High School Subjects

- Accounting
- Mathematics
- Computer Science
- Economics
- English
- Humanities
- Statistics

Famous First

Inventor John Shepherd-Barron invented the world's first automatic teller machine, now widely known as an ATM, in 1967. Shepherd-Barron was reportedly taking a bath when he invented the idea and also claims that he invented the idea of the Personal Identification Number (PIN), now widely used to access a variety of personal information. Shepherd-Barron's ATM used special checks impregnated with radioactive carbon 14 to activate the machine, though this idea would later be replaced with magnetic strips on ATM cards.

College/Postsecondary

College classes in the business and economics fields can be useful, either before becoming a bank teller or while on the job, and can lead to opportunities to move beyond teller positions. These classes may be taken in a degree program or as continuing education. It is important to note that a college degree is usually not mandatory for becoming a bank teller, though some business may list it as a requirement.

Related College Majors

- Accounting
- Business Accounting
- Finance, General
- Business, General
- Mathematics
- Management, General
- Business Administration

Adult Job Seekers

Adults seeking work can contact banks directly or check Internet job sites and classified ads listing bank teller openings. Although new tellers are trained on the job, those with little clerical or customer service experience may consider taking classes at a bank teller school in order to improve their chances of being hired. Adults without a high school diploma may need to pass the General Education Development (GED) exam.

Professional Certification and Licensure

After six months on the job, bank tellers can take the Certified Bank Teller (CBT) exam, sponsored by the American Institute of Banking (AIB). Those with certification may find more employment options in the banking field. Bank tellers can maintain their certification through continuing education every three years. Some banks will even help pay continuing education tuition.

Additional Requirements

Bank tellers need to be clean and well groomed, with good communication skills. They should be computer literate, and it is useful to be fluent in a second language. Background sales experience is also helpful for tending to customers' account concerns, as many people who invest money may need help determining which financial service would make the most sense for their particular situation.

EARNINGS AND ADVANCEMENT

According to the Bureau of Labor Statistics (BLS), bank tellers earned a median annual wage of $27,260 in 2016, with a range of between $20,000 and $37,000. Most tellers work full time, though there are part time opportunities in the field and approximately 25 percent of tellers worked part time in 2016. Advancing in the field is typically a matter of seniority and time with a specific banking institution. Individuals who wish to advance within an institution can apply for head teller positions when offered by their specific bank.

Metropolitan Areas with the Highest Employment Level in this Occupation

Metropolitan area	Employment	Employment per thousand jobs	Hourly mean wage
New York-Jersey City-White Plains, NY-NJ Metropolitan Division	20,160	3.06	$14.28
Los Angeles-Long Beach-Glendale, CA Metropolitan Division	11,680	2.77	$13.97
Chicago-Naperville-Arlington Heights, IL Metropolitan Division	10,820	2.97	$14.19
Houston-The Woodlands-Sugar Land, TX	10,590	3.61	$13.45
Dallas-Plano-Irving, TX Metropolitan Division	7,940	3.27	$13.04
Atlanta-Sandy Springs-Roswell, GA	6,340	2.48	$15.07
Washington-Arlington-Alexandria, DC-VA-MD-WV Metropolitan Division	6,130	2.46	$16.07
St. Louis, MO-IL	4,770	3.55	$13.19
Anaheim-Santa Ana-Irvine, CA Metropolitan Division	4,720	3.02	$14.39
Miami-Miami Beach-Kendall, FL Metropolitan Division	4,710	4.18	$14.48

Source: Bureau of Labor Statistics

EMPLOYMENT AND OUTLOOK

The bank teller industry is shrinking due to the popularity of online and personal money management. As consumers less often visit bank branches to work directly with tellers and manage their own accounts using online tools, there is less need for bank tellers and therefore little growth in the field. New opportunities for bank tellers arise when banks grow or open new branches. The Bureau of Labor Statistics estimates that the industry with shrink by 8 percent between 2014 and 2024 and this may create increased competition for the few remaining available positions. Bank tellers with advanced degrees may therefore have a distinct advantage in the field.

Related Occupations

- Bookkeeping, Accounting, and Auditing Clerks
- Cashiers
- Customer Service Representatives
- Information Clerks
- Loan Officers
- Receptionists

SELECTED SCHOOLS

Many colleges and universities, especially those with business schools, offer programs in business and finance. The student can also gain initial training at a technical or community college. For some of the more prominent institutions in this field, see the list of selected schools in the "Accountant" and "Finance Manager" chapters of this volume.

MORE INFORMATION

Accreditation Council for AAmerican Bankers Association
1120 Connecticut Avenue NW
Washington, DC 20036
800.226.5377
www.aba.com

Bank Administration Institute
115 South LaSalle Street, Suite 3300
Chicago, IL 60603
312.683.2464
www.bai.org

National Bankers Association
1513 P Street NW
Washington, DC 20005
202.588.5432
www.nationalbankers.org

Micah Issitt & Susan Williams/Editors

Bill & Account Collector

Snapshot

Career Cluster(s): Finance
Interests: Accounting, business, finance, solving problems, communicating with others, customer service
Earnings (Yearly Average): $35,350
Employment & Outlook: Decline in growth expected

OVERVIEW

Sphere of Work

Bill and account collectors locate and contact individuals and businesses in an attempt to collect payments on outstanding loans and/or bills, or in some cases, to arrange for the repossession of merchandise. Entities and individuals who owe money to other people or businesses are called debtors, while creditors are entities or individuals to whom money is owed by debtors. While some merchants, banks, lenders, and other institutions may operate their own collection services, the majority of bill and account collectors are employed by specialist collection agencies. Collection agencies represent creditors

to whom debts are owed. Bill and account collectors usually report to a credit or collections supervisor. Some bill and account collectors may specialize in certain sectors, such as medical or automobile debt collection.

Work Environment

Bill and account collectors usually work in an office environment. In large collection agencies, the office might generally be arranged as a call center, where each collector is equipped with a telephone headset connected to automated systems and a computer workstation.

Depending on the type of collection work being undertaken, some research may be required to locate debtors who have moved from their last known address and do not wish to be found. This involves tracking current contact information listed with other creditors, and even contacting the debtor's family members, friend, and employers (an activity known as "skip tracing").

Profile

Working Conditions: Work Indoors
Physical Strength: Light Work
Education Needs: High school diploma or equivalent
Licensure/Certification: Not Required
Opportunities For Experience: Part-time work
Holland Interest Score*: CSR, ESA

* See Appendix A

Occupation Interest

Bill and account collections may attract individuals who have an interest in finance and credit, and who are skilled or find satisfaction in interacting with people. Strong problem solving and negotiation skills are needed to help debtors formulate and commit to payment arrangements. The ability to convey empathy for the debtor while also assertively pursuing payment on behalf of the creditor can be extremely valuable in this job.

A Day in the Life—Duties and Responsibilities

Much of the bill and account collector's day is spent trying to locate and contact debtors. Although much of this work is performed via telephone, for legal and practical reasons some collectors also write letters requesting payments.

When a collector is able to speak with a debtor, they will inquire about the debtor's financial situation to assess their ability to pay their debt. The collector may be required to explain payment terms and conditions, to instruct people how to make payments, and to counsel debtors on how to seek help if they are experiencing financial hardship. He or she may work with lawyers and arrange for legal action to be undertaken against a debtor.

Bill and account collectors must often speak with people who are under financial, physical, or emotional stress, which often makes those people difficult to communicate with. As such, bill and account collectors should be prepared to encounter a range of emotions, including depression, sadness, anxiety, anger, defensiveness, and hostility. For this reason, bill and account collectors must excel at communicating with tact, diplomacy, and patience while maintaining assertiveness.

Bill and account collectors are likely to receive continual coaching and training and constructive criticism from their supervisors to improve their contact outcomes and negotiation techniques. Some collectors may be required to train and mentor others. In addition to debt collection duties, bill and account collectors will be required to participate in other office duties and activities, such as meetings and training sessions.

A bill and account collector's duties are likely to occur within normal office hours, but longer or more flexible hours may be required at times. Some collection activities are scheduled in the evenings when people are more likely to be at home. Because of this, some part-time opportunities may be available.

Duties and Responsibilities

- **Talking with customers to determine reasons for overdue accounts**
- **Preparing statements**
- **Writing reports and letters**
- **Filing and typing**
- **Locating accurate addresses for incorrect ones given on a credit application**
- **Receiving money or arranging payment at a later date**
- **Recommending legal action**
- **Repossessing merchandise**

OCCUPATION SPECIALTIES

Repossessor

Repossessors go to the homes of debtors to obtain or remove the merchandise and return it to the seller. They may be designated according to the merchandise repossessed, such as automobile repossessor.

WORK ENVIRONMENT

Relevant Skills and Abilities

Communication Skills
- Speaking effectively
- Writing concisely

Interpersonal/Social Skills
- Cooperating with others
- Working with a team
- Interacting with clients

Organization & Management Skills
- Following instructions
- Making decisions
- Managing conflict
- Performing routine work

Research & Planning Skills
- Conducting research
- Locating debtors

Technical Skills
- Handling money
- Traveling

Physical Environment

Office and call center settings predominate. Bill and account collectors in full-time employment generally work for small to large collections departments or dedicated agencies. Some bill and account collectors may work remotely from home using telecommunications technologies provided by their employer.

Human Environment

Bill and account collectors are required to communicate with people from diverse backgrounds over the telephone and in written communications. These communications are primarily about the collection of payments on outstanding debts. This demands a high degree of patience and assertiveness. Bill and account collectors generally perform their duties independently, but they are usually members of a larger team of collectors. Each debt collector must meet specific goals, such as number of calls placed per hour or reaching a certain success rate of calls. Companies typically provide financial incentives to those debt collectors who meet goals.

Technological Environment

Bill and account collectors use an assortment of telecommunications tools, from telephones to the Internet, as well computer software such as word processing, spreadsheet, and database programs. They are likely to use office equipment such as fax machines and photocopiers, since some of their duties include general administrative work.

EDUCATION, TRAINING, AND ADVANCEMENT

High School/Secondary

High school students can best prepare for a career in bill and account collections by taking courses that develop numerical skills, such as accounting, bookkeeping, economics, and applied mathematics. To develop communication skills, students should consider studies in foreign languages. Subjects such as psychology, history, legal studies, and social studies may also assist the student to develop analytical and problem-solving skills. Extracurricular activities, such as debating, may also help to the student to advance their oral communication and negotiation skills. Students can also benefit from part-time customer service work, which will give them valuable experience with how to handle customers in a variety of situations.

Suggested High School Subjects

- Bookkeeping
- English
- Foreign Language
- Typing
- Intro to Computers

- Mathematics
- Psychology

Famous First

Historians have found that the process of borrowing and lending stretches back to before recorded history and there are records to suggest that the occupation of debt collector emerged in the ancient world as well. The first record of debt collection in history comes from ancient Babylon where historians have found that there were rules governing borrowing and lending, meant to protect borrowers but also giving lenders the right to collect on delinquent accounts. It was during this ancient period that debt collectors first gained a negative public perception as unscrupulous lenders sometimes used intimidation and force to collect outstanding debts.

College/Postsecondary

Bill and accounts collection is an occupation which accommodates graduates from a diverse range of disciplines. No specific educational qualifications are required for this profession, although a good understanding of the principles of money management and consumer credit management is likely to be valued by employers.

Related College Majors

- Accounting
- Business Accounting
- Finance, General
- Business, General
- Mathematics
- Intro to Computing

Adult Job Seekers

Since there is no specific postsecondary training required, most debt collectors learn on the job. Work experience in fields such as banking, administration, clerking, policing, legal support, bookkeeping, account management, call center activities, and customer service is likely to be well-regarded by employers. Candidates may also wish to consider self-guided continuing education and professional development courses offered by independent agencies and associations, such as the Association of Credit and Collection Professionals (or ACA International). Candidates may improve their chances of employment success by becoming knowledgeable about the statutes and regulations that govern the collections industry.

Professional Certification and Licensure

Collections agencies must be appropriately licensed, but there are no formal professional certifications or licensing requirements for the bill and accounts collectors who work within these agencies.

Additional Requirements

Bill and account collection should not be confused with financial counselling. While some collectors may provide advice to debtors about debt reduction, this is not their primary function. Bill and account collectors work on behalf of the creditors to whom debtors owe money. Bill and account collectors must be conscientious about following state consumer protection laws, as well as guidelines administered under the Fair Debt Collection Practices Act (FDCPA) by the Federal Trade Commission (FTC).

EARNINGS AND ADVANCEMENT

According to the Bureau of Labor Statistics (BLS), the median annual wage for bill and account collectors was $35,350 in 2016, with a range of between $23,610 and $54,970. There are no specific ways to advance in the industry and advancement may therefore involve gaining seniority within a company and moving into management. Individuals with bachelor's degrees or higher levels of education will be more likely to qualify for leadership positions in a debt collection company.

Metropolitan Areas with the Highest Employment Level in this Occupation

Metropolitan area	Employment	Employment per thousand jobs	Hourly mean wage
Los Angeles-Long Beach-Glendale, CA Metropolitan Division	11,570	2.74	$20.66
Atlanta-Sandy Springs-Roswell, GA	9,670	3.79	$18.35
Dallas-Plano-Irving, TX Metropolitan Division	9,430	3.88	$21.26
Chicago-Naperville-Arlington Heights, IL Metropolitan Division	8,500	2.34	$18.76
New York-Jersey City-White Plains, NY-NJ Metropolitan Division	7,720	1.17	$21.08
Phoenix-Mesa-Scottsdale, AZ	7,500	3.87	$18.40
Houston-The Woodlands-Sugar Land, TX	6,390	2.18	$17.89
Anaheim-Santa Ana-Irvine, CA Metropolitan Division	5,490	3.51	$20.72
Minneapolis-St. Paul-Bloomington, MN-WI	5,030	2.63	$18.13
St. Louis, MO-IL	4,500	3.35	$15.71

Source: Bureau of Labor Statistics

EMPLOYMENT AND OUTLOOK

The Bureau of Labor Statistics estimates that the bill and account collection field with decline by approximately 6 percent between 2014 and 2024 due to consolidation, with larger debt collection companies replacing smaller companies across the nation. In addition, the advent of more accurate software for debt and account management has made is possible for a smaller number of collectors to handle a larger number of clients. Outsourcing to foreign nations where the cost of employment is lower is another reason for the decline in domestic debt collection.

Related Occupations

- Bookkeeping, Accounting, and Auditing Clerks
- Customer Service Representatives
- Financial Clerks
- Information Clerks
- Loan Officers

SELECTED SCHOOLS

Many colleges and universities, especially those with business schools, offer programs in business and finance. The student can also gain initial training at a technical or community college. For some of the more prominent institutions in this field, see the list of selected schools in the "Accountant" and "Finance Manager" chapters of this volume.

MORE INFORMATION

ACA International
P.O. Box 390106
Minneapolis, MN 55439
952.926.6547
aca@acainternational.org
www.acainternational.org

Federal Trade Commission
600 Pennsylvania Avenue NW
Washington, DC 20580
202.326.2222
www.ftc.gov

Kylie Hughes & Micah Issitt/Editors

Bookkeeper & Accounting Clerk

Snapshot

Career Cluster(s): Business, Management & Administration, Finance, Hospitality and Tourism
Interests: Accounting, finance, business management, mathematics, analyzing data
Earnings (Yearly Average): $38,390
Employment & Outlook: Decline expected

OVERVIEW

Sphere of Work

Bookkeepers and accounting clerks are responsible for administering the financial records of a business. This may include the business's payroll, invoices, expenses, receipts, and other accounting matters. While bookkeepers and accounting clerks fulfill an accounting function, they are generally not qualified accountants. A certified accountant must possess graduate qualifications and professional certification, whereas bookkeeping and clerking requires no formal qualifications.

Generally speaking, bookkeepers work for smaller businesses and handle all accounting functions, whereas accounting clerks usually work for larger companies performing particular tasks as members of an accounting team. A bookkeeper may work alone, in which case they usually interact with external financial service providers such as an auditor and tax accountant.

Bookkeeping and account clerking is a general business administration function, but many bookkeepers and accounting clerks will develop specialized industry experience as a result of the employers they work for.

Work Environment

Bookkeepers and accounting clerks can expect to work in office settings. Depending on the size and nature of the organization they serve, they may manage financial record keeping alone or as part of an accounting team. Internally, they will interact with other administrators, business support staff, and management. Externally, they may interact with customers, suppliers, vendors, wholesalers, contractors, and other service providers.

Bookkeepers and accounting clerks engaged in full-time work for an employer usually work a standard forty-hour week, although they may be required to work longer hours during a company's busy periods or to meet financial reporting deadlines. Self-employed bookkeepers may serve a number of small- to medium-sized firms, each on a part-time basis. They may work from home or on-site.

Profile

Working Conditions: Work Indoors
Physical Strength: Light Work
Education Needs: High School Diploma or Equivalent
Licensure/Certification: Not required
Opportunities For Experience: Part-time work, Military service, Internship
Holland Interest Score*: CRE, CSE, CSI, CSR

* See Appendix A

Occupation Interest

Bookkeeping and account clerking attracts people who have an interest in accounting, numbers, and business transactions. This work may also attract candidates who would like to gain entry-level experience in accounting and financial administration before committing to studies in accounting, finance, or economics.

The often meticulous and repetitive nature of bookkeeping demands sustained attention to detail. Bookkeepers and accounting clerks may spend long periods of time sitting at a desk or workstation crunching numbers and doing data entry. Therefore, attention to accuracy and the ability to meet deadlines are important.

These roles also offer potential opportunities to learn a variety of allied skills and specialist business functions, such as purchasing, quoting, budgeting, and payroll.

A Day in the Life—Duties and Responsibilities

Accounting clerks are usually members of an accounting team. As such, they may spend periods of their day working alone and with others. Bookkeepers may work as part of a team or independently. Much of the day will be spent at a desk doing financial data entry into specialized accounting and bookkeeping systems.

Bookkeepers and accounting clerks may also assist with payroll processing, invoicing and receipting, accounts payable and receivable administration, reconciling bank statements, writing checks, making bank deposits, doing petty cash reimbursements, completing forms, and preparing financial reports such as profit and loss statements or balance sheets. They may also assist in processes such as budgeting and purchasing.

They may be expected to attend meetings and to contribute to projects, groups, and committees. General administrative tasks are likely to include opening and sending mail and generating correspondence, memos, and other written communications.

Duties and Responsibilities

- **Calculating employees' wages and preparing payroll checks**
- **Recording data from sales slips, statements, check stubs, and inventory records in general ledgers, journals, or on data processing sheets or computers**
- **Preparing financial reports**
- **Balancing books**

OCCUPATION SPECIALTIES

Audit Clerk

Audit Clerks verify the accuracy of figures, calculations, and postings relating to business transactions recorded by other workers. They examine such information as expense accounts, bank records, and inventory records to verify the accuracy of the recorded data.

WORK ENVIRONMENT

Relevant Skills and Abilities

Communication Skills
- Editing written information
- Expressing thoughts and ideas
- Writing concisely

Interpersonal/Social Skills
- Cooperating with others
- Working with a team
- Working independently

Organization & Management Skills
- Following instructions
- Organizing information or materials
- Paying attention to and handling details
- Performing routine work

Research & Planning Skills
- Using logical reasoning

Physical Environment

Office settings predominate. Bookkeepers and accounting clerks are found in nearly every type of industry and business. Self-employed bookkeepers may work from home.

Human Environment

Bookkeepers and accounting clerks must be able to sustain relatively detailed and repetitive work for long periods of time. They must also be able to work collaboratively with colleagues, supervisors, managers, members of other departments, and external stakeholders such as customers and vendors.

Technical Skills

- Performing mathematical calculations
- Working with data and/or numbers
- Working with computers, digital devices, and other tools

Technological Environment

Bookkeepers and accounting clerks are expected to use specialized accounting software and systems, as well as general office computing programs. Daily operations will also demand the use of standard office technologies, including telephone, e-mail, photocopiers, and the Internet.

EDUCATION, TRAINING, AND ADVANCEMENT

High School/Secondary

High school students can best prepare for a career in bookkeeping or account clerking by taking courses in business mathematics and administration, accounting, bookkeeping, communications, and business law. Foreign languages are also increasingly valued as businesses find themselves operating in global and cross-cultural contexts.

Becoming involved in extracurricular school activities that develop business competencies will also provide students with an opportunity to develop relevant skills and learn from others prior to graduation. This could include, for example, participating in business incubation projects.

Suggested High School Subjects

- Accounting
- Communication
- Bookkeeping
- Business
- Intro to Computers
- English
- Pre-Law

- Mathematics
- Typing

Famous First

Italian mathematician Luca Pacioli, a contemporary of inventor Leonardo da Vinci, has been called the "father of bookkeeping" for his seminal work on the subject of "double-entry bookkeeping" published in 1494. Though the practice of double-entry bookkeeping is believed to have begun in the 1300s, Pacioli's mathematical study of the subject was the beginning of academic bookkeeping and accounting in the western world and established bookkeeping as a field of statistics and mathematics.

College/Postsecondary

There are no formal educational qualifications required for bookkeeping or account clerking, although an associate or bachelor's degree in accounting would be highly regarded by employers. Practical experience and knowledge of accounting and bookkeeping software is usually expected, as is an understanding of accounting methods. A large selection of nondegree programs and short courses are offered in bookkeeping.

Opportunities for career advancement will depend largely on the size and type of organization in which the candidate works and their breadth of experience. Bookkeepers and accounting clerks who wish to become accountants or financial controllers will need to complete a bachelor's degree in accounting, finance, or economics, as well as postgraduate professional certification.

Related College Majors

- Accounting
- Business Accounting
- Finance, General
- Business, General
- Mathematics

Adult Job Seekers

Adults seeking a career transition into or return to bookkeeping or account clerking are advised to refresh their skills and update their resume. A number of agencies and institutions provide self-guided continuing education and professional development modules. Candidates may make themselves more attractive to employers by gaining specialist knowledge in certain fields, such as payroll, taxation preparation, wholesale accounting, credit applications and collections, financial statement analysis, double-entry bookkeeping, and fraud prevention. Experience in relevant specialty areas or industries should be highlighted in the candidate's resume and application letter.

Networking, job searching, and interviewing are critical. Aspiring bookkeepers and accounting clerks may be well-counseled also to consider allied roles, such as payroll clerk and purchasing clerk.

Professional Certification and Licensure

There are no formal professional certifications or licensing requirements for bookkeeping and account clerking. Certification with and/or membership in national or state-based professional associations is optional.

Additional Requirements

Bookkeeping and account clerking balances the demands of data entry and transactional work with potentially more complex and strategic accounting activities. These are roles, therefore, in which there are often opportunities to learn a variety of allied skills and business functions.

EARNINGS AND ADVANCEMENT

Earnings in the bookkeeping and clerk fields depend on experience and expertise, and the average median salary for a bookkeeper or accounting clerk in 2016 was $38,390, with a range of less than $23,000 to over $59,000. Higher salaries are found in professional service companies or in the finance and insurance fields, while those working in retail or wholesale companies earn lower salaries on average. Advancement in the field generally involves applying for positions in larger or more profitable companies or gaining seniority within a company. Most bookkeepers and clerks work full time.

Metropolitan Areas with the Highest Employment Level in this Occupation

Metropolitan area	Employment	Employment per thousand jobs	Hourly mean wage
New York-Jersey City-White Plains, NY-NJ Metropolitan Division	76,210	11.57	$22.13
Los Angeles-Long Beach-Glendale, CA Metropolitan Division	56,300	13.34	$21.77
Chicago-Naperville-Arlington Heights, IL Metropolitan Division	33,130	9.10	$20.04
Houston-The Woodlands-Sugar Land, TX	29,940	10.20	$20.91
Dallas-Plano-Irving, TX Metropolitan Division	29,830	12.28	$20.43
Atlanta-Sandy Springs-Roswell, GA	26,670	10.44	$19.76
Boston-Cambridge-Newton, MA NECTA Division	22,560	12.51	$22.55
Minneapolis-St. Paul-Bloomington, MN-WI	21,590	11.30	$20.53
Nassau County-Suffolk County, NY Metropolitan Division	20,380	15.85	$21.99
Washington-Arlington-Alexandria, DC-VA-MD-WV Metropolitan Division	20,220	8.12	$23.32

Source: Bureau of Labor Statistics

EMPLOYMENT AND OUTLOOK

The Bureau of Labor Statistics estimates that opportunities for bookkeepers and accounting clerks will decline over the decade from 2014 to 2024. In 2014, there were 1.7 million professional bookkeepers and/or accounting clerks in the United States, but that number is expected to drop at least 8 percent to 1.6 million by 2024. The decline of the bookkeeping and clerk industry is primarily due to the advancement of technology. With better and more efficient accounting and computing systems available, there has been a reduced demand for full time bookkeeping services. Position that remain are often on a contract-basis, with companies hiring out bookkeeping activities rather than keeping a professional bookkeeper on staff.

Related Occupations

- Accountants and Auditors
- Budget Analysts
- Cost Estimators
- Medical Records Administrator
- Payroll Clerk
- Cashier
- Bank Teller
- Financial Clerks
- Loan Officers
- Tax Examiners and Collectors, and Revenue Agents

Related Military Occupations

- Service Branch Bookkeeper

Conversation With . . . *KAREN MILLER*

Bookkeeper/Accountant/Office Manager
New Orleans, Louisiana
Bookkeeper, $5^{1/2}$ years

1. **What was your individual career path in terms of education/training, entry-level job, or other significant opportunity?**

   I received a Bachelor's Degree in Business Administration from the University of New Orleans and went straight into a large corporation. I started as an executive assistant and I thought once I got my foot in the door I could work my way up, which I did. I spent the 10 years in human resources as a benefits clerk and then as a compensation analyst. However, I learned over the years that I really wanted to work for a small business because I felt a corporation has so much bureaucracy and I'd lost the personal touch. When I was in HR, I had to do exit interviews whenever there were layoffs and it was just a very cold process. So I joined my family's business in payphones, back before cell phones prospered. I became operations manager and ran every aspect of the business until we sold the business after the proliferation of cell phones. During this time, I found that I really enjoyed accounting, specifically working with numbers and analyzing profits. By this time I was in my 50's and wanted to "slow" down, so I started working part-time as a bookkeeper/accountant. That's what I am currently doing.

2. **What are the most important skills and/or qualities for someone in your profession?**

   The most important skills for a bookkeeper/accountant are definitely organization and attention to detail.

3. **What do you wish you had known going into this profession?**

   I always assumed the position of bookkeeper/accountant was a boring job, but I've learned that I like the process. I like entering numbers, having clean numbers, and having them balance. If I'd know that earlier, I would have gotten into it much sooner, and possibly gone for CPA accreditation.

4. **Are there many job opportunities in your profession? In what specific areas?**

   There are plenty of job opportunities in this profession. A working mother could do something as basic as part-time bookkeeping, or someone could establish a career in accounting and go as high as CFO of a major corporation. The options are very diverse in this field.

5. **How do you see your profession changing in the next five years, what role will technology play in those changes, and what skills will be required?**

   I think this profession will stay in great demand for two reasons: 1) Technology helps streamline the job greatly, but a human brain will always need to analyze the data. 2) Technology enables this job to be done remotely—such as at home—or on a part-time basis, which is a wonderful alternative for many employees.

6. **What do you like most about your job? What do you like least about your job?**

   I enjoy organizing things, and when I analyze reports and make recommendations, and when they result in favorable numbers, it is a source of pride in the job! There's nothing really that I enjoy the least. I don't mind being at a desk for hours, but I'm sure lots of people would not like that aspect of the job.

7. **Can you suggest a valuable "try this" for students considering a career in your profession?**

   When I was in college, I got a part-time job at the university in their financial services department, and that is when I became exposed to the "numbers" world. Even though my degree is not in accounting, my bachelor's degree program in business administration required that I take three different accounting courses. The rest I learned from on-the-job exposure. A real "try this" would be to use the Quickbooks accounting program in your own life for your personal finances, and get a real feel for income/expense analysis. This profession has greatly helped me plan my personal finance spending and retirement planning.

SELECTED SCHOOLS

Many colleges and universities, especially those with business schools, offer programs in finance and business administration. The student can also gain initial training through enrollment at a technical or community college. For advanced positions, a master's of business administration (MBA) with a concentration in finance is usually expected. Below are listed some of the more prominent institutions in this field.

Carnegie Mellon University
Tepper School of Business
500 Forbes Avenue
Pittsburgh, PA 15213
412.268.2268
tepper.cmu.edu

Indiana University, Bloomington
Kelley School of Business
1309 E. 10th Street
Bloomington, IN 47405
812.855.8100
kelley.iu.edu

Massachusetts Institute of Technology
Sloan School of Management
50 Memorial Drive
Cambridge, MA 02142
617.253.2659
mitsloan.mit.edu

New York University
Stern School of Business
665 Broadway, 11th Floor
New York, NY 10012
212.998.4500
www.stern.nyu.edu

University of California, Berkeley
Haas School of Business
S450 Student Services Building #1900
Berkeley, CA 94720
510.642.1421
haas.berkeley.edu

University of Michigan, Ann Arbor
Ross School of Business
701 Tappan Avenue
Ann Arbor, MI 48109
734.763.5796
michiganross.umich.edu

University of North Carolina, Chapel Hill
Kenan-Flagler Business School
Campus Box 3490, McColl Building
Chapel Hill, NC 27599
919.962.3235
www.kenan-flagler.unc.edu

University of Pennsylvania
The Wharton School
1 College Hall
Philadelphia, PA 19104
215.898.6376
www.wharton.upenn.edu

MORE INFORMATION

American Accounting Association
5717 Bessie Drive
Sarasota, FL 34233-2399
941.921.7747
info@aaahq.org
aaahq.org/index.cfm

American Institute of Certified Public Accountants
1211 Avenue of the Americas
New York, NY 10036-8775
212.596.6200
www.aicpa.org

American Institute of Professional Bookkeepers
6001 Montrose Road, Suite 500
Rockville, MD 20852
800.622.0121
www.aipb.org

Kylie Grimshaw Hughes,
updated by Micah Issitt

Budget Analyst

Snapshot

Career Cluster(s): Business, Management & Administration, Finance, Government
Interests: Economics, accounting, planning, finance
Earnings (Yearly Average): $73,840
Employment & Outlook: Slower than Average Growth Expected

OVERVIEW

Sphere of Work

A budget analyst is a professional who helps in the development and implementation of a business or government budget. Budget analysts review revenues and expenses, study the cost-effectiveness of an organization's activities, research alternative courses of action, and make recommendations for a balanced annual budget. Budget analysts play an important role in an organization's financial planning for the fiscal year. For government agencies and non-profit organizations, a budget analyst can help the group efficiently and effectively distribute funds for programs and departments. For

businesses, a budget analyst can help maximize profits and reduce expenditures.

Work Environment

The work of a budget analyst is performed primarily in an office setting. In a government agency, the analyst may work as part of a team, each member of which focuses on selected budget areas. A budget analyst frequently meets with his or her superiors, department heads, managers, and other members of the organization with insight on how the organization's money is being spent. Budget analysts normally work a regular forty-hour workweek, although during periods in which the budget is being finalized, their hours may be extended temporarily. At these peak times, the Work Environment may be somewhat stressful when budget deadlines loom.

Profile

Working Conditions: Work Indoors
Physical Strength: Light Work
Education Needs: Bachelor's Degree
Licensure/Certification: Not Required
Opportunities For Experience: Part-time work, Military service
Holland Interest Score*: CER

* See Appendix A

Occupation Interest

Budget analysts use their extensive research and analysis experience to help an organization map out its future, finding and making recommendations concerning the best financial course of action for the short- and long-term. Budget analysts are able to perceive and grasp the complete and often complex inner workings of a government agency, non-profit organization, or business in such a way that few other employees can.

A Day in the Life—Duties and Responsibilities

A budget analyst is responsible for monitoring the past, present, and short- and long-term fiscal health of an organization or government agency. He or she will research the organization's past financial activities and health, reviewing financial reports and other related documents from previous years. Additionally, the budget analyst analyzes monthly budgets for each department (or applicable business activity) to ensure that the current year's budget requirements are being followed and that no extraordinary costs or revenue drops are occurring. The budget analyst researches current trends in the marketplace, the economy, and between vendors to see if there are any trends that may positively or negatively impact the organization for which he or she works. This research includes reviewing documents and meeting with key officials and personnel for more information.

Using this past and present information, the budget analyst will put together the framework for the organization's annual spending plan for the coming fiscal year. This budget will feature revenues and profits generated from each activity in the previous year, the costs involved for those activities, the amounts the business will invest in employee pay and benefits, and any other information of importance to the organization's financial health. In addition to the annual budget, these analysts may be called upon to create smaller budgets for individual activities and projects and/or short-term programs. In each of these activities, the analyst will be focused on ensuring that investments are cost-effective—in other words, that the program will generate as much revenue as possible while costs and expenses are held to a minimum.

The budget analyst may also be called upon by executives, legislators, and other officials to present their findings and opinions about how best to proceed with financial plans. This component of a budget analyst's job may include testifying at legislative and agency hearings, speaking at board of directors meetings, or meeting directly with executives and high-level officials.

Duties and Responsibilities

- **Providing technical assistance**
- **Preparing budget reports**
- **Analyzing financial data and trends**
- **Examining budget and other financial records**
- **Reporting discrepancies**
- **Conducting seminars on new budgetary guidelines**
- **Training staff or employees**

WORK ENVIRONMENT

Physical Environment

Budget analysts generally work in office environments, either in their own individual offices or sharing open office space with other personnel. These settings will be busy, especially during periods closest to budget deadlines. Many meetings between these analysts and key personnel will take place in conference rooms and similar settings within the main office.

Relevant Skills and Abilities

Communication Skills

- Speaking effectively
- Writing concisely

Interpersonal/Social Skills

- Being able to work independently
- Working as a member of a team

Organization & Management Skills

- Paying attention to and handling details
- Performing routine tasks

Research & Planning Skills

- Analyzing information
- Conducting budget research
- Using logical reasoning

Technical Skills

- Working with data or numbers
- Working with computers, digital tools, and software
- Performing calculations

Human Environment

Although budget analysts often work independently on their individual areas of focus, they typically work in a team dynamic, particularly when putting together large government or corporate budgets. They frequently interact with one another as well as with superiors and department heads during the course of developing an annual or quarterly budget.

Technological Environment

Budget analysts typically need to have knowledge of computers and be proficient in the use of business and accounting software. Such software includes spreadsheet and database programs and word processing systems.

EDUCATION, TRAINING, AND ADVANCEMENT

High School/Secondary

High school students interested in becoming budget analysts should take courses in business and accounting, mathematics, and computer science. They may also benefit from developing better writing and communications skills.

Suggested High School Subjects

- Accounting
- Business
- Business Data Processing
- Business Law
- Business Math
- Computer Science
- English

Famous First

In 2013, controversial former intelligence agent Edward Snowden, working with investigative journalists, published a trove of documents detailing secret U.S. government activities and spending. This was the first time that the government's so-called "black budget," funds requested by the nation's more than 100 civilian intelligence agencies, was made available to the public. According to the documents revealed by Snowden, the U.S. government set aside an annual budget of $52.6 billion for secret intelligence activities, which does not account for funding spent by military agencies on intelligence. Among the spending items highlighted by the media, was $48.6 million set aside to cope with sifting through data gathered through controversial monitoring and surveillance operations.

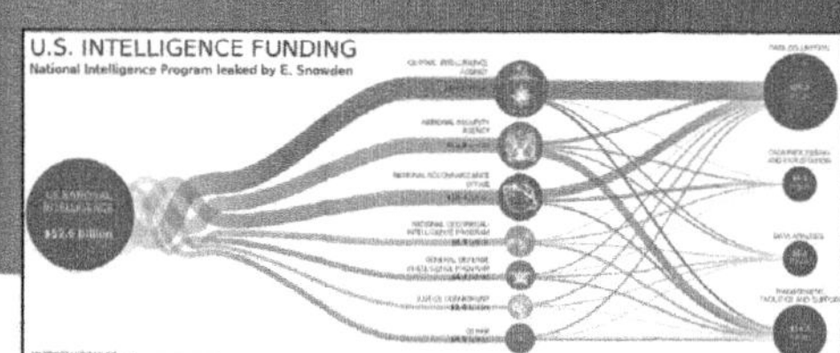

College/Postsecondary

Budget analysts generally choose to complete bachelor's degrees in business, finance, accounting, and management. Because this field is highly competitive, individuals who obtain a master's degree tend to have an edge over other candidates.

Related College Majors

- Accounting
- Business
- Business Administration & Management, General
- Finance, General

Adult Job Seekers

Individuals with an interest in becoming budget analysts will often find positions posted on government jobs websites. They may also consult with state and municipal government websites. Trade associations such as the National Association of State Budget Officers and the American Association for Budget and Program Analysis can also offer opportunities for candidates.

Professional Certification and Licensure

Federal, state, and local government budget analysts are sometimes asked to obtain training and certification through Advancing Government Accountability's Certified Government Financial Manager program. Advancing Government Accountability's program requires that the candidate have two years of financial management experience, a bachelor's degree, and twenty-four credit hours in financial management.

Additional Requirements

Government budget analysts are often called upon to testify on their research findings at legislative and agency hearings. They must therefore have the ability not only to understand the often complex nature of budgets, but be able to effectively communicate with those individuals who are not as well-versed on the subject. Additionally, budget analysts are expected to be critical thinkers; they should be able to carefully analyze a budget area for strengths and weaknesses, explore alternatives, and offer new ideas and approaches to budgets.

EARNINGS AND ADVANCEMENT

As of 2016, the median annual salary for budget analysts was estimated at approximately $73,840, with those at the lowest ten percent of the income spectrum earning less than $48,000 and those at the upper end of the spectrum earning more than $111,000. The highest salaries in the field can be found in professional organizations, followed by positions in the federal government. Individuals working in local and state government offices typically earn lower average salaries. Advancing in the field depends on a professional's specific place of employment. In some cases, analysts may be able to gain seniority within a single company or institution, qualifying for higher pay and perhaps transitioning into managerial roles. In other cases, advancing may mean accruing experience and applying for more lucrative positions with an alternate company or institution.

Metropolitan Areas with the Highest Employment Level in this Occupation

Metropolitan area	Employment	Employment per thousand jobs	Hourly mean wage
Washington-Arlington-Alexandria, DC-VA-MD-WV Metropolitan Division	4,540	1.82	$45.70
New York-Jersey City-White Plains, NY-NJ Metropolitan Division	2,700	0.41	$37.28
Los Angeles-Long Beach-Glendale, CA Metropolitan Division	1,900	0.45	$43.87
Boston-Cambridge-Newton, MA NECTA Division	1,350	0.75	$36.71
Houston-The Woodlands-Sugar Land, TX	1,260	0.43	$44.30
Baltimore-Columbia-Towson, MD	1,260	0.94	$37.90
Dallas-Plano-Irving, TX Metropolitan Division	1,000	0.41	$42.68
Chicago-Naperville-Arlington Heights, IL Metropolitan Division	910	0.25	$36.75
Atlanta-Sandy Springs-Roswell, GA	900	0.35	$35.64
San Antonio-New Braunfels, TX	840	0.86	$35.61

Source: Bureau of Labor Statistics

EMPLOYMENT AND OUTLOOK

The Bureau of Labor Statistics (BLS) estimates that the budged analyst field will grow by just 3 percent between 2014 and 2024, which is slower than the average of 6-7 percent predicted for all U.S. occupations. Cuts to federal and state spending have reduced opportunities for budget analysts specializing in governmental work. Positions will still be available through private companies, banks, and other institutions but, due to limit growth, competition for available positions will likely increase. Individuals with advanced degrees and higher levels of experience will therefore have an advantage on the job market.

Related Occupations

- Accountant
- Actuary
- Auditor
- Cost Estimator
- Energy Auditor
- Financial Analyst
- Personal Financial Advisor

Related Military Occupations

- Finance & Accounting Manager
- Management Analyst

Conversation With . . .
CLAIRE LODGE

Finance Consultant and Former Budget Analyst
Arlington, Virginia
Financial profession, 7 years
Budget analyst, 6 years

1. What was your individual career path in terms of education/training, entry-level job, or other significant opportunity?

I thought I wanted to do International Development/Development Economics. In fact, I have a B.A. in International Studies from American University and an M.S. in Development Economics from the University of Manchester in England. After graduation, however, I fell into budgeting. I had a job interview and the day-to-day tasks seemed analytical—which I liked from my economics background—but with a lot of people interaction. It seemed like a good fit for me.

To be a budget analyst, a specific degree is not needed. I'm good at math, but I think it's more important to be a logical thinker. The main thing, at least at the government agency where I worked, is writing ability and analytical skills. So, even though I went in without a budget-related educational background, I was hired and excelled.

We developed the budget by working within the department, then the Office of Management and Budget that is basically the White House budget wing, and, finally, with Congress.

2. What are the most important skills and/or qualities for someone in your profession?

Writing is really important. You have to be able to effectively write responses to inquiries from government departments and Congress and to write the agency's budget for Congress. But the other aspect of writing, which I think is sometimes taken for granted, is email writing. Tone is important. Sometimes you are giving bad news. So, even if it's only a four sentence email, you have to be willing to reread it three times to make sure nothing can be misconstrued.

Analytical skills are critical. In the federal budgeting world, there is a mantra: Come to me with solutions, not problems. My boss actually wanted three solutions. You can't come up with solutions if you don't know how to analyze the problem.

You need to be organized. If you can't multi-task and keep track of your assignments, you will not excel in this career. Oftentimes, I was working on three different assignments and something time-pressing would come up. I had to know what I could afford to put to the back burner, what couldn't be left behind, and then communicate that to my bosses.

3. What do you wish you had known going into this profession?

I asked a lot of questions in my job interviews so I knew what to expect, at least as much as one can. The interviewee should ask questions to see if the job is a good fit.

4. Are there many job opportunities in your profession? In what specific areas?

Yes. The federal government needs budget analysts, as do state and local governments.

5. How do you see your profession changing in the next five years, what role will technology play in those changes, and what skills will be required?

I think that there will always be budget analysts in the public sector. Technology has made their jobs easier. I have no idea how budget analysts were able to do what they do before computers, and really before Excel.

6. What do you like most about your job? What do you like least about your job?

Being a budget analyst is not a routine job. I might do something different every day. Also, there may be crunch times, especially in public sector budgeting where you can plan on working later than normal at times like the end of a fiscal year. The lack of daily routine was a negative only because I couldn't make plans for the same time every day.

7. Can you suggest a valuable "try this" for students considering a career in your profession?

A lot of budget analysts learn on the job. The closest "try this" would be budgeting in your own life, but that leaves out some of the big parts of the federal budgeting process such as questions from Congress, submitting your budget for approval, and working with different entities.

SELECTED SCHOOLS

Many colleges and universities, especially those with business schools, offer programs in business and finance. The student can also gain initial training at a technical or community college. For some of the more prominent institutions in this field, see the list of selected schools in the "Accountant" and "Finance Manager" chapters of this volume.

MORE INFORMATION

Advancing Government Accountability
2208 Mount Vernon Avenue
Alexandria, VA 22301
703.684.6931
www.agacgfm.org

American Association for Budget and Program Analysis
P.O. Box 1157
Falls Church, VA 22041
703-941-4300
aabpa@aabpa.org
www.aabpa.org

Government Finance Officers Association
203 N. LaSalle Street, Suite 2700
Chicago, IL 60601-1210
312.977.9700
www.gfoa.org

National Association of State Budget Officers
444 N. Capitol Street NW, Suite 642
Washington, DC 20001
202.624.5382
www.nasbo.org

Michael Auerbach,
updated by Micah Issitt

Cost Estimator

Snapshot

Career Cluster(s): Financial Services, Engineering, Construction, Financial analysis
Interests: Working with people, management, building science, mathematics, finance
Earnings (Yearly Average): $61,790
Employment & Outlook: Faster Than Average Growth Expected

OVERVIEW

Sphere of Work

Cost estimators research and analyze data to determine the cost of completing a variety of corporate projects, such as expansion, building new facilities, manufacturing a product, or corporate mergers and acquisitions. Many professional cost estimators specialize in a specific industry, such as construction or engineering, while others may work on a variety of different types of projects. In general, cost estimators prepare for their jobs by studying accounting, finance, and mathematics, but estimators also need experience in the specific field in which they work. Construction cost estimators, therefore, need

to have specific experience in the construction field to inform their estimates and so may work in construction before transitioning to cost estimation as a career.

Work Environment

Cost estimators spend time in office environments where they analyze budget information, research and compare cost information, and work with software to complete calculations and prepare estimates for clients. The specific environment for a professional cost estimator may depend on the industry in which the professional works. Estimators often visit specific sites where a client is considering a future project and may also travel to visit vendors when attempting to obtain prices for materials or other services needed for a potential project.

Profile

Working Conditions: Work Indoors
Physical Strength: Light Work
Education Needs: Bachelor's Degree, Master's Degree
Licensure/Certification: Not Required
Opportunities For Experience: Part-time work, Military service
Holland Interest Score*: CE

* See Appendix A

Occupation Interest

Those seeking to become cost estimators should have strong interest in their chosen field, such as non-profit, construction, engineering, or manufacturing, as well as interest in management, accounting, and research. Cost estimators also work directly with clients and potential vendors and should be comfortable with frequent interaction and collaboration. While some individuals may seek to become cost estimators directly, many professionals in the field first gain work experience in a specific field, such as engineering, or plumbing, before transitioning to become a cost estimator in their field.

A Day in the Life—Duties and Responsibilities

Each new project for a cost estimator begins by meeting with clients to discuss the project. For instance, in the construction industry, cost estimators must first meet with their clients to review blueprints and other plans before they can begin to create an official estimate. Cost estimators may spend time meeting with engineers, architects, and other logistics and construction professionals working on a project and may also spend time contacting vendors to obtain the cost of materials.

Research is a major part of a cost estimator's job and cost estimators must be familiar with resources for determining and calculating materials costs, labor, insurance, and other factors involved in a project.

After obtaining sufficient data, cost estimators typically use computer programs, such as accounting and spreadsheet software, to calculate costs and prepare estimates for their clients. In many cases, cost estimators may need to revisit and revise their estimates with further input from their client and creating a cost estimate may therefore involve multiple iterations. Once a project is underway, cost estimators may act as consultants and may be asked to meet with clients to recommend ways to reduce costs or to adjust their estimates to account for new developments.

Duties and Responsibilities

- **Referring to building codes and zoning laws**
- **Working with engineers, architects, and project managers**
- **Developing and explaining cost estimates to clients**
- **Consulting with clients**
- **Researching costs of materials, labor, and other aspects of specific projects**
- **Meeting with vendors and other professionals**
- **Keeping detailed records of estimates and actual costs of current and past projects**

OCCUPATION SPECIALTIES

Building Estimator

Building estimators specialize in estimating the costs of construction or architectural projects and need detailed knowledge of construction practices and techniques as well as knowledge of local codes, laws, and regulations that might affect the cost of various projects. Building estimators may have a background in accounting or mathematics or may come into the field from engineering or construction management.

Cost Engineer

Cost engineers are engineers who specialize in accounting and mathematics and specialize in estimating the profitability of engineering projects. Unlike other cost estimators, cost engineers are more likely to remain involved in a project after it begins and cost estimators and cost engineers may work together on the same projects.

Quantity Surveyor

A quantity surveyor is a financial professional who work in construction and specializes in budgeting, contracts, procurement and sourcing, and economic management. Quantity surveyors may create cost estimates as part of their job, but often also serve as project manager for various construction projects.

Manufacturing Cost Estimator

A manufacturing cost estimator specializes in the manufacturing industry and is called upon to estimate the costs of manufacturing processes, including labor and materials costs. Manufacturing cost estimators might be consulted to help calculate the cost of a new product or to evaluate the cost of an existing project and to recommend changes to the process or materials that could reduce costs.

WORK ENVIRONMENT

Physical Environment

Cost estimators frequently visit building or manufacturing sites as part of their job and may also travel to meet with prospective or current clients. Much of a cost estimator's daily work can be completed in an office environment working with digital tools and software to perform the calculations needed for their work. Cost estimators may work alongside other cost estimators or may work out of an independent office or out of their own home.

Relevant Skills and Abilities

Communication Skills

- Speaking with clients and other professionals
- Writing clear reports, letters, and emails

Interpersonal/Social Skills

- Being able to work with a team
- Working independently

Organization & Management Skills

- Meeting deadlines
- Managing employees
- Creating and maintaining detailed records

Research & Planning Skills

- Researching costs

Technical Skills

- Performing complex calculations
- Using digital software and other tools

Human Environment

Cost estimation is frequently collaborative and cost estimators typically work closely with project managers, surveyors, architects, engineers, and other individuals involved in funding and managing projects. In many cases, the calculations completed by cost estimators are complex and estimators are often called upon to explain their estimates and the estimate process to their clients and to consult with clients to provide options on a specific project. In some cases, cost estimators may be employed directly by a design, construction, or manufacturing company, while, in other cases, cost estimators may work for a cost estimation firm or may work independently.

Technological Environment

Digital technology is essential to the cost estimation field and cost estimators must be familiar with a variety of software used to perform calculations and to create estimates for their clients. Typically, cost estimators use accounting software like Intuit QuickBooks or Sage 50 Accounting Software. There are also programs specifically designed for creating financial estimates, such as IBM Costimator, used by some professionals in the field. In addition, cost estimators frequently use mobile digital tools like smartphones and tablets to keep track of data and to communicate with clients and other professionals.

EDUCATION, TRAINING, AND ADVANCEMENT

High School/Secondary

High school students interested in a career as cost estimators should focus on preparing for a bachelor's degree program in a related field, such as accounting, mathematics, or engineering. Many cost estimators transition to cost estimation from another field. For instance, cost estimators who work in electrical repair and plumbing, often work as electricians or plumbers, before becoming cost estimators. In general, high school students interested in cost estimation should study mathematics, engineering, business, and accounting.

Suggested High School Subjects

- Algebra
- Applied Math
- Applied Physics
- Engineering
- College Preparatory
- Computer Science
- Drafting
- English

- Geometry
- Graphic Arts
- Industrial Arts
- Business
- Calculus

Famous First

The American Association of Cost Engineering, formerly called the Association for the Advancement of Cost Engineering, was the first professional organization for cost estimation specialists in the United States and was formed in 1956 by a group of cost engineering experts at the University of New Hampshire. The organization provides education programs in a variety of cost engineering fields and supports technical research on cost estimation techniques and emerging digital tools.

College/Postsecondary

In general, applicants with a college degree will have an advantage in the field and prospective cost estimators are therefore advised to pursue higher education. Many cost estimators in the construction field, for instance, may first obtain degrees in engineering, building management, urban planning, or other related fields. Individuals may also prepare for a career in cost estimation by obtaining a degree in mathematics or accounting before transitioning to cost estimation.

Related College Majors

- Architecture
- Engineering, General
- Building Science
- Urban Planning
- Construction Management
- Manufacturing Management
- Industrial Design
- Business Accounting
- Finance, General
- Business, General

Adult Job Seekers

Individuals with a bachelor's degree and sufficient experience in mathematics and financial management can apply directly for jobs in cost estimation. In some cases, professional firms may provide training to applicants in the field who can learn on the job. Individuals with experience in a field, who wish to shift to cost estimation, can consider pursuing education in mathematics, accounting, or finance to supplement their existing experience and to prepare for a job in cost estimation.

Professional Certification and Licensure

There are no state or local requirements for cost estimators to obtain certification, but there are organizations, like the American society of Professional Estimators, that offer training certification programs for prospective cost estimators. Obtaining a certificate from a professional association may provide an advantage for individuals seeking employment and most certification programs are designed for professionals with at least 2 years of experience in the field. Some professional estimation companies may require prospective employees to complete training and certification programs before being hired.

Additional Requirements

Cost estimators blend practical skills in their fields, such as construction or manufacturing, with mathematics and accounting skills. Cost estimators must be fluent in digital accounting, spreadsheet, and presentation software and utilize a variety of digital tools in their work. Cost estimators should therefore be comfortable working with computers, mobile digital tools, and various software systems. For instance, individuals seeking to work as cost estimators in the construction industry may benefit from experience working with building information modeling (BIM) and smart building software systems.

Fun Fact

Figuring out how much a project is going to cost is no simple feat. Take the time in 1924 a Zane Grey novel was made into a silent film: Fourteen bison were brought in to shoot a scene on California's Catalina Island: the movie ran over budget: and the bison were left on the island…which now boasts a herd of 150.

Source: http://www.thestacygroup.com/blog/fun-fact/

EARNINGS AND ADVANCEMENT

Salaries vary in the cost estimate industry depending on the specific field and level of experience. The Bureau of Labor Statistics (BLS) estimated the media annual wage for the industry at $61,790 in May of 2016, with those at the lowest ten percent earning less than $35,000, while those at the upper 10 percent had the potential to earn over $100,000 annually. Earning potential may be higher for those working in construction and for those who have earned bachelor's degrees or higher levels of education. On an hourly scale, cost estimators earned an average of $29.71 per hour, with those at the lowest 10 percent earning around $17.00 per hour, while those at the upper 10 percent earned over $49.00 per hour.

Metropolitan Areas with the Highest Employment Level in this Occupation

Metropolitan area	Employment	Employment per thousand jobs	Hourly mean wage
New York-Jersey City-White Plains, NY-NJ Metropolitan Division	6,280	0.95	$38.01
Houston-The Woodlands-Sugar Land, TX	5,310	1.81	$35.99
Los Angeles-Long Beach-Glendale, CA Metropolitan Division	5,070	1.20	$31.45
Washington-Arlington-Alexandria, DC-VA-MD-WV Metropolitan Division	5,060	2.03	$35.89
Chicago-Naperville-Arlington Heights, IL Metropolitan Division	4,210	1.16	$34.20
Phoenix-Mesa-Scottsdale, AZ	4,060	2.10	$31.57
Atlanta-Sandy Springs-Roswell, GA	3,850	1.51	$30.60
Dallas-Plano-Irving, TX Metropolitan Division	3,490	1.44	$32.78
Seattle-Bellevue-Everett, WA Metropolitan Division	3,320	2.09	$37.65
Anaheim-Santa Ana-Irvine, CA Metropolitan Division	3,100	1.98	$36.57

Source: Bureau of Labor Statistics

EMPLOYMENT AND OUTLOOK

As of 2016, there were approximately 214,610 individuals working as professional cost estimators in the United States and the field was growing at an average rate of 9 percent annually, constituting higher than average growth compared to the 6-7 percent estimated for all U.S. occupations. Demand for cost estimators increases both as industries grow and during periods of financial constraint when it becomes more essential for companies to accurately estimate their budgets and costs for projects. Prospects for employment in specific industries, such as green technology, manufacturing, and construction, vary according to the overall state of the field. If the construction industry thrives, therefore, there will be increased demand for construction industry estimators.

Related Occupations

- Accountants
- Construction Managers
- Engineers
- Financial Analysts
- Budget Specialists
- Financial Managers
- Appraisers, Examiners, and Investigators

Related Military Occupations

- Military Engineer
- Military Cost Estimator

Conversation With . . .
LYNDA SCHNEIDER

Cost Analyst, EVM
Government Contractor, Maryland
Cost analysis field, 12 years

1. What was your individual career path in terms of education/training, entry-level job, or other significant opportunity?

I worked full-time in a bank after graduating from high school and took night classes at a community college, but I didn't get my degree because life happens: I got married and had a child. I had always wanted to go back and finish, and eventually reached a point where I couldn't move on professionally without a degree. When my son started high school, I went back to college and earned an associate degree in accounting and a bachelor's in business administration from Strayer University in Maryland. Going back to school was very good for my career.

I spent the first 20 years of my career in banking and accounting. I moved into project controls because the company I was working for consolidated accounting departments and moved my responsibilities to another state. A friend at the company called to ask if I was interested in an opening she had in the project controls department. I told her I had never done that and she said, "That's OK; you have enough experience and I can train you." Once I got into it, I really liked it.

I went on to get my certification in Earned Value Management (EVM) through the professional organization AACE International. It's a respected credential that requires study and experience, and is a certification required by many companies. It's also a requirement on many government contracts. Having that experience and Earned Value Professional (EVP) certification is a plus.

Initially I worked for a defense contractor who worked on military jets. I had the opportunity to work with people on the technical side because in project controls you talk to the people who are building these projects. It's interesting. I'm currently working on a construction project, and I went to see the building, review the project, and meet with the guys who work on it. This work gives you the opportunity to meet and talk with people who are not just crunching numbers.

We have to put out a report every month to the government that reviews project costs and schedules. For instance, I'll look at a delayed activity and ask: What's preventing you from doing this particular piece of the job? Maybe it rained and they couldn't work, or perhaps they couldn't get a particular material delivered. And I'll talk with them about costs: It looks like you're overspending in a particular area.

Why? Maybe rain delayed their schedule and they had to work overtime. I write up specific reports, called Cost Performance Reports (CPR), that must be delivered monthly to the customer.

I've worked for companies that build airplanes and satellites, and another that did research and development for vaccines. It doesn't matter what the project is, there's going to be a cost and a schedule involved.

2. What are the most important skills and/or qualities for someone in your profession?

Attention to detail, being organized and being a good communicator. I work in a fast-paced environment on numerous projects under different program managers and teams. It is essential to stay on top of the workload and keep deadlines in front of you. You must also be a team player.

3. What do you wish you had known going into this profession?

That you don't have to be a math wiz to do the job. Communication, and sometimes dealing with difficult people, are part of the job.

4. Are there many job opportunities in your profession? In what specific areas?

I can best speak to the Washington, D.C., area, where there is a lot of opportunity with government contractors.

5. How do you see your profession changing in the next five years, what role will technology play in those changes, and what skills will be required?

Specific software is used for Earned Value Management, mostly through one source but more companies are starting to offer alternatives. It will be interesting to see where the industry expands in this area.

6. What do you enjoy most about your job? What do you enjoy least about your job?

I enjoy the opportunity to interact with colleagues from many different departments and the variety of programs I'm exposed to. I least enjoy co-workers who wait until the last minute on really hectic and stressful days of pending contractual deadlines.

7. Can you suggest a valuable "try this" for students considering a career in your profession?

Look for an internship at a local company in any industry that interests you. You can learn cost analysis skills at any company that has an accounting office.

SELECTED SCHOOLS

Many colleges and universities, especially those with business schools, offer programs in business and finance. The student can also gain initial training at a technical or community college. For some of the more prominent institutions in this field, see the list of selected schools in the "Accountant" and "Finance Manager" chapters of this volume.

MORE INFORMATION

AACE International
1265 Suncrest Towne Centre Dr.
Morgantown, WV 26505
304-296-8444
web.aacei.org

American Society of Professional Estimators
2525 Perimeter Place Drive
Nashville, TN 37214
615-316-9200
www.aspenational.org

Association for the Advancement of Cost Estimating International
1265 Suncrest Towne Centre Dr.
Morgantown, WV 26505
304-296-8444
web.aacei.org

International Cost Estimating and Analysis Association
4115 Annandale Road, Suite 306
Annandale, VA 22003
www.iceaaonline.com

Micah Issitt/Editor

Credit & Loan Officer

Snapshot

Career Cluster(s): Finance, Agriculture, Food & Natural Resources, Banking
Interests: Financial trends, risk assessment, data analysis, organizing information, mathematics, sales, customer service
Earnings (Yearly Average): $38,080
Employment & Outlook: Average Growth Expected

OVERVIEW

Sphere of Work

Loan clerks, credit authorizers, and loan officers are responsible for the credit and loan activities of financial institutions. Loan clerks and credit authorizers interact directly with loan and credit applicants and interview them about their personal and financial histories. Loan officers also review and process loan and credit applications, participate in credit and loan fraud investigations, send out loan and credit approval or denial notices, respond to inquiries from loan and credit applicants, and notify customers of delinquent loans or credit accounts. They generally work under the direct supervision of credit

and loan managers, who review and authorize all final loan and credit decisions.

Work Environment

Loan clerks and credit authorizers generally work in offices and call centers at commercial banks, credit card companies, mortgage companies, savings and loan associations, and credit unions. Loan officers frequently travel from their offices at financial institutions to client homes or businesses to negotiate loan agreements. Most loan clerks, credit authorizers, and loan officers work regular forty-hour weeks, although overtime may be required during periods of peak business.

Profile

Working Conditions: Work Indoors
Physical Strength: Light Work
Education Needs: Bachelor's Degree
Licensure/Certification: Required
Opportunities For Experience: Part-time work
Holland Interest Score*: CES, CSE

* See Appendix A

Occupation Interest

Individuals attracted to the loan and credit field tend to be organized and detail-oriented people who find satisfaction in tracking financial trends and assessing risk. Those who excel in loan and credit jobs demonstrate financial and mathematical acumen, focus, responsibility, and effective time management. Loan clerks, credit authorizers, and loan officers should be knowledgeable about finance, exhibit good judgment, and have a background in customer service. Loan officers who are persuasive and have experience in sales may enjoy greater success in this field as they frequently receive a commission or bonus for the loans they close.

A Day in the Life—Duties and Responsibilities

Loan clerks perform the background research necessary to determine an applicant's eligibility for credit or a loan. They first interview loan and credit applicants about their financial history, including contact information, employer, education, debts, income, and assets. They also verify the identity of any loan co-signers, request credit ratings from credit bureaus and associations, and confirm the value of collateral (property used to ensure repayment of a loan). Once applications have been reviewed, loan clerks may be asked to send out loan and credit approval or denial notices. When a loan application is approved, the loan clerk must prepare and gather documents for the loan closing, record all related transactions, and provide repayment information to the client.

Loan officers perform more sophisticated and complex tasks in the loan application process. Depending on the size and type of the organization, they may personally interview clients and thoroughly investigate their credit histories, as a loan clerk does. Loan officers are additionally responsible for educating loan applicants about various loan and credit options, comparing credit histories of prospective borrowers, analyzing client financial statements, and reviewing and processing loan and credit applications. Under the guidance of the credit manager and institutional loan policies, the loan officer decides whether loans or credit should be extended to applicants. Once applications have been reviewed, loan officers may notify clients of loan and credit approval or denial. When a loan is approved, the loan officer calculates repayment schedules, negotiates terms, and finalizes loan transactions. Loan officers may also investigate credit fraud, prepare credit and loan history reports, create loan request summary reports for managers, and report delinquent accounts to credit agencies. Some specialize in personal or commercial loans or mortgages.

Credit authorizers determine credit eligibility and perform credit-related tasks. They receive notification of charges from vendors and keep records of customer credit and loan payments. Using this information and predefined guidelines, they determine whether a client is eligible for credit. As needed, they also prepare credit card charge plates for business and send charge statements and overdue notices to clients.

Duties and Responsibilities

- **Conducting interviews**
- **Researching credit history and other data**
- **Completing reports**
- **Researching financial data**

OCCUPATION SPECIALTIES

Credit Reference Clerk

Credit Reference Clerks verify information of applicants by contacting previous employers, credit reporting agencies and credit references.

Credit Investigator

Investigators do extensive investigations on the credit worthiness of individuals. Investigators typically go beyond the normal requirements by interviewing character witnesses, contacting neighbors of applicants, speaking with co-workers, and gathering health, social, moral and legal information.

Credit Authorizer

Credit Authorizers authorize credit purchases against a credit card holder's payment history or credit line.

Loan Interviewer

Loan interviewers or processors conduct interviews with potential clients during a loan approval process and also may assist applicants in filling out and filing forms.

WORK ENVIRONMENT

Physical Environment

Loan clerks and credit authorizers generally work in office environments in commercial banks, credit card companies, mortgage companies, savings and loan associations, and credit unions. The work of a loan clerk or credit authorizer requires sitting at a desk and using computers for long periods each day. Loan officers are employed in similar office settings but often travel locally to work with clients.

Relevant Skills and Abilities

Communication Skills
- Speaking effectively
- Writing concisely
- Writing reports
- Listening attentively

Interpersonal/Social Skills
- Being able to work independently
- Working as a member of a team
- Conducting interviews
- Meeting new people

Organization & Management Skills
- Paying attention to and handling details
- Performing routine tasks

Research & Planning Skills
- Analyzing information
- Conducting investigations

Technical Skills
- Working with data or numbers
- Working with computers, digital tools, and software

Human Environment

Loan clerks, credit authorizers, and loan officers interact with loan applicants, business owners, colleagues, and supervisors. They should be comfortable discussing financial data with clients, and must also be able to inform and instruct clients about loan procedures and options.

Technological Environment

Loan clerks and credit authorizers use computers, telephones, and Internet tools for communication. Financial analysis software and spreadsheets are other basic tools they use to complete their work. Loan officers may use scanners, PDAs, and accounting and management software in addition to basic office equipment.

EDUCATION, TRAINING, AND ADVANCEMENT

High School/Secondary

High school students interested in pursuing a career as a loan clerk, credit authorizer, or loan officer should prepare themselves by building good study habits and by developing strong mathematical skills. High school courses in bookkeeping and mathematics will provide a solid foundation for work as a credit and loan officer or college-level study in the field. High school students interested in this career path may benefit from seeking internships or part-time work with financial organizations that will familiarize them with credit procedures. Those who wish to become loan clerks or credit authorizers may find employment directly after high school, while those who intend to become loan officers should apply to college or university programs.

Suggested High School Subjects

- Accounting
- Applied Communication
- Business
- Business & Computer Technology
- Business Data Processing
- Business Law
- English
- Keyboarding
- Mathematics

Famous First

In the medieval era, most Christian churches prohibited charging interest on loans, a process known as "usury." Over the years, charging interest became a standard, legal, and accepted part of the lending process and the term usury changed. In the twenty-first century, usury refers to making unethical or immoral loans and laws in many nations prohibit the ways in which lending institutions are allowed to calculate and charge interest to protect consumer interest. In 2017, one of the most controversial debates in the lending industry involves the legality of "payday loans," which are short-term, high interest loans generally marketed towards individuals in significant financial hardship. Around the world, legislators and loan companies are debating whether the payday loan industry constitutes a form of usury within the overall lending industry.

College/Postsecondary

Postsecondary students interested in becoming loan clerks and credit authorizers should consider completing finance and credit analysis training at vocational schools or community colleges. Those who intend to become loan officers should pursue a bachelor's degree in economics, mathematics, accounting, or business. Classes in computer science, political science, and ethics may also prove useful in their future work. Postsecondary students can gain work experience and a competitive advantage in future job searches by securing internships or part-time employment with local businesses or financial organizations.

Related College Majors

- Accounting
- Business Accounting
- Finance, General
- Business, General
- Mathematics

Adult Job Seekers

Adults seeking credit and loan officer jobs have generally earned at least a high school diploma. Prospective loan officers usually have a bachelor's degree and, in some cases, a master's of business administration (MBA). Most employers also provide some job training. Adult job seekers may benefit from joining professional finance or accounting associations as a means of networking. Professional finance associations, such as the Risk Management Association, the Financial Managers Society, and the National Association of Credit Management, maintain job lists advertising open positions.

Professional Certification and Licensure

Certification and licensure is not legally required for loan clerks and credit authorizers but may be required as a condition of employment or promotion. Mortgage loan officers must obtain licensure, a process that involves education, testing, background checks, and continuing education for renewal. Options for voluntary certification in the loan and credit fields include the Risk Management Association's Credit Risk Certified (CRC) designation and the National Association of Credit Management's Certified Credit Executive (CCE), Credit

Business Fellow (CBF), and Credit Business Associate (CBA) designations. These voluntary certifications have education, experience, testing, recertification, and continuing education requirements.

Additional Requirements

Successful loan clerks and credit authorizers take the time to become knowledgeable about the profession's requirements, responsibilities, and opportunities. Integrity and professional ethics are essential qualities in loan clerks, credit authorizers, and loan officers since they have access to confidential financial information. Membership in professional finance associations can help create a sense of professional community among all loan clerks, credit authorizers, and loan officers. Loan officers must follow trends and developments in the field so they can best meet the loan and credit needs of their clients.

EARNINGS AND ADVANCEMENT

As of May 2016, the median annual wage for loan clerks was 38,630, while the median wage for credit authorizers, clerks, and checkers was closer to 36,930. Wages vary widely in the field, with those at the lowest end of the spectrum earning less than $25,000 while those at the upper end can earn more than $58,000. The path for advancement for a loan or credit clerk, investigator, authorizer, or other financial clerk depends on the company that an individual works for. In larger companies, clerks may earn higher wages with seniority or by transitioning into a managerial role. Otherwise, those seeking higher pay might need to accrue experience and then apply for higher paying positions in another company or institution.

Metropolitan Areas with the Highest Employment Level in this Occupation

Metropolitan area	Employment	Employment per thousand jobs	Hourly mean wage
Dallas-Plano-Irving, TX Metropolitan Division	10,630	4.37	$23.41
Phoenix-Mesa-Scottsdale, AZ	7,890	4.08	$20.05
Anaheim-Santa Ana-Irvine, CA Metropolitan Division	6,480	4.14	$20.66
Chicago-Naperville-Arlington Heights, IL Metropolitan Division	5,630	1.55	$21.83
New York-Jersey City-White Plains, NY-NJ Metropolitan Division	4,770	0.72	$20.42
Los Angeles-Long Beach-Glendale, CA Metropolitan Division	4,420	1.05	$22.08
Houston-The Woodlands-Sugar Land, TX	4,330	1.47	$24.74
Washington-Arlington-Alexandria, DC-VA-MD-WV Metropolitan Division	3,880	1.56	$20.53
Pittsburgh, PA	3,840	3.39	$17.94
Jacksonville, FL	3,570	5.54	$20.75

Source: Bureau of Labor Statistics

EMPLOYMENT AND OUTLOOK

The Bureau of Labor Statistics (BLS) estimates that the financial clerk field with grow by approximately 6 percent between 2014 and 2024, constituting average growth in comparison to the 6-7 percent estimated for all occupations in the U.S. However, the loan clerk field is expected to grow at a faster than average rate over the same period, with an estimated 9 percent growth due to changing lending procedures increasing the need for skilled workers in the field. However, the proliferation of online loan and credit systems, with automated checking features, will likely reduce the demand for new workers in the future and has already limited the growth of the credit authorizer, checker, and clerk field. Those with managerial and more specialized experience will likely have an advantage when applying for remaining positions in the field.

Related Occupations

- Bill and Account Collector
- Credit Manager
- Banking Clerk

Conversation With . . .
PAUL WALSH

Mortgage Officer
Mortgage Financial, Inc.
Lending profession, 24 years

1. What was your individual career path in terms of education/training, entry-level job, or other significant opportunity?

I was actually a real estate broker for five years before going into lending. The experience of buying my first home made me decide to switch careers. (I actually, in a previous life, worked in high tech). When I bought my house, my financing experience was horrendous. After I closed on the house, I kept thinking about this for two or three years. Finally, I just made the change and left the world of high tech. So, it was both the personal experience I had and the opportunity I saw that led me to get into real estate and then lending. Also, I had my bachelor's degree and to move to the next level in the world of high tech would have required a master's degree. I had a family and it just wasn't in me to pursue a master's. There's really no training required of loan officers, which has to change, it just has to. But we are licensed and required to pass two exams.

2. What are the most important skills and/or qualities for someone in your profession?

Truly, right now it's understanding exactly what the consumer wants or needs and, to some extent, protecting them from themselves. If someone wants to buy a $450,000 house and just cannot afford it, part of the job is reeling them in with realistic expectations. You have to be able to place people in the right loan program. I may get compensated more if I put someone in an FHA loan versus a Fannie Mae, but is that the best thing for them? Or the loan with the lowest interest rate may not be the least expensive. So you just really have to know what you're doing—that sounds ridiculous, but you'd be amazed how many people in this field don't know what they're doing, even with a license. You have to have good ethics. You will be required to have a criminal background check, be fingerprinted by the FBI, and submit a credit report.

3. **What do you wish you had known going into this profession?**

I wish I had known the importance of having a team and working as a team. No one person can really do the entire loan process alone. For instance, I no longer do reverse mortgages. I now know my skill set. I wish I had known that I can't be all things to all people. Right from the start, I would have chosen a specialty and stuck to it.

4. **Are there many job opportunities in your profession? In what specific areas?**

Being a mortgage officer is really a sales job. You're selling a product, and those skills will always be in demand. But the future of this business is in the world of mortgage compliance, because the government is taking mortgage compliance very, very seriously. If sales isn't your thing, I would suggest compliance.

5. **How do you see your profession changing in the next five years, what role will technology play in those changes, and what skills will be required?**

Technology is huge. I'm very old school and like to meet person to person. I'm a pen and paper guy. But many mortgage officers or loan officers and their clients nowadays never meet. They rarely even talk. You just go online and submit everything electronically. e-Mortgages and e-financing is really where this business is going. I consider that unfortunate.

6. **What do you like most about your job? What do you like least about your job?**

For me, it's always the people, and first-time homebuyers in particular. What I enjoy most is the personal interaction, and basically solving problems for people. The economy hasn't been great. If someone has excessive credit card debt or other financial problems if they have a mortgage and a home — you can use that equity to structure things and really come up with a solution to help people out of unfortunate situations.

What I enjoy least is dealing with all the regulations, though I agree wholeheartedly with it. The compliance part is very, very difficult, and the inconsistencies from lender to lender and the multitude of product guidelines or "overlays" gets complicated.

7. **Can you suggest a valuable "try this" for students considering a career in your profession?**

Team up with someone who does what I do and work with them for a summer. You'll learn things like how to look at assets and recognize risk profiles. Even with an inside position, where you're sending out verification of employment forms, you'll learn the ropes and learn industry guidelines. Over the course of a summer, someone could learn a tremendous amount about this business.

SELECTED SCHOOLS

Many colleges and universities, especially those with business schools, offer programs in business and finance. The student can also gain initial training at a technical or community college. For some of the more prominent institutions in this field, see the list of selected schools in the "Accountant" and "Finance Manager" chapters of this volume.

MORE INFORMATION

Financial Managers Society
100 W. Monroe Street, Suite 1700
Chicago, IL 60603
312.578.1300
info@fmsinc.org
www.fmsinc.org

National Association of Credit Management
Education Department
8840 Columbia 100 Parkway
Columbia, MD 21045
410.740.5560
nacm_info@nacm.org
www.nacm.org

Risk Management Association
1801 Market Street, Suite 300
Philadelphia, PA 19103-1628
215.446.4000
www.rmahq.org

Simone Isadora Flynn,
updated by Micah Issitt

Economist

Snapshot

Career Cluster(s): Agriculture, Food & Natural Resources, Finance, Government and Public Administration, Science, Engineering, Technology & Mathematics
Interests: Mathematics, banking, finance, research, analyzing data
Earnings (Yearly Average): $101,050
Employment & Outlook: Average growth expected

OVERVIEW

Sphere of Work

Economists are social scientists who study how society produces, distributes, and uses its resources. They research and analyze a wide range of economic areas, such as trade, taxation, industrial productivity, business, and employment trends. Economists study these and other areas using statistical analyses, models, and sampling techniques. Each economist tends to focus on one specific area, or sub-field, of economics.

Economists work in a number of professional capacities. Some work as advisors to government leaders, providing insight into the effects of legislation on the economy. Others are academics, teaching economic theories and concepts to postsecondary students. Major corporations and private research firms hire other economists to assess such areas as client demand, productivity, and market conditions.

Work Environment

Economists generally work in office settings in government buildings and state capitals, in colleges and universities, and at businesses and private "think tanks." In each setting, economists must use their analytical, communication, and critical thinking skills as they conduct studies of current conditions and present their findings and opinions to their superiors and other audiences.

Economists often work alone in their research, although they may work in teams in collaborative efforts to study comprehensive and complex issues. They generally work forty-hour workweeks, although they may be called upon to work extra hours when faced with project deadlines or asked to present their ideas at conferences or meetings.

Profile

Working Conditions: Work Indoors
Physical Strength: Light Work
Education Needs: Bachelor's Degree, Master's Degree, PhD
Licensure/Certification: Not Required
Opportunities For Experience: Part-time work
Holland Interest Score*: IAS

* See Appendix A

Occupation Interest

Economists have the professional ability to understand extremely complex systems that are often of great importance to world leaders, high-level business executives, and the intellectual community. Those economists who focus on microeconomics help major corporations maximize their profits while forecasting consumer demand and prices. Economists who focus on macroeconomics are invaluable to organizations and agencies that seek to understand economic growth, inflation, banking and finance, unemployment, and productivity. Because of their expertise in the many fields and subfields of economics, these individuals are often in high demand.

A Day in the Life—Duties and Responsibilities

An economist's most important duties are research and analysis. An economist must study the many elements that contribute to company or political system's operational strengths and weaknesses. The economist uses computer software to compile and organize data from consumer surveys, the media, and internal documents, such as production reports and profit and loss statements. This information helps the economist to create a comprehensive model of the subject. The data and models that an economist generates help all parties involved to understand the relationships between certain concepts and the root causes of many issues.

After the economist creates workable models and frameworks, he or she uses them to forecast conditions for the short- and long-term future. The economist may report his or her findings to help government officials draft and implement effective policy. A corporate economist can use findings to help executives determine the areas in which investments may yield the best returns. Such models enable an economics-oriented "think tank" to compile reports for the government and its corporate clients. Meanwhile, an academic economist uses such information to write scholarly articles and books while he or she conducts the typical duties of a college professor. In each situation (faculty, corporate, or government), an economist may be called upon to present his or her findings, theories, and opinions at conferences, board meetings, and hearings.

Duties and Responsibilities

- **Developing methods for collecting and processing economic and statistical data**
- **Interpreting economic and statistical data**
- **Analyzing the relationships between the supply and demand for goods and services**
- **Developing ways to control inflation, unemployment, and business cycles**
- **Planning and conducting studies to determine the need for change in business or government policy**

OCCUPATION SPECIALTIES

Agricultural Economist

Agricultural Economists study agricultural problems to determine better uses of farm resources.

Tax Economist

Tax Economists collect and study data and the effects of taxes and policies on national income and overall business activities.

Labor Economist

Labor Economists collect and interpret labor data to forecast labor trends and suggest changes in labor policies.

Industrial Economist

Industrial Economists study the organizational structure, methods of financing, production costs and techniques, and marketing policies of various types of businesses to develop improvements.

Environmental Economist

Environmental Economists assess and quantify the economic benefits of using more environmental alternatives, such as the use of renewable energy resources.

WORK ENVIRONMENT

Relevant Skills and Abilities

Communication Skills
- Speaking effectively
- Writing concisely

Interpersonal/Social Skills
- Communicating with others
- Working as part of a team
- Following directions
- Presenting information

Organization & Management Skills
- Coordinating tasks
- Making decisions
- Managing students/groups/ employees

Research & Planning Skills
- Analyzing information
- Developing evaluation strategies
- Using logical reasoning
- Paying attention to and handling details

Technical Skills
- Performing scientific, mathematical, and technical work
- Working with data and/or numbers
- Using computers and other digital tools

Physical Environment

Economists spend the majority of their time in government or private offices, classrooms (in the case of university economists), and other locations where social science research can be conducted. Additionally, they may be asked to present information to government agencies, conferences, and other venues.

Human Environment

Economists may conduct their research alone or with collaborators. In either case, economists come into contact with many different types of professionals, including corporate leaders, elected and appointed government officials, students, academic peers, and the media.

Technological Environment

Economists should be familiar with computers, including many different types of office, research, and modeling software. Such programs include basic word processing and spreadsheet systems, chart and graph generators, and specialized databases. Additionally, economists need to use other forms of basic office technology, such as cellular and smart phones, presentation technologies, personal organizers, and scanners.

EDUCATION, TRAINING, AND ADVANCEMENT

High School/Secondary

High school students who are interested in economics should take courses in economics, accounting, business, statistics, math, computer science, and data processing. As half of all professional economists work for federal, state, or local government organizations, high school students may also benefit from studying political science, social studies, government, and history. High school students interested in becoming economists may also find English and communications courses helpful preparation for report writing and public speaking responsibilities they will have as economists.

Suggested High School Subjects

- Accounting
- Algebra
- Applied Math
- Business Data Processing
- Calculus
- College Preparatory
- Composition
- Computer Science
- Economics
- English
- Geometry
- Government
- History
- Mathematics
- Political Science
- Social Studies
- Sociology
- Statistics
- Trigonometry

Famous First

Professor Elinor Ostrom, formerly a professor of economics at Indiana University, became the first woman to win a Nobel Prize in Economics in 2009 when she shared the price with economist Oliver E. Williamson for their work on political economics. Ostrom was also president of the American Political Science Association and the first woman to win the Johan Skytte Prize in politics, one of the most prestigious prizes awarded for political scientists.

College/Postsecondary

In the field of economics, advanced degrees make an individual more attractive to potential employers. Undergraduates should take courses of relevance to the field, including statistics, accounting, calculus and econometrics (the application of math and statistics to the study of finance and economics). They should also take courses in specific areas such as monetary policy, microeconomics, industrial/organizational economics, and macroeconomics. Graduate students in pursuit of their master's or doctoral degree should take more specialized courses that help hone their expertise on a particular field of economics, such as international economics, economic history, or public finance.

Related College Majors

- Economics
- Applied Economics
- Political Economics
- Macroeconomics
- Microeconomics
- Mathematics
- Statistics
- Political Science
- Management, General

Adult Job Seekers

Many economists obtain positions after college by working as interns or research assistants while they pursue a postgraduate degree. They may also gain access to job openings through professional economics associations, such as the American Economic Association, the National Association for Business Economics, or the Society of Government Economists. Professional placement services may assist candidates in pursuing available jobs.

Professional Certification and Licensure

There are no professional licensure or certification requirements for most economist positions. However, economists are encouraged to become members of a relevant professional association.

Additional Requirements

Economists must be detail-oriented, which help them compile high volumes of data. Additionally, economists' research skills should be finely tuned – they should be able to conduct interviews, develop and administer surveys, and use a wide range of media to study trends and conditions in the field of focus. An economist should also have strong written and spoken communications skills, which enable them to create coherent reports and present findings to many different types of audiences.

Fun Fact

The annals of economists include such notable names as Adam Smith and Karl Marx. But did you know fabled Irish playwright George Bernard Shaw and three fellow Fabian Society members founded the London School of Economics in 1895? The left-leaning Fabian Society still exists, and is Britain's oldest think tank.

Source: http://www.lse.ac.uk/ and www.fabians.org.uk

EARNINGS AND ADVANCEMENT

The median annual wage for economists in the United States was $101,050 in May of 2016, with an estimated range of $55,000 for those at the lowest ten percent of the field, to salaries of over $181,000 for those at the upper end of the spectrum. Higher salaries are typically found in the finance and insurance industries, as well as in the federal government. Advancing in economics is a matter of seniority and expertise. Those whose work attracts attention might be able to command higher salaries from their employers or to qualify for positions with higher-paying companies or organizations.

Metropolitan Areas with the Highest Employment Level in this Occupation

Metropolitan area	Employment	Employment per thousand jobs	Hourly mean wage
Washington-Arlington-Alexandria, DC-VA-MD-WV Metropolitan Division	8,790	3.53	$60.29
Boston-Cambridge-Newton, MA NECTA Division	1,180	0.65	$52.22
Los Angeles-Long Beach-Glendale, CA Metropolitan Division	420	0.10	$71.05
New York-Jersey City-White Plains, NY-NJ Metropolitan Division	390	0.06	$66.60
Dallas-Plano-Irving, TX Metropolitan Division	380	0.15	$57.29
Atlanta-Sandy Springs-Roswell, GA	340	0.13	$52.21
Houston-The Woodlands-Sugar Land, TX	340	0.12	$71.51
Chicago-Naperville-Arlington Heights, IL Metropolitan Division	290	0.08	$54.61
San Francisco-Redwood City-South San Francisco, CA Metropolitan Division	240	0.22	$54.78
Minneapolis-St. Paul-Bloomington, MN-WI	230	0.12	$36.56

Source: Bureau of Labor Statistics

EMPLOYMENT AND OUTLOOK

The Bureau of Labor Statistics (BLS) estimates that jobs in economics will grow by 6 percent between 2014 and 2024, constituting average growth in comparison to the 6-7 percent projected for all occupations in the United States. While demand for economists is expected to remain stable, opportunities for economists in federal positions will likely to decline due to overall reductions in state and federal budgets. As competition for available positions intensifies, those with advanced degrees will likely fare better on the job market and PhD's in the field are becoming more common even at lower-level economics positions.

Related Occupations

- Actuary
- Financial Analyst
- Management Analyst & Consultant
- Market Research Analyst
- Mathematician
- Operations Research Analyst
- Securities Sales Agent
- Sociologist
- Statistician
- Urban & Regional Planner

Related Military Occupations

- Military Economics Researcher

Conversation With . . .
SANDRA BLACK

Professor of Economics, University of Texas
Austin, Texas
Economist, 20 years

1. What was your individual career path in terms of education/training, entry-level job, or other significant opportunity?

When I started college, I didn't know what I wanted to do. I was good at math, but didn't know how you would actually use math in the real world. When I took my first economics class, it really resonated: the idea of supply and demand really made sense to me.

I graduated from the University of California at Berkeley with a BA in economics. I wanted to move to the East Coast, so I worked at a consulting firm in Boston for a year. But I didn't like being a research assistant —there was a lot of boring work like data entry and data checking—and went back to school. In graduate school, my research focused on labor economics, and I received my Ph.D. from Harvard University in 1997. My first job was at the Federal Reserve Bank of New York.

I always thought it would be great to be a professor, but the Federal Reserve Bank had a lot of aspects that made it more appealing at the time. For example, I could do research, but I could also help with other responsibilities of the Federal Reserve Bank, such as banking oversight and macroeconomic policy. I worked there for four years and really liked it, but decided I ultimately wanted to becomes a professor and do research full-time. I then moved to UCLA, where I was an assistant, then associate (with tenure) and, finally, full professor. In 2010, I became a Professor of Economics at the University of Texas, where I currently hold the Audre and Bernard Rapoport Centennial Chair in Economics and Public Affairs.

I had expected to settle in at UT, but an unexpected opportunity arose, so I decided to try something new. I took a leave of absence and moved to Washington D.C. to serve on President Barack Obama's Council of Economic Advisers from 2015 until January 2017. Government and policy work was so interesting and it provides a way for academics to make their research more relevant. I think it would be great if more academics went into policy.

People tend to think of economics as taxes, or growing the economy. But a lot of economics is understanding human decision-making. It can be about making investments not just in plants and equipment but in individuals themselves, or their children. My research has looked at such issues as how investments of money or education impact kids in the long run, or how resources are allocated within a family. Economics is broadening as a field, and now economics includes fields such as the economics of education, crime and family. Economics provides a nice framework for thinking about things.

2. **What are the most important skills and/or qualities for someone in your profession?**

   Self-motivated, hard-working, curious, likes to learn, good analytic/math skills.

3. **What do you wish you had known going into this profession?**

   I knew you could be a professor as a Ph.D economist, but I didn't know about all the other types of jobs. I also didn't really know what a professor does, and how much it varies across different schools. I knew professors taught, but wasn't aware how important research was to their job.

4. **Are there many job opportunities in your profession? In what specific areas?**

   There are, relatively speaking. Academic jobs, government jobs, private sector consulting jobs, banking jobs. A lot of firms like people with skills in economics. High tech companies like Amazon and Google hire economists to evaluate their data because we tend to be good at that. Consulting firms hire economists. For example, a lawyer might hire an economist to testify in an anti-trust case.

5. **How do you see your profession changing in the next five years, what role will technology play in those changes, and what skills will be required?**

   We are definitely in an era of "big data," which means programming skills are increasingly useful. Amazon, Google, Uber ... they all hire economists to evaluate their data. The availability of this data creates jobs for economists.

6. **What do you enjoy most about your job? What do you enjoy least about your job?**

   I like working with students and junior faculty, doing research (especially collaboratively) and I like the flexibility of my schedule. Overall, I think I am pretty lucky—there aren't many things I really dislike about my job. The work can be isolating and projects can extend for a long period of time; writing one paper can take a year. You must be self-motivated.

7. Can you suggest a valuable "try this" for students considering a career in your profession?

I would suggest looking at journals like the Journal of Economic Perspectives and see if there are topics you are really interested in. This journal writes summary pieces of research in particular areas, but they are relatively readable. If you find topics in economics that really interest you, you should consider pursuing it. You need to really like economics!

SELECTED SCHOOLS

Many colleges and universities, especially those with business schools, offer programs in economics. The student can also gain initial training through enrollment at a technical or community college. For advanced positions, a master's of business administration (MBA) with a concentration in economics is usually expected. Below are listed some of the more prominent institutions in this field.

Carnegie Mellon University
Tepper School of Business
500 Forbes Avenue
Pittsburgh, PA 15213
412.268.2268
tepper.cmu.edu

Indiana University, Bloomington
Kelley School of Business
1309 E. 10th Street
Bloomington, IN 47405
812.855.8100
kelley.iu.edu

Massachusetts Institute of Technology
Sloan School of Management
50 Memorial Drive
Cambridge, MA 02142
617.253.2659
mitsloan.mit.edu

New York University
Stern School of Business
665 Broadway, 11th Floor
New York, NY 10012
212.998.4500
www.stern.nyu.edu

University of California, Berkeley
Haas School of Business
S450 Student Services Building #1900
Berkeley, CA 94720
510.642.1421
haas.berkeley.edu

University of Michigan, Ann Arbor
Ross School of Business
701 Tappan Avenue
Ann Arbor, MI 48109
734.763.5796
michiganross.umich.edu

University of North Carolina, Chapel Hill
Kenan-Flagler Business School
Campus Box 3490, McColl Building
Chapel Hill, NC 27599
919.962.3235
www.kenan-flagler.unc.edu

University of Pennsylvania
The Wharton School
1 College Hall
Philadelphia, PA 19104
215.898.6376
www.wharton.upenn.edu

MORE INFORMATION

American Economic Association
2014 Broadway, Suite 305
Nashville, TN 37203
615.322.2595
aeainfo@vanderbilt.edu
www.vanderbilt.edu/AEA

National Association for Business Economics
1233 20th Street NW, Suite 505
Washington, DC 20036
202.463.6223
www.nabe.com

NABE Foundation Americans for the Arts Scholarships:
www.nabefoundation.com/ourPrograms.html

Society of Government Economists
P.O. Box 77802
Washington, DC 20013
202.643.1743
www.sge-econ.org

Michael Auerbach,
updated by Micah Issitt

Estate & Tax Planner

Snapshot

Career Cluster(s): Financial Services, Accounting
Interests: Financial planning, working with people, financial analysis, accounting, mathematics
Earnings (Yearly Average): $90,530
Employment & Outlook: Much Faster Than Average Growth Expected

OVERVIEW

Sphere of Work

Estate and tax planners are personal financial advisors specializing in helping individuals manage their taxes and to plan for the dispensation of an estate after death. The term "estate" refers to a person's wealth and property and individuals sometimes plan for the dispensation of their material possessions and remaining wealth after death. Estate planners help to ensure that an individual's assets are dispersed according to the wishes of the deceased and also help to plan for any expenses or debts that remain after an individual's death.

Personal financial advice, and tax and estate planning in specific, are typically luxury services marketed towards wealthy clients. As such, earnings in the field are high in comparison to time needed to complete work.

Work Environment

Estate and tax planning specialists spend most of their time working indoors, in office environments. Though most work full time, time working may increase dramatically during tax season or after a client's death, with periods of less work between. While most of an estate planner's work can be completed in an office, or out of the professional's home, estate and tax planners may also visit clients in their homes and/or offices and may therefore need to travel for their work, especially when meeting with new clients.

Profile

Working Conditions: Work Indoors
Physical Strength: Light Work
Education Needs: Bachelor's Degree, Master's Degree
Licensure/Certification: Not Required
Opportunities For Experience: Part-time work
Holland Interest Score*: ECS

* See Appendix A

Occupation Interest

Estate and tax planners typically work independently and are responsible for marketing their services to prospective clients. Individuals seeking work in the field need to be enterprising and comfortable advertising themselves to clients and should also be comfortable interacting with clients regularly. When not meeting with clients, tax and estate planners work independently and those seeking work in the field should therefore be self-motivated and enjoy solving problems and analysis. Estate and tax planning involves accounting and individuals should therefore have an interest in finance and mathematics.

A Day in the Life—Duties and Responsibilities

Estate and tax planners typically spend part of a typical day working directly with their clients or meeting with new potential clients to market their services. When meeting with clients, the professional must clearly explain the services he or she can offer and must obtain detailed information about their potential clients' needs and financial goals. Estate and tax planners also help to advice clients about legal and financial issues surrounding death and the dispersal of their estate and so must be familiar with relevant federal and local laws.

For existing clients, personal tax and estate advisors monitor their clients' finances regularly to determine if changes in income, savings, or other factors necessitates any subsequent changes to the financial plan developed with their clients. During this process, the financial advisor may contact their existing clients to recommend changes to their estate or tax planning, such as new investments, ways to increase tax savings, or to help their clients understand changes to laws related to taxes and inheritance. After a client's death, the estate planner meets with members of the family, legal professionals, and others to discuss the dispensation of his or her client's estate and helps to ensure that the client's wishes are met.

Duties and Responsibilities

- **Marketing services to potential clients**
- **Meeting with clients to discuss goals and potential services**
- **Monitoring client's financial accounts, investments, and other aspects of an estate**
- **Research changes in tax codes or laws related to inheritance**
- **Working with lawyers and creditors after a client's death**
- **Meeting with family or other beneficiaries**

OCCUPATION SPECIALTIES

Estate Lawyer

An estate lawyer is a legal professional who specializes in inheritance and financial planning for after death. Estate lawyers may help clients to handle legal issues related to the dispersal of their estate and may also function as personal financial advisors, helping clients to financially plan for their death and subsequent distribution of their assets.

Certified Financial Planner

A certified financial planner is a financial advisor who has completed a certification course in financial planning, which typically includes training in retirement, taxes, investments, and estate planning.

Tax Accountant

A tax accountant is a professional accountant specializing in helping individuals or institutions to navigate the tax process. Tax accountants can also serve as personal financial advisors, helping clients to manage savings, investment, taxes, and estate planning.

WORK ENVIRONMENT

Physical Environment

Estate and tax specialists typically work in office environments and some work out of their own homes or a home office. In some cases, personal financial advisors may work in an office as part of a financial team or in a firm that specializes in financial planning. In some cases, estate and tax planners may travel to meet with clients, beneficiaries or family members, or other professionals involved in the dispersal of a client's estate.

Relevant Skills and Abilities

Communication Skills
- Creating reports and documentation for clients
- Explaining complex information to clients

Interpersonal/Social Skills
- Meeting with clients, beneficiaries, and other professionals
- Working independently

Organization & Management Skills
- Managing investments and assets
- Creating and maintaining detailed records

Research & Planning Skills
- Researching changes in tax/inheritance law
- Researching investments

Technical Skills
- Working with accounts and monitoring client finances
- Using digital software and other tools

Human Environment

Estate and tax planning is a collaborative discipline in which the professional must work closely with his or her clients to determine the clients' needs. Estate and tax planners spend much of their time meeting with clients in person or communicating via email or telephone. Depending on the individual's specialization, estate and tax specialists may work with other professionals including accountants, investment advisors, other financial advisors, or legal professionals. In addition, estate and tax specialists must have excellent communication skills as they are responsible for helping their clients to understand complex financial and legal issues surrounding taxes and estate planning.

Technological Environment

Estate and tax planners regularly use computers and other digital tools in their work. Knowledge of word processing and spreadsheet software is important for research, planning, and providing information to clients. With the advent of cloud based sharing, financial professionals regularly use virtual programs to manage and share documents with their clients. There are also a variety of software programs designed specifically for financial planning, such as Oracle E-Business Suite Financials, and the Finance Logix Retirement Planner, that may be useful to specialists in the field. As estate and tax specialists are typically responsible for their own advertising and marketing, professionals may benefit from a basic knowledge of web and social media marketing.

EDUCATION, TRAINING, AND ADVANCEMENT

High School/Secondary

High school students interested in careers in estate or tax planning should plan to pursue higher education as most professional financial advisors have at least a Bachelor's Degree in a related field. In addition, due to higher-than-average pay and increasing demand, financial advising in a competitive field and individuals with graduate degrees or post-college certification in accounting or finance will have an advantage on the job market.

Suggested High School Subjects

- Algebra
- Applied Math
- College Preparatory
- Computer Science
- English
- Composition
- Business
- Marketing

Famous First

The most basic level of estate planning is the preparation of a will, which is a legal document that describes how an individual would like his or her estate to be handled after death. While some evidence suggests that wills were used in ancient Egypt, thousands of years before the practice appeared in western culture, the modern will and testament has its origins in Roman law. After the Norman Conquest, English society developed complex laws regarding wills, testaments, and estates, and these laws became more complex over time, thus creating the need for legal experts who could help citizens to navigate the laws surrounding the dispensation of their estates.

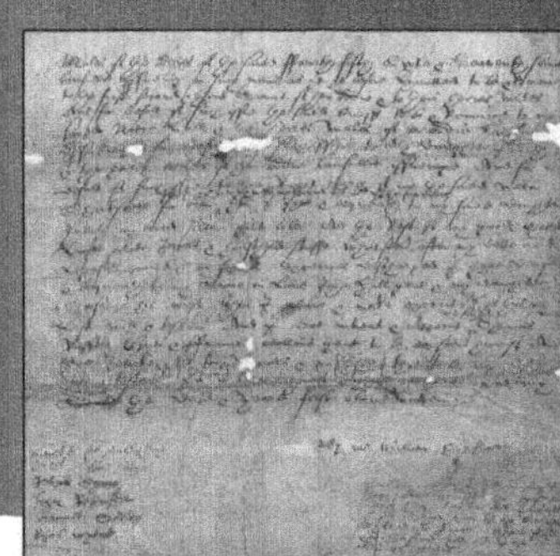

College/Postsecondary

Tax and estate specialists typically have at least an undergraduate degree, but there is some variation in training within the field. Individuals planning to work as personal financial advisors may choose to study finance or accounting or may pursue legal training to become a tax or estate- attorney. Though prospective tax/estate specialists have options for choosing an undergraduate degree, experience in finance, investing, business, marketing, and accounting are essential in the field and students should tailor their education to gain experience in these fields.

Related College Majors

- Business Accounting
- Finance, General
- Business, General
- Financial Management
- Economics, General
- Business Economics
- Business Administration
- Financial Analysis

Adult Job Seekers

Individuals with a bachelor's degree or higher and sufficient work experience can choose to market their own services as a personal financial advisor. Alternatively, those seeking to become tax and estate consultants may begin their careers by seeking work with a professional tax/estate advisor. In firms offering financial planning assistance, new advisors work alongside experienced senior advisors during a training period that can last as long as a year. Those working independently will need to invest time in marketing and advertising as they build a client network.

Professional Certification and Licensure

While there are no specific licenses required to work as a tax and estate specialist, financial advisors who wish to make investments on behalf of their clients must be registered with the Securities and Exchange Commission (SEC), the branch of the federal government charged with monitoring and regulating the investment and financial market. In addition, individuals who wish to sell insurance policies to their clients must register with state insurance boards. Some tax and estate specialists can choose to participate in certification programs to become a Certified Public Accountant (CPA) or Certified Financial Planner (CFP). These certification programs accept students who have at least a bachelor's degree and have at least 3 years of work experience in their field. AS the personal financial advisor market is highly competitive, individuals who complete CPA or CFP training may have an advantage when seeking clients or employment with an established financial firm.

Additional Requirements

Because the issues surrounding tax and estate planning can be sensitive and personal, professionals in the field benefit from having excellent interpersonal skills and the ability to explain complex financial subjects to clients who may have little knowledge of the field. Researching investments and other resources for their clients requires careful analysis and tax and estate specialists must be proficient in research and have detailed knowledge of local and federal regulations. In addition, precise, careful calculations are essential and professionals therefore benefit from advanced skills in mathematics.

Fun Fact

His name was Trouble and he was a little white dog that inherited $12 million when his owner—real estate investor and hotelier Leona Helmsley—died. A judge later reduced the Maltese's share of the estate to $2 million.

Source: https://cityroom.blogs.nytimes.com/2007/08/29/leona-helmsleys-unusual-last-will/

EARNINGS AND ADVANCEMENT

There are no available estimates for earnings specifically in the tax and estate planning field, but the Bureau of Labor Statistics (BLS) has collected data on the personal financial advisor field as a whole and estimated that the median annual pay for the field was $90,530 in May of 2016. While individuals at the lower end of the income spectrum for the field earned less than $41,000 annually, financial advisors can in some cases earn incomes of over $200,000 per year depending on their specialty. Advisors who specialize in brokering contracts and investments earn higher than average salaries, with a median of $101,750 in 2016. Professionals in the field looking to advance can pursue advanced certification or might return to education to pursue a post-graduate degree in accounting, finance, or business administration. For those working within a firm, experience and building a client list may lead to increased salary.

Metropolitan Areas with the Highest Employment Level in this Occupation

Metropolitan area	Employment	Employment per thousand jobs	Hourly mean wage
New York-Jersey City-White Plains, NY-NJ Metropolitan Division	25,490	3.87	$76.27
Chicago-Naperville-Arlington Heights, IL Metropolitan Division	10,650	2.93	$57.17
Los Angeles-Long Beach-Glendale, CA Metropolitan Division	6,730	1.59	$68.11
Boston-Cambridge-Newton, MA NECTA Division	5,640	3.13	$47.92
San Francisco-Redwood City-South San Francisco, CA Metropolitan Division	4,500	4.22	$77.60
Atlanta-Sandy Springs-Roswell, GA	4,430	1.73	$59.67
Houston-The Woodlands-Sugar Land, TX	3,550	1.21	$52.67
Anaheim-Santa Ana-Irvine, CA Metropolitan Division	3,450	2.21	$59.67
Dallas-Plano-Irving, TX Metropolitan Division	3,360	1.38	$64.75
Phoenix-Mesa-Scottsdale, AZ	3,320	1.72	$51.33

Source: Bureau of Labor Statistics

EMPLOYMENT AND OUTLOOK

The BLS estimates that the personal financial advice industry will grow by more than 30 percent between 2014 and 2024, constituting much faster than average growth in comparison to the 6-7 percent annual growth for all U.S. occupations. This growth will be especially high for those who specialize in estate and tax planning due to a demographic shift in the United States that has resulted in a larger population of elderly Americans. In addition, the shift from employer-based retirement/estate services to personal retirement and estate services has increased the demand for financial managers and advisors. Though financial advice is a highly competitive field, rapid sustained growth in the field has led to widespread opportunities for new professionals in the field. As the field grows, individuals with certification or advanced degrees are likely to have a significant advantage.

Related Occupations

- Accountants
- Budget Analysts
- Financial Managers
- Insurance Sales Agents
- Securities, Commodities, and Financial Services Sales Agents
- Financial Analysts

Related Military Occupations

- Military Financial Assistant

Conversation With . . .
KYLE P. GERMAN, CRPC

Partner, Harbor Financial Group
Annapolis, Maryland
Financial planner, 18 years

1. What was your individual career path in terms of education/training, entry-level job, or other significant opportunity?

I'm a practical person. I've always been interested in finance and the movement of money. This career path has provided me with an opportunity to make a nice living doing something I enjoy. However, I knew I could take an understanding of finance with me into many fields.

So, I took business and finance courses in college, and earned a bachelor's degree from West Virginia University. These classes in no way prepared me for a career as a personal financial advisor. We spent our time studying the theory behind the numbers as opposed to the practical application.

2. What are the most important skills and/or qualities for someone in your profession?

You need to be a people person because you will spend your days meeting with individuals and families, learning about their goals, their concerns, what drives them.

You will not be micromanaged, so you need self-motivation. You need to be creative when prospecting for new clients to set yourself apart from the thousands of other smart young people trying to build a financial planning practice. So, for instance, bring coffee to a business (even if it's a construction company that starts at 5:30) so you can meet people.

Lastly, you must have a thick skin! You will be told "no" thousands of times.

3. What do you wish you had known going into this profession?

I wish had asked for help. My best advice is to offer to help an experienced advisor. This will provide you with an opportunity to learn from someone who's done it and potentially provide you with a future business partner.

4. Are there many job opportunities in your profession? In what specific areas?

Financial advisors are in demand, for two reasons:

First off, baby boomers are retiring and shifting their retirement nest eggs from company 401K savings plans to individual IRAs. This represents the largest transfer of wealth the country has ever seen. And when people retire, they need help managing their money.

Second, this profession has high turnover because it's tough to get started. At my first job, thirty other people started at the same time. Our sole responsibility was to study for the Series 7 Exam, which is basically the stockbroker's exam. We had one month to pass the test. Then we had two weeks to study and complete the Series 66—the state securities law exam—and then we moved on to the Life and Health Exam, which is for insurance. If you failed, you were out. I quickly learned the exams were the easy part. Only two of us were left by the end of the second year. Not all firms have the same exam requirements, but all will expect you to bring in new clients right away.

If you stick with it and get through the years of hard work, it's amazing how lucrative this field can be. Trust me when I say you will work harder than most for less money for ten to fifteen years (depending how successful you are) and then, once you've built your practice, you'll work less than most for more money.

5. How do you see your profession changing in the next five years, what role will technology play in those changes, and what skills will be required?

Clients, especially younger clients, want immediate online access to their statements on their smart phones. They would rather text or email than come in for a meeting. This is all based on efficiency. If you don't adapt to work with them, they'll find someone who will.

That said, in-person meetings build trust. Older clients may be dealing with life's complexities such as illness or death and other matters that have greater consequences than what a young person is typically facing.

6. What do you enjoy most about your job? What do you enjoy least about your job?

I most enjoy the relationships I develop with my clients. A lot of my meetings take place around the dinner table. Clients share every aspect of their lives. This leads to a very close relationship that often lasts a lifetime.

I least like the stress that comes with managing a client's total financial nest egg. When the market drops, or two premier economists have completely opposing viewpoints, managing a portfolio is a big responsibility.

7. Can you suggest a valuable "try this" for students considering a career in your profession?

Pick a company, follow it on the stock market, watch it fluctuate and try to figure out why. I had one college course that really stuck with me and probably the only one that had any practical application to what I do. We bought a hypothetical stock portfolio at the beginning of the semester, explained why we liked the stock, and reported weekly on our transactions. Did we sell it and why? Did we keep it and why? We were graded on the rationale behind our moves.

Also, find a financial advisor you can interview or shadow. Offer to bring coffee or lunch. After all, you need to get used to asking for a meeting!

SELECTED SCHOOLS

Many colleges and universities, especially those with business schools, offer programs in business and finance. The student can also gain initial training at a technical or community college. For some of the more prominent institutions in this field, see the list of selected schools in the "Accountant" and "Finance Manager" chapters of this volume.

MORE INFORMATION

National Association of Estate Planners & Councils
1120 Chester Avenue, Suite 470
Cleveland, OH 44114
866-226-2224
www.naepc.org

National Institute of Certified Estate Planners
2125 West Zartman Road
Kokomo, Indiana 46902
765-453-4300
www.nicep.org

North American Securities Administrators Association
750 First Street NE, Suite 1140
Washington, DC 20002
202-737-0900
www.nasaa.org

Financial Industry Regulatory Authority
1735 K Street
Washington DC, 20006
301-590-6500
www.finra.org

U.S. Securities and Exchange Commission
100 F Street, NE
Washington, DC 20549
www.sec.gov

Micah Issitt/Editor

Financial Analyst

Snapshot

Career Cluster(s): Business, Management & Administration, Finance
Interests: Mathematics, risk assessment, financial trends, data analysis
Earnings (Yearly Average): $81,760
Employment & Outlook: Faster Than Average Growth Expected

OVERVIEW

Sphere of Work

Financial analysts, also referred to as investment analysts, financial planners, financial officers, and financial managers, are responsible for the financial investments of businesses, corporations, nonprofit organizations, and government entities. Financial analysts provide diverse financial analysis services, which may include reviewing financial statements and advising organizations about the best investment options, such as stocks, bonds, and commodities. Financial analysts generally work within or alongside management and accounting departments. While most

businesses employ a single financial analyst to oversee investments, financial institutions such as commercial banks, insurance companies, securities firms, mortgage companies, pension funds, and savings and loan associations employ multiple financial analysts to direct their internal investments and those of clients, investors, and customers.

Work Environment

Financial analysts work in offices and are often required to travel to attend annual meetings and stockholder meetings. Depending on employer and particular job description, a financial analyst may telecommute from a home office, visit client offices, or work on a full-time basis in an employer's office. A financial analyst may work as a full-time member of a finance team or as a term-of-project consultant. A financial analyst's Work Environment is filled with technology, including computers and accounting software programs.

Profile

Working Conditions: Work Indoors
Physical Strength: Light Work
Education Needs: Bachelor's Degree, Master's Degree
Licensure/Certification: Required
Opportunities For Experience: Part-time work, Military service, Internship
Holland Interest Score*: CIE

* See Appendix A

Occupation Interest

Individuals attracted to the financial analysis profession tend to be ambitious, organized, persuasive, decisive, and detail-oriented people who find satisfaction in tracking financial trends and assessing risks. Those individuals who excel as financial analysts possess financial and mathematical acumen, intense focus, responsibility and ethics, and effective time management. Financial analysts should enjoy finance and informed risk-taking and have a background in risk assessment.

A Day in the Life—Duties and Responsibilities

The daily duties and responsibilities of financial analysts vary by job specialty and employer. Areas of financial analysis job specialization include buy side financial analysts, sell side financial analysts, risk analysts, portfolio managers, fund managers, and ratings analysts. Buy side analysts assist mutual funds, hedge funds, insurance companies, and endowed organizations with developing investment strategies and implementing investment decisions. Sell side financial analysts assist banks and securities dealers with promoting and selling stocks, bonds, and other investment vehicles. Risk analysts assess the risks associated with investment decisions and work to reduce losses by diversifying the portfolio and selling stocks and bonds as needed. Portfolio managers oversee financial teams and the health of financial investments. Fund managers oversee hedge funds and mutual funds and communicate investment decisions and strategies to investors. Ratings analysts assess the likelihood that businesses will pay their debts. Based on these assessments, ratings analysts forecast the default risk. In addition to job specialization, all financial analysts specialize in particular geographic regions or industries.

Regardless of geography or industry specialization, financial analysts use spreadsheets to track financial data, analyze financial data to make investment decisions, and track trends in technology and politics that may affect the finance industry. They recommend investment options, create investment portfolios for individuals and businesses, set securities prices, prepare investment reports for business owners and investors, and advise clients or employers about when to best hold, sell, or trade securities.

In addition to the tasks described above, organizations may also require financial analysts to select, implement, and troubleshoot financial software systems. They must stay up to date with regulatory and ethical issues and news in finance by reading finance industry journals and participating in industry associations. Financial analysts employed by learning organizations also participate in ongoing discussions of work teams, workflows, dynamics, and best practices.

Duties and Responsibilities

- **Analyzing financial information to assist an organization in making investment decisions**
- **Recommending both the type and timing of investments to an organization to create the potential for successful investing**
- **Presenting oral and written presentations regarding business, industry, and economic trends**
- **Evaluating and comparing the quality of different investment possibilities in any industry**
- **Staying up to date with the latest developments in the financial industry**

OCCUPATION SPECIALTIES

Portfolio Manager

Portfolio Managers supervise a team of financial analysts and help guide companies in building their investment portfolios.

Fund Manager

Fund Managers manage mutual funds or hedge funds for their clients.

Risk Manager

Risk Managers analyze the investment decisions of their clients and determine how to grow profits through diversifying and hedging.

Ratings Analyst

Ratings Analysts determine the ability of companies that issue bonds to repay their debts.

WORK ENVIRONMENT

Physical Environment

Financial analysts generally work in office environments. The work of a financial analyst requires sitting at a desk and using computers and phones for long periods each day. Occasionally, financial analysts who work independently will be asked to travel to visit other institutions or businesses.

Human Environment

Financial analysts interact with financial teams, business owners, employees, clients, and stockholders. Financial analysts should be comfortable attending meetings, giving frequent speeches, persuading clients, listening to client concerns and opinions, and supervising and directing employees.

Relevant Skills and Abilities

Communication Skills

- Speaking effectively
- Writing concisely
- Listening attentively
- Reading and comprehension
- Persuasive speaking and presentation skill

Interpersonal/Social Skills

- Working with others
- Being able to work independently
- Having good judgment
- Listening to client needs

Organization & Management Skills

- Coordinating tasks
- Making decisions
- Managing resources and finances
- Managing time
- Paying attention to and handling details
- Organizing information, data, or materials

Research & Planning Skills

- Using logical reasoning
- Researching economic trends
- Developing strategies for conducting evaluations

Technical Skills

- Performing scientific, mathematical, and technical work
- Working with data and/or numbers

Technological Environment

Financial analysts communicate by telephone and Internet. They use computers, financial analysis software, and spreadsheets to research, monitor, analyze, and present financial data.

EDUCATION, TRAINING, AND ADVANCEMENT

High School/Secondary

High school students interested in pursuing a career as a financial analyst should prepare themselves by building good study habits as well as an ease with numbers and mathematical functions. High school-level study of bookkeeping and mathematics will provide a strong foundation for college-level study of finance. Due to the diversity of financial analyst responsibilities and given that employers in this field tend to value practical experience, high school students interested in this career path may benefit from seeking internships or part-time work with financial organizations.

Suggested High School Subjects

- Accounting
- Algebra
- Applied Communication
- Applied Math
- Bookkeeping
- Business
- Business & Computer Technology
- Business Law
- Business Math
- College Preparatory
- Computer Science
- Economics
- English
- Government
- Keyboarding
- Mathematics
- Merchandising
- Political Science
- Psychology

- Social Studies
- Sociology
- Speech
- Statistics

Famous First

Financial analyst Benjamin Graham, known for his 1949 book *The Intelligent Investor*, was a financial analyst who pioneered a research and analysis approach to investing. Graham's research and writings on the subject have since become standard sources for those learning about trading and managing financial assets and Graham's techniques produced some of the most successful financial investors in history.

College/Postsecondary

Postsecondary students interested in becoming financial analysts should complete a bachelor's degree in economics, finance, statistics, mathematics, or accounting. Courses in computer science, political science, psychology, and ethics may also prove useful in their future work. Postsecondary students can gain work experience and potential advantage in their future job searches by securing internships or part-time employment with local businesses or financial organizations.

Related College Majors
- Accounting
- Business
- Business Administration & Management, General
- Business/Managerial Economics
- Economics, General
- Finance, General
- International Economics
- Mathematical Statistics

Adult Job Seekers

Adults seeking financial analyst jobs have generally earned a bachelor's degree and, in some cases, a master's of business administration (MBA). Adult job seekers may benefit from joining professional finance or accounting associations as a means of professional networking. Professional finance and accounting associations, such as the Association for Investment Management and Research and the Society of Financial Service Professionals, generally maintain job lists advertising open accounting positions.

Professional Certification and Licensure

Certification and licensure is not legally required for financial analysts but may be required as a condition of employment or promotion. Options for voluntary financial analyst certification include the CFA Institute's Chartered Financial Analyst (CFA) and Certificate in Investment Performance Measurement (CIPM) designations, and the American Academy of Financial Management's (AAFM) Financial Analyst, Risk Management, and Financial Planning designations. These voluntary certifications require education, experience, testing, employer sponsorship, recertification, and continuing education. Those interested in becoming certified should be aware that the Financial Industry Regulatory Authority (FINRA), which is the licensing agency of the securities and finance industry, does not approve or endorse any particular professional financial certification or designation. Certification must be sponsored by one's employer, so when a financial analyst moves to a new company, he or she must go through a recertification process.

Additional Requirements

Individuals who find satisfaction, success, and job security as financial analysts will be knowledgeable about the profession's requirements, responsibilities, and opportunities. They should be able to stay focused on the same project for several hours at a time in order to make informed decisions. They should also be detail-oriented, organized, analytical, and sensitive to their clients' needs and opinions. Financial analysts must exhibit integrity and professional ethics as professionals in this role have access to confidential financial information and influence the financial health of individuals and businesses. Membership in professional finance associations is encouraged among all financial analysts as a means of building professional community.

EARNINGS AND ADVANCEMENT

According to the Bureau of Labor Statistics (BLS), the median annual wage for financial analysts was $81,760 in 2016. Those at the lower end of the analyst income spectrum earn closer to $50,000, while those at the upper end can earn over $165,000. The highest salaries in the industry can be found in financial, investment, securities, and commodity management firms, followed by positions in professional services companies. Some financial analysts, such as those working as fund managers, may be compensated based on how well their investment advice pays out for investors. Earnings in the field are therefore tied to the health of the economy. In times of economic growth, analysts may be able to command higher salaries and increased opportunities means that financial analysts may be able to seek out higher-paying positions.

Metropolitan Areas with the Highest Employment Level in this Occupation

Metropolitan area	Employment	Employment per thousand jobs	Hourly mean wage
New York-Jersey City-White Plains, NY-NJ Metropolitan Division	47,190	7.17	$64.00
Chicago-Naperville-Arlington Heights, IL Metropolitan Division	10,610	2.92	$45.45
Boston-Cambridge-Newton, MA NECTA Division	9,990	5.54	$47.90
Washington-Arlington-Alexandria, DC-VA-MD-WV Metropolitan Division	9,390	3.77	$46.58
Houston-The Woodlands-Sugar Land, TX	8,040	2.74	$46.68
Los Angeles-Long Beach-Glendale, CA Metropolitan Division	8,010	1.90	$47.05
San Francisco-Redwood City-South San Francisco, CA Metropolitan Division	7,300	6.84	$68.19
Dallas-Plano-Irving, TX Metropolitan Division	7,000	2.88	$45.66
Atlanta-Sandy Springs-Roswell, GA	5,800	2.27	$39.12
Minneapolis-St. Paul-Bloomington, MN-WI	22,310	11.68	$43.06

Source: Bureau of Labor Statistics

EMPLOYMENT AND OUTLOOK

In 2014, financial analysts held approximately 277,600 jobs and the Bureau of Labor Statistics estimates that the field will grow by 12 percent over the decade from 2014 to 2024, constituting much faster than average growth when compared to the 6-7 percent estimated for all U.S. occupations during this same period. The increasing complexity of investment opportunities, both domestically and in expanding international markets, has created increased demand for qualified financial analysts and the overall growth of multinational business has also inspired growth in the field. In general, the financial analysis field is closely tied to the health of the overall economy though economic declines can also lead to new opportunities for analysts to help companies and organizations manage limited resources. Competition is high in the field and those with advanced degrees and specialization may fare better on the job market.

Related Occupations

- Accountant
- Actuary
- Auditor
- Budget Analyst
- Economist
- Financial Manager
- Insurance Sales Agent
- Insurance Underwriter
- Personal Financial Advisor
- Real Estate Sales Agent
- Securities Sales Agent

Related Military Occupations

- Finance and Accounting Manager

Conversation With . . .
CLIFFORD ROSSI, PhD

Professor of Finance & Executive in Residence,
University of Maryland, College Park, Maryland
Financial risk manager, 25 years
Professor of finance, 7 years

1. What was your individual career path in terms of education/training, entry-level job, or other significant opportunity?

I double majored in economics and public policy at the University of Denver thinking I would have a career in government. I graduated during a recession and went to work for a small solar energy research center as a purchasing manager. Two people there steered me to Cornell University, where I earned a master's degree and a PhD in quantitative finance.

I never needed a PhD to do the job I ended up doing: financial risk management. But my doctorate gave me the structure to think critically in a deep way. Several years into my career, management realized I could translate the technical to a non-technical audience. That made me a valuable commodity. After that, my career went a completely different way; I went into management and rose up the ranks. I advise my students: find what differentiates you from the competition.

After earning my PhD, I started in government at the U.S. Treasury Department, moved into quasi-government doing risk management at mortgage-finance programs Fannie Mae and Freddie Mac, then went into private banking. A pivotal moment came in 1996 when Freddie Mac asked me to write an automated underwriting scorecard. I convinced the Federal Housing Administration commissioner that this was a great way to go. That's when management realized: This guy shouldn't just do statistical work; he needs to be a voice for how to use these models.

By the end of 2003, I had plateaued. A headhunter helped me get into the private sector, working for Countrywide Mortgage. It was a relatively smaller institution at the time and they were looking to grow significantly. I had to create their risk management function. When I left, I was Managing Director and Chief Risk Officer.

I moved on to Washington Mutual (WaMu)—then the country's largest savings and loan—as Chief Credit Officer, but was there only seven months. I left because I was dissatisfied with the bank's direction. This was 2007, as the financial crisis unfolded. I had interviewed with Citigroup when I interviewed at WaMu, and they still wanted me to work for them. It was a good move. Soon after, WaMu suffered the largest failure in the nation's financial history.

I became Managing Director and Chief Risk Officer for the Consumer Lending Group. It was the best job I ever had, overseeing 700 people at a prestigious institution. I came on under a new CEO who embraced risk management as he guided the bank through the crisis and its aftermath. I stayed two years, working out of the headquarters in New York. This was a highly stressful time. My job also became more global and demanded extensive travel.

My banking career gave my wife and me the earnings and flexibility to decide how we wanted to live our lives, so when an interesting opportunity arose to shift gears and return home, I took it.

In 2009, I joined the faculty of the University of Maryland's Robert H. Smith School of Business as a full-time professor. Now, I teach graduate students part-time and have become Chief Economist for Radian Guarantee, a large mortgage insurance company in Philadelphia.

2. What are the most important skills and/or qualities for someone in your profession?

You need some degree of analytical skill, critical thinking skills, and financial software skills—the ability to mine or extract data and manipulate and analyze it. You have to be able to communicate effectively and you need to be a team player. Risk management is an art and a science, though, so you've also got to have intuition, knowledge and judgment.

3. What do you wish you had known going into this profession?

I wish I had known that risk management wasn't viewed as an equal partner in the banking profession at the time I was there. It's become more of a focus for banks since the crisis.

4. Are there many job opportunities in your profession? In what specific areas?

If any area of banking is growing, it's risk management. It's a great career. It's at the vortex of everything a bank is about: strategy, analytics, consumers, wealth management—you can work in any part of the business.

5. How do you see your profession changing in the next five years, what role will technology play in those changes, and what skills will be required?

With the advent of high-end computing software, the risk management function has become highly quantitative and model-based and the profession is more aligned with actuarial science. Technology will continue to make our profession more quantitative.

6. **What do you enjoy most about your job? What do you enjoy least about your job?**

   In my career in private finance, I enjoyed improving our bank's risk profile and infrastructure.

   I detested some of the power-play issues that surround high-level management, such as passive-aggressive behavior from peers, or being ignored. I don't suffer fools lightly.

7. **Can you suggest a valuable "try this" for students considering a career in your profession?**

   Attend an event at the local chapter of a professional association for risk management. People are likely to share their stories and help you understand what it is to be a financial risk manager.

SELECTED SCHOOLS

Many colleges and universities, especially those with business schools, offer programs in business and finance. The student can also gain initial training at a technical or community college. For some of the more prominent institutions in this field, see the list of selected schools in the "Accountant" and "Finance Manager" chapters of this volume.

MORE INFORMATION

American Academy of Financial Management
1670-F E. Cheyenne Mountain Blvd.
Box 293
Colorado Springs, CO 80906
504.495.1748
www.aafm.us

CFA Institute
560 Ray C. Hunt Drive
Charlottesville, VA 22903-2981
800.247.8132
info@cfainstitute.org
www.cfainstitute.org

Financial Industry Regulatory Authority
1735 K Street
Washington, DC 20006
301.590.6500
www.finra.org

Financial Managers Society, Inc.
100 West Monroe Street, Suite 1700
Chicago, IL 60603
800.275.4367
info@fmsinc.org
www.fmsinc.org

Offers webinars for professional development:www.fmsinc.org/content.aspx?id=96&linkidentifier=id&itemid=96

Society for Risk Analysis
1313 Dolley Madison Boulevard
Suite 402
McLean, VA 22101
703.7901745
sra@burkinc.com
www.sra.org

Presents the SRA Awards for achievements or excellence in risk analysis policy: www.sra.org/about_awards_descriptions.php

Simone Isadora Flynn,
updated by Micah Issitt

Financial Examiner

Snapshot

Career Cluster(s): Financial Services, Accounting
Interests: Financial planning, data analysis, working with people, accounting, government
Earnings (Yearly Average): $79,280
Employment & Outlook: Faster Than Average Growth Expected

OVERVIEW

Sphere of Work

Financial examiners are finance specialists who help organizations, including both governments and corporations, to review their financial status while adhering to local laws and regulations. There are two general categories of financial examination: consumer compliance, which involves monitoring the behavior of financial organizations/institutions to protect consumer interest, and risk scoping, which involves helping financial institutions to plan for possible future losses that could endanger the function of the organization.

Work Environment

Financial examiners typically work in office environments and spend much of their time using computers and other digital tools to evaluate data and prepare presentations and financial reports for their clients or employers. Much of a financial examiner's work can be completed independently, but, during a financial review, examiners may work with legislators, consumer advocates, financial managers, and accountants.

Profile

Working Conditions: Work Indoors
Physical Strength: Light Work
Education Needs: Bachelor's Degree
Licensure/Certification: Not Required
Opportunities For Experience: Part-time work, On the Job Training
Holland Interest Score*: EC

* See Appendix A

Occupation Interest

Financial examination can be considered a branch of accounting that deals with federal and state regulations and financial institutions. Whether working in risk scoping or consumer compliance, financial examiners help consumers by helping to prevent financial institutions from engaging in activities that can negatively affect clients or investors and so financial examiners should have an interest in public welfare. In addition, financial examiners are investigators and should have a strong interest in research, mathematics, and evaluation.

A Day in the Life—Duties and Responsibilities

A typical day for a financial examiner might involve meeting with financial managers and other representatives of financial institutions. Examiners might also spend part or most of a typical day reviewing a financial institution's transactions, including expense accounts and the records created by banks and loan institutions to comply with financial regulations. In some cases, examiners might interview personnel or customers when conducting an investigation. Examiners might also spend time reviewing meetings held within financial institutions to better understand how the institutional management.

During and after an examination, examiners create and present reports to managers and other officials detailing the findings of the investigation and presenting options for changes that the institution might need to make to comply with laws and regulations. Financial examiners are also responsible for keeping up with the latest regulatory changes and might spend time studying new regulations and determining how changes in the law will affect local institutions. Senior examiners might also spend time mentoring or training new personnel as financial examiners typically receive on the job training.

Duties and Responsibilities

- **Researching new regulations and laws**
- **Reviewing financial transactions and management**
- **Training junior examiners**
- **Creating, presenting, and explaining reports**
- **Meeting with finance professionals**
- **Maintaining detained records of examinations**

OCCUPATION SPECIALTIES

Risk Scoping Specialist

A risk scoping specialist is a financial examiner who specializes in evaluating the performance of financial institutions like banks and other lending, finance institutions. Risk scoping specialists evaluate the performance of bank/financial managers and executives and may also review the accounts of financial institutions to ensure that the institution has sufficient capital to avoid risks that could adversely affect the institution and its customers.

Consumer Compliance Specialist

Consumer compliance experts help to ensure that financial institutions meet state and federal laws regarding consumer protection. Examiners in consumer compliance help consumers by investigating "predatory loan" practices and companies and also enforce federal non-discrimination policies that apply to banks and loan organizations.

Financial Manager

A financial manager is a specialist in finance, taxation, and accounting who helps to manage an organization's financial operation. Financial managers may conduct detailed examinations to ensure that their organization is complying with state and federal laws and to monitor the organization's financial health.

Financial Management Officer

A financial management officer is a financial manager who works in the military, overseeing the financial management of a military branch or group. Financial management officers perform many of the same functions as financial examiners, reviewing costs and accounts to ensure that the organization meets legal standards and protects the welfare of personnel.

Financial Examination Administrator

A financial examiner administrator works in a financial examination firm or other institution that employs financial examiners and manages the work of other examiners. Administrators are typically financial examiners who have advanced to take on a management role within their institution or organization and are responsible for overseeing and reviewing the work of other professionals in the field.

WORK ENVIRONMENT

Physical Environment

Financial examiners typically do most of their work in office environments utilizing technological tools. In some cases, examiners may travel to different financial institutions to analyze data on site or to interview members of an organization's staff, while in other cases examiners may remain in a single office and review data sent to them from institutions undergoing an examination.

Relevant Skills and Abilities

Communication Skills
- Interviewing and meeting with financial professionals
- Writing clear communications and reports

Interpersonal/Social Skills
- Working with other professionals in a team environment
- Interviewing finance professionals and managers

Organization & Management Skills
- Meeting deadlines
- Creating and maintaining detailed records

Research & Planning Skills
- Researching and evaluating data
- Scheduling meetings, reviews, and evaluations
- Researching changes in applicable laws and regulations

Technical Skills
- Performing complex calculations
- Using software and digital communication tools

Human Environment

Examiners may work alone or in offices with other financial examiners or other finance specialists. In some cases, financial examiners may be responsible for meeting with clients or managers of financial institutions to obtain information for an analysis, to explain and discuss the results of a completed or in-progress analysis, or to recommend changes to the institution's policies or practices. In some cases, examiners may work with other examiners or accountants or may be responsible for managing the work of other examiners working for an institution.

Technological Environment

Financial examiners make extensive use of computers, digital devices, and accounting software and individuals seeking work as examiners should be familiar with financial analysis and accounting software. In addition, there are specific, highly specialized software programs, like Oversight Insights On Demand, and the System for Electronic Rate and Form Filing SERFF, that are designed specifically to monitor compliance in financial institutions. Financial examiners also need to have skill with word processing and spreadsheet software for creating and delivering reports on their examinations.

EDUCATION, TRAINING, AND ADVANCEMENT

High School/Secondary

High school students interested in a career in financial examination should prepare to pursue a bachelor's degree in a related field, such as accounting or finance. Preparatory classes in accounting, mathematics, and business administration will also benefit candidates for professional positions. Classes in public speaking, composition, and business/technical writing will also help prepare students for careers in the field as financial examiners must be capable of preparing and presenting clear, detailed reports on their examinations.

Suggested High School Subjects

- Applied math
- Accounting
- Mathematics
- Algebra
- Statistics
- Composition
- Introduction to Computers
- Public speaking
- Technical writing
- Critical thinking

Famous First

In 1963, Roland W. Burris became the first African American to work as a financial examiner when he took a job for the Office of the Comptroller of the Currency (OCC) as a bank examiner. Burris, who obtained a political science degree from Southern Illinois University and later a law degree from Howard University, had difficulty finding work as a lawyer in Chicago after graduation, but was fortunate to find a job with the OCC, becoming the first African American to work for the organization. After spending only a year with the OCC, Burris went on to work for the Department of General Services under Governor Dan Walker, and later ran for election as governor in Illinois.

College/Postsecondary

Most financial examiners have at least a bachelor's degree and many specialize in accounting or other financial fields before transitioning to careers as financial examiners. Those looking to advance in the field or to become financial examination supervisors or administrators, might also consider pursuing a postgraduate degree in finance or accounting. Classes in economics, governance, and politics will also be helpful as examiners are charged with balancing institutional goals and public policy.

Related College Majors

- Finance, General
- Accounting
- Certified Public Accounting (CPA)
- Economics
- Business
- Business management
- Financial management
- Financial analysis

Adult Job Seekers

Those with degrees in finance, economics, accounting or related fields can apply for open positions as financial examiners. Typically, examiners receive on-the-job training under the supervision of senior examiners until they are ready to work independently. Individuals with degrees in economics, finance, or business, who do not have direct experience in accounting might consider returning to adult education to increase their familiarity with accounting principles and practices.

Professional Certification and Licensure

There are not specific certificates or licenses needed to become a financial examiner, but many professionals in the field choose to obtain professional certification in accounting. For instance, many financial examiners and administrators obtain Certified Public Accountant (CPA) certification to increase their chances of being hired or to advance within their field. Individuals with experience in various types of accounting, such as forensic, business, and/or tax accounting typically have an advantage when seeking employment. Organizations like the Federal Deposit Insurance Corporation (FDIC), employ financial examiners and can provide guidance on the basic parameters for employment in the field.

Additional Requirements

Financial examiners need to have excellent skill with mathematics in order to handle the advanced calculations needed to examine an organization's financial practices and history. In addition, financial examiners must be skilled with critical thinking and analysis and must have excellent attention to detail when conducting their analyses. Financial examiners should also be comfortable in meetings and speaking with financial professionals and should be able to write clear, concise reports detailing the findings of their examinations.

Fun Fact

E-commerce fraud is most likely to occur late at night: transactions that occur at 2 A.M. are 50 percent more likely to be fraudulent than those that take place during business hours, while those that take place at 4 A.M. are 100 percent more likely to be fraudulent.

Source: https://blog.siftscience.com/2013/five-ecommerce-fraud-facts/

EARNINGS AND ADVANCEMENT

According to the Bureau of Labor Statistics, the median annual wage for financial examiners in the United States was estimated at $79,280 in May of 2016. The highest wages in the field were found in federal government positions, where examiners earned an average wage of more than $115,000. Examiners at the lowest 10 percent of the income spectrum earned less than $46,000, while those at the highest 10 percent earned wages of over $148,000. After obtaining work experience, individual can advance in the field by applying for higher-paying positions in other organizations or by applying for a position as a manager or administrator who oversees other financial examiners in an institution or organization. Financial examiners who start in state government or local organizations can also attempt to advance by accruing experience and applying for positions in corporations or in federal positions.

Metropolitan Areas with the Highest Employment Level in this Occupation

Metropolitan area	Employment	Employment per thousand jobs	Hourly mean wage
New York-Jersey City-White Plains, NY-NJ Metropolitan Division	5,570	0.85	$55.02
Charlotte-Concord-Gastonia, NC-SC	1,530	1.32	$43.56
Washington-Arlington-Alexandria, DC-VA-MD-WV Metropolitan Division	1,490	0.60	$55.57
Chicago-Naperville-Arlington Heights, IL Metropolitan Division	1,440	0.40	$50.21
Boston-Cambridge-Newton, MA NECTA Division	1,350	0.75	$48.90
Los Angeles-Long Beach-Glendale, CA Metropolitan Division	1,240	0.29	$46.78
Minneapolis-St. Paul-Bloomington, MN-WI	1,170	0.61	$44.66
Dallas-Plano-Irving, TX Metropolitan Division	1,070	0.44	$45.71
St. Louis, MO-IL	1,060	0.79	$35.55
San Francisco-Redwood City-South San Francisco, CA Metropolitan Division	1,010	0.95	$60.01

Source: Bureau of Labor Statistics

EMPLOYMENT AND OUTLOOK

In 2014, the Bureau of Labor Statistics (BLS), estimated that there were 38,200 individuals employed as financial examiners in the United States. In addition, the BLS found that the financial examination field was growing by an average of 10 percent annually, which is considered higher than average growth when compared to the 6-7 percent growth for all occupations in the United States. Demand for financial examiners has risen due to more stringent guidelines on financial institutions and a proliferation of new regulations. In the finance and insurance industries, for instance, the field is growing at a much faster than average rate, with an estimated 16 percent annual growth expected between 2014 and 2024. Demand for financial examiners increases during periods of financial instability as there is a greater need to enforce regulations.

Related Occupations

- Accountants
- Financial Analysts
- Budget Specialists
- Financial Managers
- Appraisers, Examiners, and Investigators
- Budget Analysts
- Loan Officers
- Personal Financial Advisors
- Tax Examiners and Collectors and Revenue Agents

Related Military Occupations

- Financial Management Officer

Conversation With . . .
JIM KATTMAN, CFE

Managing Director, Noble Consulting Services, Inc.
Indianapolis, Indiana
Insurance regulation, 21 years

1. What was your individual career path in terms of education/training, entry-level job, or other significant opportunity?

In high school, I wasn't sure what I wanted to do but options in business seemed most intriguing, and accounting seemed a good entryway into the business world. I earned a bachelor's degree from Indiana University. I thought public accounting would give me exposure to different areas and when I went to work at a local Certified Public Accounting (CPA) firm in Indianapolis, it did. I worked on different types of accounts, and found insurance through a client. I moved over to Anthem Life Insurance Company of Indiana and did statutory reporting for a year before becoming an examiner performing statutory examinations for the Indiana Department of Insurance, which regulates all life and health, HMO, property and casualty insurers in Indiana. This includes nationally significant insurers.

Five years later, I took the opportunity to join Noble Consulting Services, Inc., which works or has worked with 15-20 state insurance departments in its 20-year history. But, in this specialized industry, we maintain relationships with most state insurance departments in the country.

States are responsible for regulating insurance companies. In my current role, I'm responsible for quality control for examination reports provided to state insurance departments. I am part of the team responsible for firm-wide controls and procedures related to examinations.

2. What are the most important skills and/or qualities for someone in your profession?

Being an insurance examiner requires technical knowledge and skill in applying laws and regulations to real-world situations, along with advanced written and oral communication ability.

It's important to be able to interact with different personalities and understand what people are saying because you're always talking with people who are experts in their different fields.

3. **What do you wish you had known going into this profession?**

The importance of building and maintaining relationships has time and again proven to be a valuable tool and resource. In a career such as this that requires technical skill and knowledge—and probably advanced degrees or designations—the pool of people pursuing the same or similar careers is likely to be limited in a regional or even national scope. That means you are likely to work with the same people and good relationships are critical.

4. **Are there many job opportunities in your profession? In what specific areas?**

Yes. Insurance is a highly specialized and regulated industry. The technical skills and knowledge required are in demand—especially in the accounting, finance, and legal areas—even as the insurance industry experiences consolidation in certain areas. In my field of expertise, there are in-house analyst functions and field-examination functions within state insurance departments. The roles within state insurance departments are diverse, meaning people with careers in many insurance-related fields may find themselves qualified to work in insurance regulation.

5. **How do you see your profession changing in the next five years, what role will technology play in those changes, and what skills will be required?**

Working remotely is rapidly increasing, which cuts down on the expense of travel. The ability to share information and documents electronically in real time has a real impact on what we do. Software improvements in functions such as customer relations management, or even keeping time and expense records, require technical knowledge of these programs and applications.

6. **What do you enjoy most about your job? What do you enjoy least about your job?**

I enjoy the opportunity to work with diverse and interesting people in many parts of the country. The relationships built over the years are important and rewarding and the perspective that comes from engaging with these people is interesting.

Working with people across the country means travel is often involved. Some travel is a great way to see parts of the country that you otherwise might not see. But over time, and as your life changes, travel can mean time away from family and friends. Everyone's situation is different and that can place travel requirements in a positive or negative light.

7. **Can you suggest a valuable "try this" for students considering a career in your profession?**

There may be intern opportunities with state insurance departments. Some independent consulting firms such as Noble offer intern opportunities throughout the year. This is a great way for students and recent graduates to better understand the work involved.

SELECTED SCHOOLS

Many colleges and universities, especially those with business schools, offer programs in business and finance. The student can also gain initial training at a technical or community college. For some of the more prominent institutions in this field, see the list of selected schools in the "Accountant" and "Finance Manager" chapters of this volume.

MORE INFORMATION

Federal Deposit Insurance Corporation (FDIC)
Washington D.C.
877-275-3342
www.fdic.gov

Consumer Financial Protection Bureau (CFPB)
1625 Eye Street N.W.
Washington, D.C. 20006
855-411-2372
www.consumerfinance.gov

Society of Financial Examiners
7044 South 13th Street
Oak Creek, WI 53154
414-908-4930
www.sofe.org

Office of the Comptroller of the Currency
400 7th Street SW, Suite 3E-218
Washington, D.C. 20219
877-275-3342
www.occ.gov

Association of Certified Fraud Examiners
716 West Ave
Austin, TX 78701-2727
800-245-3321
www.acfe.com

Micah Issitt/Editor

General Manager & Top Executive

Snapshot

Career Cluster(s): Business, Management & Administration, Government & Public Administration
Interests: Communicating with others, managing personnel, communication, time management
Earnings (Yearly Average): $103,950
Employment & Outlook: Average growth expected

OVERVIEW

Sphere of Work

General managers and top executives are responsible for making strategic business decisions to ensure that their organizations run smoothly and profitably. They occupy the very top tier of management and, as such, bear the ultimate responsibility to the owners and stakeholders for the organization's performance. Highly compensated, they are expected to provide a corresponding level of leadership and direction to other senior executives and managers, as well as to formulate and communicate high-level policy. General managers and top executives in private enterprises may be known by more specific job

titles, such as president, chief executive officer, or director. In the non-profit and government sectors, they may have job titles such as agency director, chief, or superintendent.

Work Environment

General managers and top executives usually spend most of their work day in office environments. Typically, they have their own office or suite of offices close to other members of the organization's executive management team. General managers and top executives can expect to spend a considerable amount of time traveling away from home, especially if their organization is national or multinational. They are frequently expected to put in as many hours as required to fulfill their duties. As a result, many top executives work sixty or more hours a week, including evenings, weekends, and holidays.

Profile

Working Conditions: Work Indoors
Physical Strength: Light Work
Education Needs: Bachelor's Degree, Master's Degree, PhD
Licensure/Certification: Not Required
Opportunities For Experience: Part-time work, Military service, Internship
Holland Interest Score*: ESR

* See Appendix A

Occupation Interest

This occupation suits people who combine technical knowledge and abilities relevant to the industry they work in with sophisticated business and leadership skills and the desire and commitment needed to effectively run an organization. They must have the experience, foresight, and ability to develop an organization's strategic direction by taking into account the competitive environment, market opportunities and challenges, micro- and macroeconomics, sociopolitical factors, resource requirements, and operations. Strong analytical abilities and the capacity to set goals for short- and long-term planning are a must in this profession. This job usually requires long hours and a level of responsibility that may cause stress.

A Day in the Life—Duties and Responsibilities

A top executive's day may be dedicated to dealing with one issue or a wide variety of issues. It is likely, however, that a significant proportion of the day will be spent communicating with others, either one-on-one or in group meetings. The general manager is likely to schedule regular meetings with key staff and committees about issues such as budgets, financial results, sales forecasts, and special projects. He or she will meet regularly with the key staff who report to them. This may include, for example, the chief financial officer, human resources director, operations director, sales and marketing directors, and any other key staff. The general manager is likely to delegate duties as needed to his or her support staff, as well as task them with special projects, research, and analysis. Individuals in this position are additionally responsible for developing lower-level employees into future managers.

The organization's top executives may also be involved at a strategic level in special projects and initiatives. Depending on the type of organization, this may include, for example, crisis and reputation management, new product development and launches, mergers and acquisitions, site openings and closures, strategic operational and logistic changes, and policy development.

The general manager is responsible for reporting to the company's board of directors, owners, and investors. In the case of publicly listed companies, this includes shareholders. The general manager is responsible for ensuring that the company fulfills its legal and fiduciary responsibilities. In doing so, the general manager makes a personal guarantee to the company's board and shareholders that the information provided in official legal and financial reports is accurate and reliable.

Duties and Responsibilities

- **Analyzing data and setting goals**
- **Meeting with other professionals**
- **Directing operations**
- **Overseeing executives and other employees**
- **Managing organizational budgets**

OCCUPATION SPECIALTIES

Chief Executive Officer/President

Chief Executive Officers/Presidents decide policies and direct operations of organizations.

Department Store Manager

Department Store Managers direct activities, formulate and implement policies for sales and other departments.

Bank President

Bank Presidents plan and direct policies and practices of banks or other financial institutions.

Special Agent

Special Agents recruit sales agents and coordinate agencies and home offices of insurance companies.

College President

College Presidents plan and direct the administration of a school, college or university.

School Superintendent

School Superintendents direct and coordinate the administration of school systems.

Police Chief

Police Chiefs direct and coordinate the activities of a municipal police department.

Harbor Master

Harbor Masters direct and coordinate the activities of a harbor police force.

Library Director

Library Directors plan and administer library services with the approval of a board of directors.

WORK ENVIRONMENT

Relevant Skills and Abilities

Communication Skills
- Speaking effectively
- Writing concisely
- Presenting information
- Giving speeches

Interpersonal/Social Skills
- Being able to work independently
- Working as a member of a team
- Motivating others

Organization & Management Skills
- Paying attention to and handling details
- Making decisions

Research & Planning Skills
- Analyzing information
- Solving problems
- Researching market and industry developments

Technical Skills
- Using computers and digital tools

Physical Environment

General managers and top executives usually work from their own office, which tends to be pleasant and well-appointed. The general manager's physical environment will be influenced by the size and type of employer and the industry in which they operate.

Human Environment

This role involves a great amount of interaction with others. General managers and top executives must possess advanced oral and written communication skills, including the ability to collaborate, negotiate, and resolve conflict. They must be able to conduct themselves with diplomacy and tact and interact confidently with powerful people.

Technological Environment

Daily operations may demand the use of standard office technologies, including computers, telephones, e-mail, photocopiers, and the Internet. General managers and top executives are supported by an executive secretary or administrative team who completes much of the more routine paperwork and requests. The technology used by someone in this position can vary depending on the industry. Increasingly, general managers may use cloud based and virtual communication and data management tools and may use mobile digital tools for communication and management activities.

EDUCATION, TRAINING, AND ADVANCEMENT

High School/Secondary

High school students can best prepare for a career as a general manager and top executive by taking courses in applied communication subjects such as business writing as well as computer science. Foreign languages may also be beneficial. Courses that develop general business skills may include accounting, entrepreneurship, bookkeeping, business management, and applied mathematics. Administrative skills may be developed by taking subjects such as business computing and typing. Becoming involved in part-time administrative or clerical work after school or during the weekends builds people skills and is a helpful way to begin learning about business operations and management. Leadership experience can be developed through taking part in extracurricular activities.

Suggested High School Subjects

- Applied Communication
- College Preparatory
- Composition
- Computer Science
- English
- Mathematics
- Economics
- History
- Public Speaking

Famous First

In 1889, American entrepreneur Anna Bissell became the first woman in the U.S. to serve as Chief Executive Officer (CEO) of an American company when she took over for her husband Melville as head of the Bissell Sweeper Company. Before becoming CEO, Bissell reportedly worked in different facets of the company, including traveling to promote and sell Bissell products across the nation. By 1899, Bissell had led the Bissell Sweeper Company to become the largest cleaning technology company in the world. Bissell became one of the first companies to offer full pension plans and workers compensation to her employees and, by 1899, Anna Bissell was among the wealthiest and most powerful women in the world.

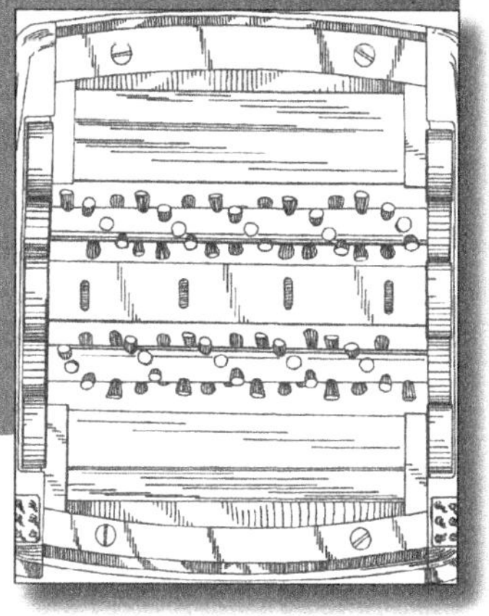

Postsecondary

In keeping with the level of responsibility of the position, most employers expect their general managers and top executives to possess postsecondary qualifications. The minimum requirement is considered to be a bachelor's degree in business or another relevant field. A master's degree in business administration is sometimes, but not always, considered to be a requirement. Because this position is extremely results-oriented, some individuals earn more advanced degrees, while others advance as a result of proving their abilities through on-the-job experience.

Related College Majors

- Aviation Management
- Business
- Business Administration & Management, General
- Education Administration & Supervision, General
- Enterprise Management & Operation
- Entrepreneurship
- Finance, General
- General Retailing & Wholesaling Operations & Skills
- Sport & Fitness Administration/Management
- Travel-Tourism Management

Adult Job Seekers

Adults seeking a career as a general manager and top executive should emphasize any prior management experience or advanced knowledge of the core competencies of business management, such as financial management, human resource management, operations, and sales and marketing. Adult job seekers may need to supplement their current skill set by taking classes in relevant areas. Candidates should keep in mind that many companies promote their existing managers into top executive positions. Networking, job searching, and interviewing are, therefore, critical, and this should include registering with executive recruitment agencies.

Professional Certification and Licensure

There are no formal professional certifications or licensing requirements for general managers and top executives. Professional associations offer general manager certifications and some industry authorities require staff to hold special licenses. The American Management Association (AMA) and National Management Association (NMA) provide certificate programs in a range of specialty areas, as well as general management.

Additional Requirements

The workload and pressures placed on general managers and top executives are often relentless or intense, so these individuals should be highly motivated, confident, and able to thrive under pressure. Work/life balance may be difficult to achieve or maintain in such a demanding and responsible role, which often requires a great commitment of time and energy.

Fun Fact

A 2016 study of 261 top corporate executives concluded that 21 percent of them had traits of psychopaths. In the general population, the rate of psychopathology is one in 100 people.

Source: http://www.telegraph.co.uk/news/2016/09/13/

EARNINGS AND ADVANCEMENT

According to the Bureau of Labor Statistics (BLS), the median annual wage for general managers in 2016 was $114,850, while the median wage for top executives was closer to $180,000 annually. Salaries range widely in the field depending on the professional's specific field. For instance, top executives earn salaries ranging from less than $69,000 to well over $208,000, while general and operations managers earn salaries ranging from less than $44,000 at the low end to more than $200,000 for the highest paid positions. Advancing also depends largely on the specific field and level of competition. In some cases, general managers can advance to top executive positions within a company or institution. Professionals in upper management can also advance by accruing experience and applying for more lucrative or higher level positions in another company/institution.

Metropolitan Areas with the Highest Employment Level in this Occupation

Metropolitan area	Employment	Employment per thousand jobs	Hourly mean wage
New York-Jersey City-White Plains, NY-NJ Metropolitan Division	111,740	16.97	$81.48
Chicago-Naperville-Arlington Heights, IL Metropolitan Division	76,760	21.10	$61.50
Los Angeles-Long Beach-Glendale, CA Metropolitan Division	70,520	16.71	$65.33
Atlanta-Sandy Springs-Roswell, GA	60,130	23.55	$59.90
Washington-Arlington-Alexandria, DC-VA-MD-WV Metropolitan Division	58,160	23.35	$72.17
Houston-The Woodlands-Sugar Land, TX	47,800	16.29	$72.56
Boston-Cambridge-Newton, MA NECTA Division	38,280	21.23	$71.21
Dallas-Plano-Irving, TX Metropolitan Division	36,510	15.03	$70.14
Phoenix-Mesa-Scottsdale, AZ	32,210	16.64	$49.56
Minneapolis-St. Paul-Bloomington, MN-WI	28,920	15.14	$55.23

Source: Bureau of Labor Statistics

EMPLOYMENT AND OUTLOOK

In general, the upper management industry is growing at an average rate, with 6 percent growth expected between 2014 and 2024, while the BLS expects 6-7 percent average growth for all occupations. Consolidation of larger corporations reduces opportunities for chief executives and upper level managers, while expansion into overseas markets has created new opportunities for executives with experience in foreign commerce and international business. The overall expansion of virtual business has also created significant growth in the industry. In general, with average growth, competition for upper management jobs will remain significant and applicants with higher levels of experience and with advanced degrees will continue to enjoy a significant advantage when seeking employment.

Related Occupations

- City Manager
- Computer & Information Systems Manager
- Education Administrator
- Financial Manager
- Human Resources Specialist/ Manager
- Information Technology Project Manager
- Management Analyst & Consultant
- Medical & Health Services Manager
- Online Merchant
- Postmaster & Mail Superintendent
- Public Administrator
- Public Relations Specialist
- Retail Store Sales Manager

Related Military Occupations

- Law Enforcement & Security Officer
- Law Enforcement & Security Specialist
- Military Police

Conversation With . . .
EDWARD BREINER

CEO/President (retired)
Schramm, Inc.
West Chester, Pennsylvania
CEO, 10 years

1. What was your individual career path in terms of education/training, entry-level job, or other significant opportunity?

The only reason I went to college was because I got recruited to play football. I majored in sociology and dropped out after a year because I quit football. I had no idea what I was doing or why and then I worked in a foundry for nine months, which was hot, dirty intense work. That's when I decided that I was going to go back to college. I borrowed money to pay for it and asked about the number one employment opportunity and the college told me that 90 percent of accountants got a job. So I graduated from Bloomsburg University of Pennsylvania with a B.S. in accounting.

I started out after graduation as a cost accountant at Ingersoll Rand, a manufacturing company in New Jersey, where I had worked summers. My father worked there, and I never would have gotten the summer job if it wasn't for him, but from there it was up to me. After a few years, I ended up at a Texas plant that became headquarters for the entire division. I worked in pretty much every aspect of the business. I made a lot of lateral moves, which turned out to be to my benefit. While I was in Texas, I got my MBA at the University of Dallas

After 22 years, I left to go to Schramm, which was a competitor. It was a family-owned business and the principal was looking for someone to come in and do a buyout and he recruited me. It was hard to leave Ingersoll Rand because I was in a very good position, but the company was changing. At Schramm, I came in as a vice president. It was handshake; there weren't any guarantees on the acquisition that I was recruited to do. It took a while because the owner wanted to sell, but he didn't really want to sell. But after a few years and lots of back and forth, a team of managers, including me, put in a little bit of money and the bank lent us a lot of money, and we bought most of his ownership share. I became CEO in 2004-2005. In 2012, we sold to a private equity firm and within months, the business went south in terms of revenue. It was a struggle for a couple of years. I had told them I was going to leave. They decided I had checked out already, so, in 2014, I got fired at the Peninsula, which is a very pricey hotel in Manhattan. But they wanted me to stay on as a board member because I had all the contacts and actually understood business. So, I'm still there as a director.

2. What are the most important skills and/or qualities for someone in your profession?

I would put listening first. Particularly in today's world, a collaborative style of management is necessary. Second is bias to action. In other words, don't sit around and wait for somebody else to do it. If something's broke, fix it. And, third, a willingness to take risks.

3. What do you wish you had known going into this profession?

I wish I had known how boring accounting was. Accounting was a great background for understanding a business, but I really wasn't suited to sitting at a desk and crunching numbers all day.

4. Are there many job opportunities in your profession? In what specific areas?

With an accounting degree, there are a lot of opportunities. Once you understand a balance sheet, income statement and cash flow, and you get down to understanding where the cash comes from and where it goes, you can manage the business. It doesn't matter if it's General Electric or a street vendor in Mumbai.

5. How do you see your profession changing in the next five years? What role will technology play in those changes, and what skills will be required?

I would be intimidated in the next 10 years if I didn't understand the foundations of information technology, artificial intelligence and, from a marketing standpoint, the role of social media.

6. What do you enjoy most about your job? What do you enjoy least about your job?

Taking aim at an objective and working together and succeeding and also failing and living through that and still keeping friendships and dignity. We really did have a very collaborative, open style of working together. It's a cliché, but it was the people.

I did not like firing people and unfortunately, I did it many times. My business was mining and oil and gas and the swings in the commodities market are severe. So, you had to grow businesses and shrink businesses. It is part of the nature of cyclical businesses, but you really felt that you had failed these people.

7. Can you suggest a valuable "try this" for students considering a career in your profession?

There's nothing like team sports to teach you how to work with others, how to accept defeat, how to fail together and win together. The good thing about internships is exposure, to see what it is that people do.

SELECTED SCHOOLS

Many colleges and universities, especially those with business schools, offer programs in finance and business administration. The student can also gain initial training through enrollment at a technical or community college. For advanced positions, a master's of business administration (MBA) with a concentration in finance is usually expected. Below are listed some of the more prominent institutions in this field.

Carnegie Mellon University
Tepper School of Business
500 Forbes Avenue
Pittsburgh, PA 15213
412.268.2268
tepper.cmu.edu

Indiana University, Bloomington
Kelley School of Business
1309 E. 10th Street
Bloomington, IN 47405
812.855.8100
kelley.iu.edu

Massachusetts Institute of Technology
Sloan School of Management
50 Memorial Drive
Cambridge, MA 02142
617.253.2659
mitsloan.mit.edu

New York University
Stern School of Business
665 Broadway, 11th Floor
New York, NY 10012
212.998.4500
www.stern.nyu.edu

University of California, Berkeley
Haas School of Business
S450 Student Services Building #1900
Berkeley, CA 94720
510.642.1421
haas.berkeley.edu

University of Michigan, Ann Arbor
Ross School of Business
701 Tappan Avenue
Ann Arbor, MI 48109
734.763.5796
michiganross.umich.edu

University of North Carolina, Chapel Hill
Kenan-Flagler Business School
Campus Box 3490, McColl Building
Chapel Hill, NC 27599
919.962.3235
www.kenan-flagler.unc.edu

University of Pennsylvania
The Wharton School
1 College Hall
Philadelphia, PA 19104
215.898.6376
www.wharton.upenn.edu

MORE INFORMATION

Business and Professional Women's Foundation
1718 M Street NW, #148
Washington, DC 20036
202.293.1100
foundation@bpwfoundation.org
www.bpwfoundation.org

Career Advancement Scholarship Program
www.free-4u.com/bpw-career_advancement_scholarship_program.htm

National Management Association
2210 Arbor Boulevard
Dayton, OH 45439
937.294.0421
nma@nma1.org
www.nma1.org

Various national awards; eligibility is contingent on membership
www.nma1.org/Awards/NMA_Awards.html#National_Awards

Kylie Hughes & Micah Issitt/Editors

Insurance Claims Adjuster and Examiner

Snapshot

Career Cluster(s): Business, Management & Administration, Finance
Interests: Investigation, risk assessment, solving problems, helping others
Earnings (Yearly Average): $63,670
Employment & Outlook: Slower than average growth expected

OVERVIEW

Sphere of Work

Insurance claims adjusters and examiners, also referred to as insurance claims investigators, insurance claims assessors, insurance claims analysts, and liability assessors, are responsible for investigating and settling claims that insurance policyholders have made to their insurance companies. Adjusters visit the scene of an accident, injury, or natural disaster and estimate the cost of the damage done. They

write reports recommending whether the claim should be approved or not. Examiners are very similar to adjusters, although in some companies they may follow up on adjusters' work by checking their reports for accuracy and to ensure that the adjuster has followed the insurance company's procedures properly. Adjusters and examiners may be independent agents or employed by insurance companies.

Work Environment

Insurance claims adjusters and examiners work in offices writing and evaluating claims reports as well as in the field investigating claims and inspecting damaged property. They visit claimants and insurance policyholders at their homes, accident scenes, hospitals and rehabilitation facilities, and automobile repair shops. Insurance claims adjusters and examiners may work a forty-hour week or in an on-call capacity responding to claims as they are made. They may be expected to work overtime during busy times or when responding to emergencies or natural disasters that affect many people at once. When investigating claims in the field, especially in the aftermath of an event like a tornado or a fire, insurance claims adjusters and examiners may be exposed to physical hazards.

Profile

Working Conditions: Work Indoors
Physical Strength: Light Work
Education Needs: Associate's Degree, Bachelor's Degree
Licensure/Certification: Required
Opportunities For Experience: Part-time work, Internship
Holland Interest Score*: ESC

* See Appendix A

Occupation Interest

Individuals attracted to the insurance claims adjuster and examiner profession tend to be organized, diplomatic, and detail-oriented people who find satisfaction in resolving questions and helping people in times of need. Those individuals who excel as insurance claims adjusters and examiners exhibit traits such as responsibility, time management, composure under pressure, attention to detail, and a desire to help. Insurance claims adjusters and examiners should enjoy insurance work and have a background in investigation and risk assessment.

A Day in the Life—Duties and Responsibilities

The daily duties and responsibilities of insurance claims adjusters and examiners will vary with job specialty and employer. Areas of insurance claims specialization include claims adjusters, appraisers, examiners, and investigators. Insurance claims adjusters and examiners investigate and settle property damage, liability, and bodily injury claims. Insurance companies encourage insurance claims adjusters and examiners to settle claims without legal arbitration whenever possible.

When they receive claims, insurance claims adjusters and examiners may begin work by reviewing insurance policies to determine what type and amount of coverage applies to the claim. They may travel to the site of damaged property and confirm the cause and extent of the damage; they may interview people involved in the incident, including policyholders, witnesses, first responders (police, firemen, and paramedics), and physicians. They gather information and records related to the incident, such as police reports, and work with appraisers, colleagues, and relevant professionals, such as builders or auto mechanics, to determine the extent of the damage. Providing emotional and customer service support to customers is a very important aspect of processing claims, especially since customers may have experienced a personal loss or a significant loss of property due to the event. Claims adjusters and examiners may assist policyholders with various requests, and communicate with them about the process of investigating the claim. If a widespread natural disaster occurs, the adjuster may be sent to assist local residents with the filing of their claims before the evaluation process begins.

When the initial work is complete, insurance claims adjusters and examiners prepare the claim report and attempt to negotiate a monetary settlement with the policyholder. Most of the time this is successful, but if the claimant contests the company's decision regarding a claim, sometimes claims adjusters and examiners must initiate legal proceedings if an out-of-court settlement cannot be reached. The final claims report is submitted by the adjuster or examiner to supervisors at the insurance company. Examiners are also responsible for checking the accuracy of adjusters' reported findings and for confirming that adjusters followed correct procedures while investigating the claim or claims.

All insurance claims adjusters and examiners should stay up to date with regulatory and ethical issues and news in the insurance industry by reading insurance industry journals and participating in insurance industry associations.

Duties and Responsibilities

- Determining the amount of damage
- Determining if the claim is covered by a policy
- Interviewing or corresponding with the person making the claim
- Inspecting property damage or loss
- Consulting police, fire, and medical reports and records
- Preparing a detailed report of findings
- Recommending necessary legal action
- Testifying in court on contested claims
- Preparing and maintaining files on clients' policies
- Making adjustments to existing policies, such as change in type or amount of coverage

WORK ENVIRONMENT

Physical Environment

Insurance claims adjusters and examiners work in office environments as well as in the field investigating claims and visiting damaged property and injured people. Insurance claims adjusters and examiners generally must be physically able to drive as well as walk over potentially rough terrain damaged by flood, winds, earthquakes, and fire.

Relevant Skills and Abilities

Communication Skills
- Speaking effectively
- Speaking and communicating persuasively
- Writing concisely
- Conducting interviews

Interpersonal/Social Skills
- Being able to work independently
- Working as a member of a team
- Cooperating with others

Organization & Management Skills
- Making decisions
- Paying attention to and managing details

Research & Planning Skills
- Developing evaluation strategies
- Researching information relevant to claims

Technical Skills
- Working with data or numbers
- Using computers and other digital tools

Human Environment

Insurance claims adjusters and examiners interact with insurance policyholders, lawyers, doctors, automobile repair mechanics, business owners, and coworkers and supervisors. Insurance claims adjusters and examiners should be comfortable meeting with policyholders and industry professionals and show good judgment, objectivity, and tact when responding to policyholders.

Technological Environment

Insurance claims adjusters and examiners use computers, telephones, tape measures, cameras, calculators, Internet communication tools, insurance business software programs, and spreadsheets to complete their work.

EDUCATION, TRAINING, AND ADVANCEMENT

High School/Secondary

High school students interested in pursuing a career as an insurance claims adjuster or examiner should prepare by building good study habits. High school–level study of sociology, bookkeeping, and mathematics will provide a strong foundation for work as an insurance claims adjuster and examiner or for college-level study in the field. High school students interested in this career path will benefit from seeking internships or part-time work with insurance businesses or investigators.

Suggested High School Subjects

- Applied Communication
- Bookkeeping
- Business
- Business Law
- Computer Science
- Economics
- English
- Keyboarding
- Mathematics
- Psychology
- Statistics

Famous First

Many insurance investigators work as independent contractors who specialize in investigation and hire out their services to insurance companies. Insurance investigation gained popularity as a career due to the radio drama, *Yours Truly, Johnny Dollar*, which explored the adventures of a private investigator, billed as "America's fabulous freelance insurance investigator." The stories were formatted such that each act related to a different entry in Dollar's expense account he used while working a case, and each episode began with Dollar being contacted by an insurance company executive asking him to investigate a suspicious claim. The series lasted for 12 years and was among the most popular private detective serials before the advent of television.

College/Postsecondary

Postsecondary students interested in becoming insurance claims adjusters and examiners should work toward an associate's or bachelor's degree in economics, finance, statistics, or accounting. Coursework in computer science, political science, and ethics may also prove useful in their future work. Postsecondary students can gain work experience and potential advantage in their future job searches by securing internships or part-time employment with local insurance businesses.

Related College Majors

- Accounting
- Banking
- Business Accounting
- Finance, General
- Business, General

Adult Job Seekers

Adults seeking insurance claims adjuster and examiner jobs have generally earned an associate's or bachelor's degree. Some insurance claims adjuster and examiner jobs require extensive experience and on-the-job training. Adult job seekers should educate themselves about the educational and professional requirements of the organizations where they seek employment. Adult job seekers will benefit from joining professional insurance associations as a means of professional networking. Professional insurance associations, such as the National Association of Professional Insurance Agents, the Independent Automotive Damage Appraisers Association, the Insurance Institute of America, and the National Association of Independent Insurance Adjusters, generally maintain job lists advertising open positions in the field.

Professional Certification and Licensure

Certification is not legally required for insurance claims adjusters and examiners but may be required as a condition of employment or promotion. Extensive options for voluntary insurance claims adjuster and examiner certification exist within the insurance industry. These voluntary credentials or designations have education, experience, testing, employer sponsorship, recertification, and continuing education requirements. Licensing requirements for insurance claims adjusters and examiners vary significantly by state. At least sixteen states require insurance claims adjusters to hold a license earned through satisfying an education requirement or passing an examination. Some states award licenses directly to insurance companies or businesses rather than individual insurance adjusters. Insurance claims adjusters and examiners should contact the agency that oversees insurance in their home state for specific licensing requirements.

Additional Requirements: Successful insurance claims adjusters and examiners adhere to strict codes of professional ethics. Professionals in this occupation have access to confidential information and can influence the financial futures of individuals and businesses. Membership in professional insurance associations is encouraged among all insurance claims adjusters and examiners as a means of building professional community.

Additional Requirements

Individuals seeking to become claims adjusters should have good communication skills and should enjoy or be comfortable engaging in frequent conversations and meetings. In addition, as insurance adjusters are responsible for investigation, candidates for positions in the field should be inquisitive and capable with research and study.

EARNINGS AND ADVANCEMENT

According to the Bureau of Labor Statistics (BLS), the median annual wage for claims adjusters, investigators, and examiners was $63,680 in May 2016. Salaries in the field range from a lower level of below $37,000 to an upper end of over $95,000 and many of the higher wage positions in the field can be found in federal or governmental positions. Advancing in the field is typically a matter of gaining experience within a position and then moving to senior level positions that may involve some management expertise. Individuals can also use experience gained at one company or organization to apply for higher paying jobs with an alternate employer.

Metropolitan Areas with the Highest Employment Level in this Occupation

Metropolitan area	Employment	Employment per thousand jobs	Hourly mean wage
New York-Jersey City-White Plains, NY-NJ Metropolitan Division	11,170	1.70	$34.90
Chicago-Naperville-Arlington Heights, IL Metropolitan Division	8,440	2.32	$32.42
Phoenix-Mesa-Scottsdale, AZ	7,270	3.76	$27.57
Los Angeles-Long Beach-Glendale, CA Metropolitan Division	7,260	1.72	$33.79
Dallas-Plano-Irving, TX Metropolitan Division	6,930	2.85	$34.57
Atlanta-Sandy Springs-Roswell, GA	5,970	2.34	$29.41
Riverside-San Bernardino-Ontario, CA	5,430	3.99	$19.66
Tampa-St. Petersburg-Clearwater, FL	5,300	4.19	$29.35
Boston-Cambridge-Newton, MA NECTA Division	4,480	2.49	$33.69
Baltimore-Columbia-Towson, MD	4,370	3.26	$34.36

Source: Bureau of Labor Statistics

EMPLOYMENT AND OUTLOOK

While the insurance adjustment and claims industry is still growing in the 2010s, growth has slowed, and the Bureau of Labor Statistics estimates only 3 percent growth between 2014 and 2024, which is slower than the average of 6-7 percent expected for all occupations in the United States over the same period. Growth in the field is based primarily on growth in the health insurance agency and federal changes to laws regarding health insurance may therefore have a significant impact on growth in the industry overall. Continued growth is expected in part because the cost of medical care continues to rise, thereby placing increased pressure on insurance providers to investigate and adjust claims. In addition, climate change has increased the frequency of natural disasters, such as floods, fires, and tropical storms, and this has increased demand for home and property insurance, resulting in the expansion of the insurance industry. However, even as demand for private and company insurance increases, outsourcing of jobs combined with automation within the insurance agency will reduce the expansion of jobs in the industry. For instance, many insurance companies now handle claims through an online automated system and thus have reduced need for personnel to handle various stages of the claims process.

Related Occupations

- Appraisers and Assessors of Real Estate
- Automotive Service Technicians and Mechanics
- Insurance Underwriter
- Personal Financial Advisor
- Fire Inspectors
- Construction and Building Inspectors

Conversation With . . .
MARY ANNE MEDINA

Director of Business Development & Training,
One Call Claims, Orlando, Florida
Insurance adjuster, 25-plus years

1. What was your individual career path in terms of education/training, entry-level job, or other significant opportunity?

After I graduated from college, I taught for a year. Several people in my family worked in claims. It was during a time when the industry was under pressure to hire women. I went to work for a large adjusting firm that had its own training facility, so I got a lot of training. It intrigued me to be able to move into a position with so many benefits and a company vehicle and room for promotions and the ability to learn many aspects of the industry: property claims, catastrophe claims, casualty, litigation. I eventually moved to upper management.

Prior to the job that I have now, I was vice president of Vale Training Solutions, which is a training facility for adjusters. My career path was to go out and experience everything in the field, then bring it back and train others. It came full circle.

2. What are the most important skills and/or qualities for someone in your profession?

I think communication is probably the priority. If you're a catastrophe adjuster, you're dealing with someone who's been devastated and lost their home. You need to be able to guide them through the process. Or if you're called to testify, you have to be able to communicate in a courtroom. You have to be able to communicate with different cultural groups. We constantly get calls for what we call "soft skills." The new people coming in aren't used to not sending that instant text and their writing skills to communicate and explain are not there.

And secondly, being organized. Being an adjuster, especially a catastrophe adjuster, can be very demanding— trying to see everyone and return every call and every email and get people back on their feet.

You have to genuinely like people. If you can't deal with confrontation, it's not for you. You have to be empathetic. It may seem like a mild fender bender to you, but to this grandma who's never had an accident in her life, it's major

3. **What do you wish you had known going into this profession?**

   I wish I had known how physically demanding the job can be. When it's 105 degrees and you're putting a 70-pound ladder up on a roof 10 times a day or you're going through a commercial building that's been burned and you can't breathe because there's soot in your nasal passages, it's tough. When you go to a catastrophe, you're hoping you can find a hotel room; there may be no water or power. And it's emotionally demanding. I've seen things that I'll never forget. I had a claim for a family in Miami where during the height of a storm—and of course, they blamed themselves, they didn't board the windows up—well, a piece of the window came through and hit their 9-year-old across the chest and he bled to death. Things like that really do impact you.

4. **Are there many job opportunities in your profession? In what specific areas?**

   Yes. No matter what happens with the economy, there are still tornadoes and storms and car accidents and people falling down in grocery stores.

5. **How do you see your profession changing in the next five years? What role will technology play in those changes, and what skills will be required?**

   Technology constantly changes and you have to keep up. Drones can fly over and take pictures for adjusting purposes. We already have satellite capability in areas where the roof is too steep or you can't get to the area. You can examine damage, get in your car, dial your cell phone and update a voice-activated diary: 'Went to Mrs. Jones home, she had 6 feet of water' and Mrs. Jones can log into her claim and see what's going on.

   Everything is fast, fast, fast, but now customers are saying, "I got this estimate and I don't understand it." I really see a shift in realizing that fast is not always better, that you can't replace human contact.

6. **What do you enjoy most about your job? What do you enjoy least about your job?**

   Meeting people and helping people. It's a tough industry. I've always looked at it as really helping people get their lives back together.

   For a while, what I liked least was the travel. I was missing a lot of the joys of life: my kids, my husband. Catastrophe adjusters can be gone for long periods and you can't get that time back.

7. **Can you suggest a valuable "try this" for students considering a career in your profession?**

   There are claims offices located pretty much everywhere. Go in and talk to an adjuster. There's so much out there that you can read, like Claims Magazine and Claims Management Magazine.

SELECTED SCHOOLS

Many colleges and universities, especially those with business schools, offer programs in business and finance. The student can also gain initial training at a technical or community college. For some of the more prominent institutions in this field, see the list of selected schools in the "Accountant" and "Finance Manager" chapters of this volume.

MORE INFORMATION

Independent Insurance Agents and Brokers of America
127 S. Peyton Street
Alexandria, VA 22314
800.221.7917
www.iiaa.org

Independent Automotive Damage Appraisers Association
P.O. Box 12291
Columbus, GA 31917–2291
800.369.4232
www.iada.org

Insurance Institute of America
720 Providence Road, Suite 100
Malvern, PA 19335-0716
800.644.2101
customerservice@TheInstitutes.org
www.aicpcu.org

National Association of Independent Insurance Adjusters
P.O. Box 807
Geneva, IL 60134
630.208.5002
naiia@hilltek.com
www.naiia.com

National Association of Insurance and Financial Advisors
2901 Telestar Court
Falls Church, VA 22042-1205
877.866.2432
www.naifa.org

National Association of Professional Insurance Agents
400 N. Washington Street
Alexandria, VA 22314
703.836.9340
web@pianet.org
www.pianet.com

Simone Isadora Flynn & Micah Issitt/Editors

Mergers & Acquisitions Professional

Snapshot

Career Cluster(s): Financial Services, Law, Accounting, Economics, Business
Interests: Financial planning, investment, analysis, accounting, business, research
Earnings (Yearly Average): $81,760
Employment & Outlook: Faster Than Average Growth Expected

OVERVIEW

Sphere of Work

Mergers and acquisitions (M&A) professionals help companies grow by either merging with or purchasing another company. The merger and acquisition process is complex and involves identifying and solving a variety of personnel, management, financial, legal, and logistical problems. Professionals who specialize in helping companies with the M&A process need to be skilled in law, accounting, oversight, personnel management, negotiation, and financial analysis and

specialists in the field may come from a variety of backgrounds, such as business, accounting, financial analysis, or a number of other fields.

Work Environment

Mergers and acquisitions take place through meetings and M&A specialists may therefore spend much of their time meeting with managers, owners, and company representatives both when trying to arrange a merger or acquisition and when negotiating the details of an existing or continuing M&A process. Mergers and acquisitions professionals usually work in office environments and typically work full time, though overtime is common in the field. In addition, M&A specialists may be asked to travel frequently, either to engage in meetings or to survey facilities. M&A professionals also spend time on financial analysis and thus typically need access to digital tools and computers.

Profile

Working Conditions: Work Indoors
Physical Strength: Light Work
Education Needs: Bachelor's Degree
Licensure/Certification: Not Required
Opportunities For Experience: Part-time work, Military service
Holland Interest Score*: CIE

* See Appendix A

Occupation Interest

Individuals seeking to become mergers and acquisitions specialists should be interested in solving complex problems and brokering agreements as professionals in the field serve to facilitate communication and cooperation between merging corporations. As mergers and acquisitions professionals also spend much of their time conducting research, prospective professionals should be interested in general economics, finance, and business and should be comfortable conducting detailed, comprehensive analyses of financial data. In addition, M&A is a management activity, and professionals with interest in project and personnel management will be more likely to enjoy working on merger and acquisition projects.

A Day in the Life—Duties and Responsibilities

A typical day for a mergers and acquisitions professional depends on the state of a current merger or acquisition project. Before a company can merge with another corporation, or can acquire another business, researchers must first identify companies that might be good candidates for a potential merger or acquisition and this typically involves complex research on financial trends and companies. Mergers and acquisitions specialists may be asked to participate in this process by reaching out to representatives of companies to propose a potential merger or acquisition. Once appropriate companies have been identified, the M&A specialist must engage in due diligence, which involves conducting a detailed financial analysis of all companies involved in the merger or acquisition process. This stage is essential to determining if the merger or purchase is beneficial for the specialist's client and to identify any problems that may occur during the process.

Once a company has been identified and the M&A specialist, or team, has conducted their initial financial analysis, M&A professionals then work on structuring the deal, which may involve meeting with management, accountants, and financial professionals on both sides, organizing and guiding contract negotiations, and arranging financing for the purchase or merger. Once a deal has been created and agreed upon by responsible parties on both sides, M&A professionals may be involved in various activities needed to guide both companies through the process, which may include addressing management, financial, and legal issues before the merger or acquisition can proceed. After the completion of a deal, M&A professionals might still be needed to address contract issues or financial issues that arise over time and M&A specialists will conduct post-merger or acquisition analyses to evaluate the effect of the project on the companies involved.

Duties and Responsibilities

- **Researching companies for potential mergers and/or acquisitions**
- **Meeting with accountants, financial managers, and ownership**
- **Creating and explaining financial and profit/liability analyses**
- **Participating in negotiations, meetings, and legal processes**
- **Solving problems that arise during the merger or acquisition process**
- **Conducting post-merger/acquisition analyses**

OCCUPATION SPECIALTIES

Mergers & Acquisitions Attorney

Mergers and acquisitions attorneys are legal professionals who specialize in helping corporations with the legal issues involved in the merger and acquisition process. M&A attorney's may specialize in corporate or financial law and need to be adept at navigating state and federal regulations as well as handling legal issues related to contract disputes.

Risk Assessment Specialist

A risk assessment specialist is a financial professional who helps determine the financial risks involved in various corporate activities and helps advise companies in how to avoid or reduce risk. Risk assessment specialists may be accountants or financial specialists or may have background in law.

Mergers and Acquisitions Manager

An M&A manager is a mergers and acquisitions specialist who helps to manage to M&A process, often overseeing a team that may include legal professionals, financial planners, budget specialists, and accountants.

WORK ENVIRONMENT

Physical Environment

Mergers and acquisitions professionals typically work indoors in office environments. Mergers and acquisitions specialists typically work full time, but, depending on the specifics of the position and the stage of the merger/acquisition process, overtime work is often necessary. Mergers and acquisitions professionals may also be asked to travel to attend meetings with company managers/owners/or representatives or to visit a company's physical facilities as part of their research on potential merger/acquisition projects. Depending on the industry and field, M&A professionals may travel within a certain geographic area or may need to travel longer distances or internationally during a specific merger or acquisition project.

Relevant Skills and Abilities

Communication Skills

- Participating in meetings and negotiations
- Creating and presenting financial analyses to clients

Interpersonal/Social Skills

- Being able to work with a team

Organization & Management Skills

- Meeting deadlines
- Creating and maintaining detailed records

Research & Planning Skills

- Conducting corporate research
- Planning and Implementing timelines

Technical Skills

- Performing detailed financial analyses
- Using digital software and other tools

Human Environment

The mergers and acquisitions process is complex and typically involves a team of professionals working together to complete the process. Mergers and acquisitions teams may include financial analysts, budget specialists, accountants, and legal professionals who assist at various stages in the process. In addition, M&A specialists work closely with managers and corporate financial specialists representing all companies involved in the project and must be comfortable communicating and negotiating both in person and via telephone, email, and other digital communication channels.

Technological Environment

M&A specialists may use a variety of digital tools to complete their job, including software for accounting and financial analysis. In many cases, meetings and negotiations take place, in part, via email or telephone and M&A specialists need to be proficient with computer and basic mobile communications. In some cases, M&A specialists may need to learn to operate software systems unique or specialized to a specific business. Additionally, M&A professionals need to keep detailed records and typically use word processing and spreadsheet software to organize and store data on their projects.

EDUCATION, TRAINING, AND ADVANCEMENT

High School/Secondary

High school students interested in a career handling mergers and acquisitions should focus on preparing for a bachelor's degree in business, accounting, or a related field. In addition, students can prepare for a career in M&A by taking classes in related subjects, such as mathematics, public speaking, composition, and business.

Suggested High School Subjects

- Applied Math
- College Preparatory
- Computer Science
- English
- Business
- Calculus
- Accounting
- Public Speaking
- Economics
- History

Famous First

In some cases, when companies acquire competitors or merge with other leading companies, the M&A process can lead to the formation of a monopoly, in which a single company or small number of companies come to control all or most business in a certain market. Lawmakers in many countries have long attempted to prevent or limit monopolization in the public interest, as monopolies often lead to corporate exploitation of consumers as limited competition means that consumer costs can grow rapidly. The first monopoly recorded in western culture occurred in ancient Greece where a Grecian merchant named Thales successfully predicted the expansion of the olive oil market and, through acquisition, obtained a monopoly on olive presses, essentially inventing the modern process of investing in futures.

College/Postsecondary

Most professionals specializing in M&A obtain a minimum of a bachelor's degree in a related field, such as finance, business, or accounting. A typically career path for a future M&A specialist might involve obtaining an undergraduate degree followed by a graduate degree in finance or a Masters of Business Administration degree. Individuals interested in the legal aspects of mergers and acquisitions might consider pursuing a law degree with a focus on corporate or finance law.

Related College Majors

- Business Accounting
- Finance, General
- Business, General
- Financial Management
- Financial Law
- Business Management
- Marketing

Adult Job Seekers

Individuals with training an experience in law, accounting, business, and/or finance can apply for open positions in mergers and acquisitions. Individuals with experience in business who do not have specific training in finance or accounting can attempt to qualify for positions in the field by seeking adult education in business accounting or finance. In many cases, mergers and acquisitions professionals will receive on-the-job training working under other M&A professionals and participating in meetings, contract negotiations, and research.

Professional Certification and Licensure

While there are no required certifications or licenses for individuals working in mergers and acquisitions, training in accounting and finance is essential in the field and prospective M&A professionals can increase their chances on the job market by seeking out Certified Public Accountant (CPA) or Certified Financial Analyst (CFA) training from an appropriate educational institution.

Additional Requirements

Mergers and acquisitions can be a stressful and complicated process and professionals in the field must be adept at negotiation and problem solving. In addition, M&A professionals must be fluent with investigation and research as detailed research is needed to investigate accounts, company structure, and other factors that influence the success or failure of a merger or acquisition process.

Fun Fact

Hmmm ... Haagen Daz ice cream. It's owned by Nestlé, the same company that decided on an acquisition of weight loss giant Jenny Craig several years ago. But in 2013, when Nestlé decided to "shed some extra pounds,." it sold Jenny Craig.

Source: http://www.minyanville.com/business-news/editors-pick/

EARNINGS AND ADVANCEMENT

Salaries for M&A specialists vary widely depending on level of experience, seniority, and specific role in the merger and acquisition process. Mergers and acquisitions can be seen as a subfield of financial analysis or can be seen as a branch of corporate accounting. The Bureau of Labor Statistics estimated the average annual salary in the financial analysis field at $81,760 in 2016, with those at the upper end of the spectrum earning more than $165,000, while those at the lower end of the spectrum earned closer to $50,000. Accountants and auditors earned less, on average, than financial analysts, with an average annual pay of $68,150 in May of 2016. In addition to regular annual pay, M&A specialists often earn bonuses after a successful merger or acquisition is completed. Professionals in the field can advance by earning work experience and seniority or can apply for positions with higher paying firms or companies.

Metropolitan Areas with the Highest Employment Level in this Occupation

Metropolitan area	Employment	Employment per thousand jobs	Hourly mean wage
New York-Jersey City-White Plains, NY-NJ Metropolitan Division	47,190	7.17	$64.00
Chicago-Naperville-Arlington Heights, IL Metropolitan Division	10,610	2.92	$45.45
Boston-Cambridge-Newton, MA NECTA Division	9,990	5.54	$47.90
Washington-Arlington-Alexandria, DC-VA-MD-WV Metropolitan Division	9,390	3.77	$46.58
Houston-The Woodlands-Sugar Land, TX	8,040	2.74	$46.68
Los Angeles-Long Beach-Glendale, CA Metropolitan Division	8,010	1.90	$47.05
San Francisco-Redwood City-South San Francisco, CA Metropolitan Division	7,300	6.84	$68.19
Dallas-Plano-Irving, TX Metropolitan Division	7,000	2.88	$45.66
Atlanta-Sandy Springs-Roswell, GA	5,800	2.27	$39.12
Minneapolis-St. Paul-Bloomington, MN-WI	5,790	3.03	$43.06

Source: Bureau of Labor Statistics

EMPLOYMENT AND OUTLOOK

The Bureau of Labor Statistics estimated that there were more than 281,610 professionals working as financial analysts in 2016 and the field was growing by an average of 12 percent per year, marking faster than average growth compared to the 6-7 percent for all U.S. occupations. Growth in the industry has been driven, in part, by the expansion of overseas markets and the potential for companies to conduct business over wider geographical areas. Despite growth, mergers and acquisitions is a prestigious field within the broader financial analysis field and there is significant competition for available positions. Individuals with advanced degrees, certification in financial techniques, and higher levels of management, business, work experience will have an advantage in the job market.

Related Occupations

- Accountants
- Financial Managers
- Corporate Lawyers
- Budget Analysts
- Personal Financial Advisors
- Securities, Commodities, and Financial Services Sales Agents

SELECTED SCHOOLS

Many colleges and universities, especially those with business schools, offer programs in finance and business administration. The student can also gain initial training through enrollment at a technical or community college. For advanced positions, a master's of business administration (MBA) with a concentration in finance is usually expected. Below are listed some of the more prominent institutions in this field.

Carnegie Mellon University
Tepper School of Business
500 Forbes Avenue
Pittsburgh, PA 15213
412.268.2268
tepper.cmu.edu

Indiana University, Bloomington
Kelley School of Business
1309 E. 10th Street
Bloomington, IN 47405
812.855.8100
kelley.iu.edu

Massachusetts Institute of Technology
Sloan School of Management
50 Memorial Drive
Cambridge, MA 02142
617.253.2659
mitsloan.mit.edu

New York University
Stern School of Business
665 Broadway, 11th Floor
New York, NY 10012
212.998.4500
www.stern.nyu.edu

University of California, Berkeley
Haas School of Business
S450 Student Services Building #1900
Berkeley, CA 94720
510.642.1421
haas.berkeley.edu

University of Michigan, Ann Arbor
Ross School of Business
701 Tappan Avenue
Ann Arbor, MI 48109
734.763.5796
michiganross.umich.edu

University of North Carolina, Chapel Hill
Kenan-Flagler Business School
Campus Box 3490, McColl Building
Chapel Hill, NC 27599
919.962.3235
www.kenan-flagler.unc.edu

University of Pennsylvania
The Wharton School
1 College Hall
Philadelphia, PA 19104
215.898.6376
www.wharton.upenn.edu

MORE INFORMATION

CFA Institute
Charlottesville, VA
434-951-5499
www.cfainstitute.org

Association of Professional Merger and Acquisition Advisors (APMAA)
534 Cypress Bend
Oldsmar, FL 34677
813-252-0456
www.apmaa.com

Financial Industry Regulatory Authority (FINRA)
1735 K Street
Washington DC, 2006
301-590-6500
www.finra.org

Micah Issitt/Editor

Personal Financial Advisor

Snapshot

Career Cluster(s): Business, Management & Administration Finance, Customer Service
Interests: Working with others, financial planning, finance, commodities and securities, banking
Earnings (Yearly Average): $90,530
Employment & Outlook: Much faster than average growth expected

OVERVIEW

Sphere of Work

Personal financial advisors help direct, plan, and manage the financial investments of individuals. They are also sometimes referred to as wealth managers, private or personal bankers, personal investment analysts, personal financial planners, or personal financial managers. Personal financial advisors review financial statements and advising individuals about the best investment options, such as stocks, bonds, and commodities. In addition, personal financial advisors provide guidance

and direction for their clients on matters of insurance, retirement, education financing, and tax law. Personal financial advisors may be self-employed or employed by financial institutions, such as commercial banks, insurance companies, securities firms, mortgage companies, pension funds, and savings and loan associations.

Work Environment

Personal financial advisors work in offices and are often required to travel for work. Depending on clients, employer, and particular job description, a personal financial advisor may telecommute from a home office, visit client offices as a contractor, or work on a full-time basis in an employer's office. A personal financial advisor may work as a full-time member of a financial services team or a term-of-project consultant. Personal financial advisors use technology constantly throughout the workday, including computers, the Internet, and accounting software programs.

Profile

Working Conditions: Work Indoors
Physical Strength: Light Work
Education Needs: Bachelor's Degree
Licensure/Certification: Not Required
Opportunities For Experience: Part-time work, Internship
Holland Interest Score*: ECS

* See Appendix A

Occupation Interest

Individuals attracted to the personal financial advisor profession tend to be ambitious, organized, outgoing, and detail-oriented people who find satisfaction in tracking financial trends and assessing risks. Those who excel as personal financial advisors exhibit traits such as financial and mathematical acumen, focus, analytical thought, honesty, responsibility, effective time management, and a sense of ethics. They should enjoy finance and possess good judgment and risk assessment skills.

A Day in the Life—Duties and Responsibilities

The daily duties and responsibilities of personal financial advisors vary with job specialty and employer. Areas of personal financial advisor job specialization include tax law, retirement, education financing, insurance, and investments.

During a typical workday, personal financial advisors may market and promote financial services to clients, travel to meet with prospective clients, assess clients' attitude toward financial risk, and advise clients on investment options. Some of the most important work done by personal financial advisors is to assess the health of a client's financial holdings or portfolio, help clients plan for their dependents' education costs, advise clients on matters of retirement and estate planning (wills and trusts), and advise clients about when to best hold, sell, or trade assets and securities. Personal financial advisors also work with clients to determine insurance needs and purchase appropriate amounts and types of insurance to cover eventualities and help them choose appropriate financial teams that include accountants and lawyers. In the course of generating recommendations for clients, personal financial advisors use spreadsheets to track financial data, track trends in technology and politics that may affect the finance industry, and analyze those data to make informed investment decisions that take into account a client's short-term versus long-term goals.

Personal financial advisors may periodically attend annual stockholder or shareholder meetings for businesses in which clients own shares. More frequently, they prepare investment reports for business owners and investors.

In addition, all personal financial advisors should stay up to date with regulatory and ethical issues and news in finance by reading finance industry journals and participating in industry associations.

Duties and Responsibilities

- **Meeting with clients**
- **Preparing financial plans and strategies**
- **Reviewing and altering financial plans for clients**
- **Answering questions and explaining financial data**
- **Researching investment opportunities**
- **Recommending strategies for investments**

OCCUPATION SPECIALTIES

Private Banker

Private Bankers are personal financial advisors who specifically work with clients who have a lot of money to invest.

WORK ENVIRONMENT

Relevant Skills and Abilities

Communication Skills

- Speaking effectively
- Writing concisely
- Listening attentively
- Reading
- Persuading others

Interpersonal/Social Skills

- Being able to work independently
- Working as a member of a team
- Cooperating with others
- Representing clients

Organization & Management Skills

- Paying attention to an handling details
- Making critical decisions
- Coordinating tasks
- Organizing information and data

Research & Planning Skills

- Analyzing information
- Using logical reasoning
- Developing sales strategies
- Gathering financial data

Physical Environment

Personal financial advisors generally work in office environments. The work of a general financial advisor requires sitting at a desk and using computers and phones for long periods each day.

Human Environment

Personal financial advisors interact with clients, lawyers, banks, accountants, business owners, and stockbrokers. Personal financial advisors should be comfortable leading meetings and consultations with clients.

Technological Environment

Personal financial advisors use computers, telephones, Internet communication tools,

Technical Skills
- Working with data or numbers
- Working with computers, digital tools, and software

financial analysis software, and spreadsheets to complete their work.

EDUCATION, TRAINING, AND ADVANCEMENT

High School/Secondary

High school students interested in pursuing a career as personal financial advisor should prepare themselves by building good study habits and by developing an ease with numbers and mathematical functions. High school classes in bookkeeping and mathematics will provide a strong foundation for college-level study in the field. Due to the diversity of personal financial advisor responsibilities, high school students interested in this career path may benefit from seeking internships or part-time work with financial organizations.

Suggested High School Subjects
- Accounting
- Algebra
- Applied Communication
- Applied Math
- Bookkeeping
- Business
- Business & Computer Technology
- Business Law
- Business Math
- College Preparatory
- Computer Science
- Economics
- English
- Government

- Keyboarding
- Mathematics
- Merchandising
- Political Science
- Psychology
- Social Studies
- Sociology
- Speech
- Statistics

Famous First

Vincent Logan, of the Osage Nation, is a pioneer in financial advice tailored to the needs of Native American populations in the United States. Logan formed one of the first Native American-owned and operated financial advice firms, Nations Group Advisors, LLC, based on New York City. Logan advises Native Americans on investment strategies and works with Native-owned businesses around the nation and, in 2014, was selected to serve as the U.S. government's Special Trustee for American Indians through the U.S. Department of Interior.

College/Postsecondary

Postsecondary students interested in becoming personal financial advisors should work towards a bachelor's degree in economics, finance, statistics, mathematics, or accounting. Courses in computer science, political science, and ethics may also prove useful in their future work. Postsecondary students can gain work experience and potential advantage in their future job searches through internships or part-time employment with local businesses or financial organizations.

Related College Majors

- Accounting
- Business
- Business Administration & Management, General
- Business/Managerial Economics
- Economics, General

- Finance, General
- International Economics
- Mathematics
- Statistics, General

Adult Job Seekers

Adults seeking personal financial advisor jobs have generally earned a bachelor's degree and, in some cases, a master's of business administration (MBA). Adult job seekers may benefit from joining professional finance or accounting associations as a means of professional networking. Professional finance and accounting associations, such as the Financial Planning Association, the Investment Management Consultants Association, and the Society of Financial Service Professionals, generally maintain job lists advertising open accounting positions.

Professional Certification and Licensure

Certification is not legally required for personal financial advisors but may be required as a condition of employment or promotion. Professional organizations, such as the Certified Financial Planner Board of Standards, the CFA Institute, and the American Academy of Financial Management, offer certifications for personal financial advisors. Certification options include Certified Financial Planner (CFP), Chartered Financial Analyst (CFA), Certificate in Investment Performance Measurement (CIPM), Financial Analyst, Risk Management, and Financial Planning credentials. These voluntary credentials or designations have education, experience, testing, employer sponsorship, recertification, and continuing education requirements.

Personal financial advisors who buy or sell stocks and bonds need to be licensed stockbrokers. Individuals can become licensed stockbrokers by passing the General Securities Registered Representatives Examination (commonly referred to as the Series 7 exam) from the Financial Industry Regulatory Authority. Candidates should be aware that the Financial Industry Regulatory Authority, which is the licensing agency of the securities and finance industry, does not rank, promote, or endorse any particular professional financial certification or designation above any other.

Additional Requirements

Successful financial advisors will be knowledgeable about the profession's requirements, responsibilities, and opportunities. Since personal financial advisors have access to confidential financial information and influence the financial health of individuals and businesses, they must adhere to strict codes of professional ethics. Membership in professional finance associations is encouraged among all personal financial advisors as a means of building professional community.

EARNINGS AND ADVANCEMENT

The Bureau of Labor Statistics (BLS) estimates the median annual wage for personal financial advisors at $90,530 in May 2016. Salaries range widely in the field, with those at the lower end of the income spectrum regularly earning less than $40,000, while those at the upper end can earn over $200,000. Bonuses are common in the field, especially for those working in financial services firms, and the annual salary for an advisor may therefore increase depending on how well the advisor earns revenue for his or her clients or on how well the advisor's company fares in a given year or financial quarter. Some personal financial advisors charge by the hour, while others work on a yearly salary. Advancing in the field depends on an advisor's position. In a financial firm, an advisor may gain seniority and work experience, eventually attracting more lucrative clients. For independent advisors, advancement is a matter of marketing and advertising to attract clients.

Metropolitan Areas with the Highest Employment Level in this Occupation

Metropolitan area	Employment	Employment per thousand jobs	Hourly mean wage
New York-Jersey City-White Plains, NY-NJ Metropolitan Division	25,490	3.87	$76.27
Chicago-Naperville-Arlington Heights, IL Metropolitan Division	10,650	2.93	$57.17
Los Angeles-Long Beach-Glendale, CA Metropolitan Division	6,730	1.59	$68.11
Boston-Cambridge-Newton, MA NECTA Division	5,640	3.13	$47.92
San Francisco-Redwood City-South San Francisco, CA Metropolitan Division	4,500	4.22	$77.60
Atlanta-Sandy Springs-Roswell, GA	4,430	1.73	$59.75
Houston-The Woodlands-Sugar Land, TX	3,550	1.21	$52.67
Anaheim-Santa Ana-Irvine, CA Metropolitan Division	3,450	2.21	$59.67
Dallas-Plano-Irving, TX Metropolitan Division	3,360	1.38	$64.75
Phoenix-Mesa-Scottsdale, AZ	3,320	1.72	$51.33

Source: Bureau of Labor Statistics

EMPLOYMENT AND OUTLOOK

The personal financial advisor career field is one of the fastest growing facets of the job market, with as much as 30 percent growth expected between 2014 and 2024, which is much faster than the 6-7 percent growth expected for all U.S. occupations during this same period. The growth of the personal financial advisor market is primarily due to the advancing age of the nation's largest generations and increased demand for advisors to help elderly consumers manage assets and prepare for retirement. Overall, the retirement market has shifted, with more and more consumers using personal retirement accounts as fewer employers offer work-based pensions. However, the advancement of personal investment technologies, online trading, and other tools that allow consumers to handle their own finances and investments may stall growth in the personal financial advisor field in the future.

Related Occupations

- Accountant
- Actuary
- Auditor
- Budget Analyst
- Cost Estimator
- Financial Analyst
- Financial Manager
- Insurance Claims Adjuster and Examiner
- Insurance Sales Agent
- Insurance Underwriter
- Purchasing Agent
- Real Estate Sales Agent
- Stockbroker

Related Military Occupations

- Finance & Accounting Manager

Conversation With . . .
PAUL S. VIREN

Financial Planner, Viren & Associates
Spokane, WA
Financial planner, 24 years

1. What was your individual career path in terms of education/training, entry-level job, or other significant opportunity?

I'm a product of a liberal arts education. I graduated with degrees in psychology and religion, and I use those two skills in my practice more than I use the financial part. I did ministry work for a couple of years, but decided it wasn't for me. I got into sales and worked in a variety of positions and ended up working at a university here in Spokane in the development office. That's how I first discovered estate planning, trying to helping alumni make a bequest or a gift to the university in a legacy way. I fell in love with that whole concept. That goes back about 30 years.

I got into this profession through an insurance company, the Principal Financial Group, which had a training program that helped you get licensed and offered a lot of classes. Financial planning is a very, very difficult professional to break into because there's lots of licensing, lots of failure, lots of commission types of arrangements. After about six years, I matured out of The Principal and became an independent financial planner, doing fee-based work. Throughout that whole time, estate planning has been a cornerstone of my success and my passion for helping people in preparing for their future. I find it's a helpful starting point to motivate clients. At our first meeting, I tell them there are five documents that are universally needed: a will, power of attorney for health care, power of attorney for finances, and a living will. The fifth one is probably the most important one: a handwritten love letter to your husband or your child and other family members or friends. Usually that last item is what gets people to realize they better take care of these things.

The journey of finding a career is not always a straight line. It can take several different kinds of jobs. That was my experience until I finally found the job I love, the one I'm doing now. Along the way, I learned different skill sets that I incorporate into my work.

2. **What are the most important skills and/or qualities for someone in your profession?**

   Being empathetic and listening are really important skills to build a relationship with a client. The profession requires a lot of technical expertise, but many people who are good technical people are horrible relationship-building people. Many times, you're dealing with people who have just gotten married or just lost a loved one or just had child or lost their child or started a business or sold their business. As people go through those chapters, that's where we enter in.

   I really gravitate toward educating my clients on the world of finances. A lot of people don't know what they don't know when they go to their financial investment person. To have at least a basic understanding is important. Especially when there's a stressful point in a market cycle and there's the usual moment of panic, talking people off the edge of the roof is important, but you have to have that trust. You don't build trust by being a good technician; you build trust by being empathetic and listening.

3. **What do you wish you had known going into this profession?**

   I wish I had known how rewarding it would be because I would have gotten into it sooner. It's so challenging to get through the first few years of this profession.

4. **Are there many job opportunities in your profession? In what specific areas?**

   Every time I open up a professional journal, the headlines are screaming that we're all getting older and there's nobody behind us. The average age is 58 or older—it's crazy. So I think there's huge opportunity over the next 5, 10 years.

5. **How do you see your profession changing in the next five years? What role will technology play in those changes, and what skills will be required?**

   The robo-advice that's out there is going to help some people, because we want an app on our phone. The problem with a financial planner app is it's cookie cutter. It doesn't do the empathetic listening or ask good questions. And people like experiences … we like the Starbucks experience versus coffee out of a machine.

6. **What do you enjoy most about your job? What do you enjoy least about your job?**

   I'm passionate about helping clients and being part of their lives and helping them achieve their goals.

   We are a profession that is very, very heavily regulated. The regulation has gotten so onerous.

7. Can you suggest a valuable "try this" for students considering a career in your profession?

Get an internship with a brokerage firm or an insurance company. If nothing else, most of those places, if they're good, will help you with communication skills, which is code for selling skills. Try to find a mentor, that person who's willing to take a little bit of time to help you.

SELECTED SCHOOLS

Many colleges and universities, especially those with business schools, offer programs in finance and business administration. The student can also gain initial training through enrollment at a technical or community college. For advanced positions, a master's of business administration (MBA) with a concentration in finance is usually expected. Below are listed some of the more prominent institutions in this field.

Carnegie Mellon University
Tepper School of Business
500 Forbes Avenue
Pittsburgh, PA 15213
412.268.2268
tepper.cmu.edu

Indiana University, Bloomington
Kelley School of Business
1309 E. 10th Street
Bloomington, IN 47405
812.855.8100
kelley.iu.edu

Massachusetts Institute of Technology
Sloan School of Management
50 Memorial Drive
Cambridge, MA 02142
617.253.2659
mitsloan.mit.edu

New York University
Stern School of Business
665 Broadway, 11th Floor
New York, NY 10012
212.998.4500
www.stern.nyu.edu

University of California, Berkeley
Haas School of Business
S450 Student Services Building #1900
Berkeley, CA 94720
510.642.1421
haas.berkeley.edu

University of Michigan, Ann Arbor
Ross School of Business
701 Tappan Avenue
Ann Arbor, MI 48109
734.763.5796
michiganross.umich.edu

University of North Carolina, Chapel Hill
Kenan-Flagler Business School
Campus Box 3490, McColl Building
Chapel Hill, NC 27599
919.962.3235
www.kenan-flagler.unc.edu

University of Pennsylvania
The Wharton School
1 College Hall
Philadelphia, PA 19104
215.898.6376
www.wharton.upenn.edu

MORE INFORMATION

Certified Financial Planner Board of Standards
1425 K Street, NW, Suite 500
Washington, DC 20005
800.487.1497
mail@CFPBoard.org
www.cfp.net

Financial Industry Regulatory Authority
1735 K Street
Washington DC, 20006
301.590.6500
www.finra.org

Financial Managers Society
100 W. Monroe Street, Suite 1700
Chicago, IL 60603
312.578.1300
info@fmsinc.org
www.fmsinc.org

Financial Planning Association
7535 E. Hampden Avenue, Suite 600
Denver, CO 80231
800.322.4237
www.fpanet.org

Investment Management Consultants Association
5619 DTC Parkway, Suite 500
Greenwood Village, CO 80111
303.770.3377
imca@imca.org
www.imca.org

Society for Risk Analysis
1313 Dolley Madison Boulevard, Suite 402
McLean, VA 22101
703.790.1745
www.sra.org

Simone Isadora Flynn,
updated by Micah Issitt

Portfolio Manager

Snapshot

Career Cluster(s): Financial Services, Accounting
Interests: Financial planning, research, data analysis, working with people, mathematics
Earnings (Yearly Average): $90,530
Employment & Outlook: Faster Than Average Growth Expected

OVERVIEW

Sphere of Work

A portfolio manager is a financial analyst or financial advisor who helps clients manage their portfolios, which are collections of assets and other financial investments. A person's financial portfolio might include stock investments, property, savings, and other assets and portfolio managers help their clients to create and manage investments and to understand investment strategies and practices. Depending on their specialization, portfolio managers may also be known as investment managers, asset managers, or financial advisors, but portfolio managers are also analysts

who develop detailed knowledge of various types of investments and help clients, and the position is therefore a combination of financial analyst and advisor.

Work Environment

Portfolio managers typically work in office environments, using digital tools to research and manage investments and other assets for their clients. In some cases, portfolio managers may work for a company offering various types of investment opportunities, such as stock investments, hedge funds, and pension plans. Other portfolio managers may work independently, serving as general financial advisors and analysts for their clients. Depending on the specific position, portfolio managers may work as part of a financial team that may include accountants, investment sales associates, and financial managers, while other portfolio managers may work independently.

Profile

Working Conditions: Work Indoors
Physical Strength: Light Work
Education Needs: Bachelor's Degree, Master's Degree
Licensure/Certification: Required for some positions
Opportunities For Experience: Part-time work
Holland Interest Score*: CIE

* See Appendix A

Occupation Interest

Financial advisors and analysts should have interest in economics, accounting, and mathematics, as much of their job focuses around interpreting shifts in the financial market and the global economy. Portfolio management might appeal to individuals concerned with accruing personal wealth as the occupation is typically lucrative, especially for those working in prestigious firms. Success in the job requires that managers work closely with their clients to help their clients achieve their financial goals and portfolio managers should therefore be comfortable interacting frequently with their customers and should have good interpersonal skills.

A Day in the Life—Duties and Responsibilities

A typical day for a portfolio manager may involve meeting with existing or prospective clients to discuss possible investments, strategies, and other factors of the current financial enviornment. When meeting with clients, portfolio managers must determine the best way to handle each client's financial goals, based on the client's timeframe, preferences for risk in investments, expectations about returns, and on the general state of the investment market. With this information, portfolio managers recommend investments to their clients and, if an agreement is reached, the manager may then make investments for his or her clients. For existing clients, portfolio managers monitor market conditions and the status of their clients' portfolios to determine if any changes need to be made to each client's portfolio. Some portfolio managers may create investment packages for their clients directly, while others may focus on managing investments made by the clients directly.

Much of a portfolio manager's job involves research, as portfolio specialists need to maintain detailed knowledge about financial markets and economic trends. Changes in laws, regulations, or in the overall economic market, may necessitate meeting with clients to explain subsequent changes to their investment portfolios or to present new opportunities. Portfolio managers might also spend part of a typical day creating documentation about the various investments and any stock trades that he or she has been involved in, in an effort to adhere to regulatory agencies that monitor for fraud and other violations of trade regulations. Portfolio managers might also spend time working with other financial professionals, such as sales associates and accountants, as part of creating portfolios for their clients.

Duties and Responsibilities

- **Researching changes in financial laws and regulations**
- **Learning about new investment opportunities**
- **Marketing services to potential clients**
- **Explaining investments, economic policies, and other factors to clients**
- **Maintaining portfolios for existing clients**
- **Working with sales associates to purchase services for clients**
- **Purchasing or selling stocks, securities, and other investments for clients**

OCCUPATION SPECIALTIES

Hedge Fund Manager

Hedge fund managers are responsible for managing hedge funds, which are investment pools of security investments for individual or institutional clients. Hedge fund investment is typically considered an advance form of securities investment marketed primarily to wealthy clients and institutions.

Money Manager

Money managers collect funds from a pool of investors to collectively invest in securities like stocks, bonds, or other assets, a type of investment known as a "mutual fund." By using mutual funds, money managers make advanced investments available to independent clients who would not otherwise be able to invest in professionally managed portfolios.

Financial Analyst

A financial analyst researches economic conditions and provides advice to companies and investors on how to benefit from investments in various financial markets. Chartered Financial Analysts are required to pass a regulated test to demonstrate their knowledge of accounting, economics, and other aspects of finance.

Personal Financial Advisor

Personal financial advisors are financial specialists who help investors and institutions to develop financial strategies. Financial advisors may help their clients to set up and manage investments and other assets and differ from financial analysts in that they specialize in helping clients, rather than researching advanced economic trends.

WORK ENVIRONMENT

Relevant Skills and Abilities

Communication Skills
- Speaking with clients and other professionals
- Writing clear information for clients

Interpersonal/Social Skills
- Being able to work with a team
- Working independently

Organization & Management Skills
- Creating and maintaining documentation for clients
- Maintaining legal and regulatory records

Research & Planning Skills
- Researching economic trends
- Researching investment opportunities

Technical Skills
- Performing complex calculations
- Using digital software and other tools

Physical Environment

Portfolio managers typically work in office environments and may either work independently or alongside other financial specialists in an investment firm or other financial institution. Some portfolio managers work directly for banks or investment companies, while others may work for institutions, helping to manage collective retirement or corporate investments. In some cases, portfolio managers may need to travel to meet with their clients and some managers may attend professional development conferences or professional conferences discussing economic or investment trends.

Human Environment

Portfolio managers are responsible for learning about and helping their clients reach their financial goals and so portfolio managers spend considerable time interacting with clients. In addition, portfolio managers may frequently interact with investment sales associates, accountants, and other financial managers during the course of their work. Though client interactions are a major part of the job, managers also spend much of their time working independently and researching economic trends and developments that may affect their clients' investment portfolios.

Technological Environment

Increasingly, financial management and investments are handled via virtual digital technology and portfolio managers need to be fluent in web-based and digital financial tools. Specialized financial planning software, such as the Wealth Tec Foundations suite, Oracle E-Business Suite Financials, or Ibbotson Portfolio Strategist, are also available to help portfolio managers track investments and other assets. In addition, portfolio managers used mobile technology and computers to share information with their clients and to communicate with clients and other professionals in the field. Portfolio managers may also frequently use other digital office tools such as work processing, spreadsheet, and accounting software. When sharing data and documentation with clients and regulatory agencies, portfolio managers may use digital file transfer services or programs.

EDUCATION, TRAINING, AND ADVANCEMENT

High School/Secondary

High school students interested in becoming portfolio managers should prepare for higher education as entry level positions in the field typically require candidates to have at least a bachelor's degree. High school students can prepare for a career in finance by studying mathematics, economics, and business. In addition, classes in computer science, English, composition, and public speaking are helpful for those looking to work in business or finance. In some high schools, students may be able to take advantage of more specific courses teaching rudimentary accounting and financial management.

Suggested High School Subjects

- Algebra
- Applied Math
- College Preparatory
- Computer Science
- English

- Business
- Economics
- Law
- Public Speaking

Famous First

Pioneering investment specialist Harry Markowitz wrote an article in the March 1952 edition of the *Journal of Finance*, entitled "Portfolio Selection," in which Markowitz detailed some of the research to that point on how to manage risk and use analysis to build investment portfolios. Up to that point, stock investment was more akin to gambling, and Markowitz attempted to introduce a more scientific, mathematically grounded approach to the practice. This was the beginning of modern portfolio management and led to a wealth of new theories and developments in the field as experts analyzed and expanded on Markowitz' work.

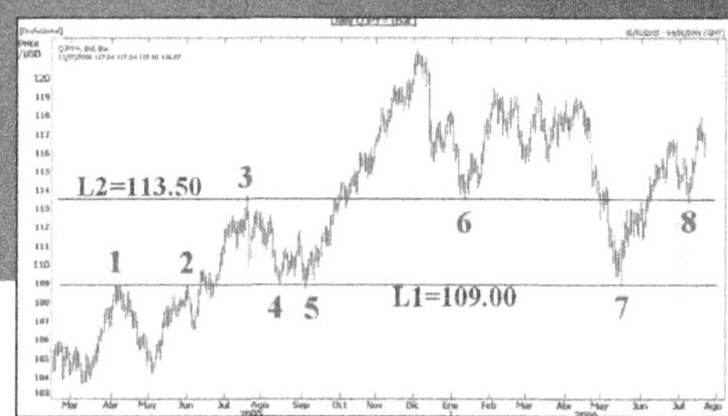

College/Postsecondary

While many entry-level portfolio management or financial advisor/analyst positions may only require a bachelor's degree, individuals with postgraduate degrees and/or professional certification may have an advantage when looking for jobs in the field. College students preparing for a career as a financial analyst, advisor, or specifically as a portfolio manager, should focus on economics, finance, business, and/or accounting, but should also take classes in computer science, technical writing, and critical thinking.

Related College Majors

- Financial Management
- Accounting, General
- Economics, General
- Economic Analysis
- Business Accounting
- Finance, General
- Business, General
- Mathematics, General
- Law, General

- Corporate Law
- Financial Law

Adult Job Seekers

Individuals with a bachelor's degree or higher in a related field can apply for open positions in portfolio management. Once hired, financial advisors and portfolio managers may spend as long as a year training under a senior advisor, analyst, or manager. During this time, professionals meet with clients, build networks of contacts, and learn the rudiments of creating and managing portfolios.

Professional Certification and Licensure

Many portfolio managers buy and sell stocks, bonds, investment policies, or other assets for their clients and must therefore obtain relevant licenses from the state. There are specific licenses for individuals who purchase and sell various types of investments and a portfolio manager might therefore need several different licenses to sell a variety of products. In addition, portfolio managers who work with the public must be registered with the federal Securities and Exchange Commission, the branch of the federal government responsible for regulating the financial industry. While professional certification is not required, some financial analysts/advisors choose to pursue certification as a Chartered Financial Analyst (CFA), a Certified Financial Planner (CFP), or a Certified Public Accountant (CPA). CFO, CFA, and CPA students are typically required to have a Bachelor's Degree and to have spent time working in the field before they are considered eligible for a certification program. To complete the program, students study accounting, finance, economics, financial law, and other subjects and must pass a state certification exam.

Additional Requirements

Portfolio managers are both financial advisors, as they help clients and institutions to make informed investment decisions and manage assets for their clients, and also financial analysts who are expected to maintain specialized knowledge of economic conditions and trends. Portfolio managers must therefore be adept at working with clients and also at research and analysis. Individuals seeking to enter the field should therefore have good interpersonal skills, as well as the ability to work independently on complex problems.

Fun Fact

Sveriges Riksbank, Sweden's central bank, was formed in 1668. It's thought to be the world's oldest, arriving on the planet 245 years before the U.S. Federal Reserve.

Source: http://www.bankrate.com/finance

EARNINGS AND ADVANCEMENT

The Bureau of Labor Statistics (BLS) estimates the average annual salary for financial advisors at approximately $90,530, with a range of under $40,000 to over $200,000 at various levels. Financial analysts earn slightly lower wages on average, with a median of $81,760 in 2016, and a range of between $50,000 and over $160,000. Depending on the specifics of their field and industry, portfolio managers can therefore earn anywhere from around $40,000 to over $200,000 annually. Advancing in the field is depending on the manager's specific position. Those working within investment or financial firms may advance in both pay and seniority over time working for the same company or by applying for more advanced or prestigious positions with other institutions. Advancement in the field might also involve personally marketing and advertising to attract new and more lucrative clients.

Metropolitan Areas with the Highest Employment Level in this Occupation

Metropolitan area	Employment	Employment per thousand jobs	Hourly mean wage
New York-Jersey City-White Plains, NY-NJ Metropolitan Division	47,190	7.17	$64.00
Chicago-Naperville-Arlington Heights, IL Metropolitan Division	10,610	2.92	$45.45
Boston-Cambridge-Newton, MA NECTA Division	9,990	5.54	$47.90
Washington-Arlington-Alexandria, DC-VA-MD-WV Metropolitan Division	9,390	3.77	$46.58
Houston-The Woodlands-Sugar Land, TX	8,040	2.74	$46.68
Los Angeles-Long Beach-Glendale, CA Metropolitan Division	8,010	1.90	$47.05
San Francisco-Redwood City-South San Francisco, CA Metropolitan Division	7,300	6.84	$68.19
Dallas-Plano-Irving, TX Metropolitan Division	7,000	2.88	$45.66
Atlanta-Sandy Springs-Roswell, GA	5,800	2.27	$39.12
Minneapolis-St. Paul-Bloomington, MN-WI	5,790	3.03	$43.06

Source: Bureau of Labor Statistics

EMPLOYMENT AND OUTLOOK

In 2016, there were 281,610 professional financial analysts in the United States and an estimated 201,850 personal financial advisors. The BLS estimates that the financial analysis field is growing by an average of 12 percent per year, marking higher than average growth in comparison to the 6-7 percent annual growth for all occupations in the United States. The personal financial advisor field is growing at an average rate of 30 percent per year, making it one of the fastest growing facets of the financial industry. In part, growth in the financial advisor field has been stimulated by an aging population and an increased focus on retirement planning and investment. This demographic change will also create opportunities for portfolio managers working with both investment and fund companies and directly with individual clients. Though there are likely to be ample opportunities in the field, individuals with advanced degrees or advanced certification will likely have an advantage on the job market.

Related Occupations

- Budged Analysts
- Financial Managers
- Personal Financial Advisors
- Securities, Commodities, And Financial Services Sales Agents
- Accountants
- Financial Analysts

Related Military Occupations

- Military Investment Manager

SELECTED SCHOOLS

Many colleges and universities, especially those with business schools, offer programs in finance and business administration. The student can also gain initial training through enrollment at a technical or community college. For advanced positions, a master's of business administration (MBA) with a concentration in finance is usually expected. Below are listed some of the more prominent institutions in this field.

Carnegie Mellon University
Tepper School of Business
500 Forbes Avenue
Pittsburgh, PA 15213
412.268.2268
tepper.cmu.edu

Indiana University, Bloomington
Kelley School of Business
1309 E. 10th Street
Bloomington, IN 47405
812.855.8100
kelley.iu.edu

Massachusetts Institute of Technology
Sloan School of Management
50 Memorial Drive
Cambridge, MA 02142
617.253.2659
mitsloan.mit.edu

New York University
Stern School of Business
665 Broadway, 11th Floor
New York, NY 10012
212.998.4500
www.stern.nyu.edu

University of California, Berkeley
Haas School of Business
S450 Student Services Building #1900
Berkeley, CA 94720
510.642.1421
haas.berkeley.edu

University of Michigan, Ann Arbor
Ross School of Business
701 Tappan Avenue
Ann Arbor, MI 48109
734.763.5796
michiganross.umich.edu

University of North Carolina, Chapel Hill
Kenan-Flagler Business School
Campus Box 3490, McColl Building
Chapel Hill, NC 27599
919.962.3235
www.kenan-flagler.unc.edu

University of Pennsylvania
The Wharton School
1 College Hall
Philadelphia, PA 19104
215.898.6376
www.wharton.upenn.edu

MORE INFORMATION

National Association of Active Investment Managers
6732 W. Coal Mine Ave. #446
Littleton, CO 80123
888-261-0787
www.naaim.org

Academy of Certified Portfolio Managers
PO Box 1322
New York, New York 10025
212-854-8404
www.academyofcpm.org

CFA Institute
Charlottesville, VA
434-951-5499
www.cfainstitute.org

Financial Industry Regulatory Authority (FINRA)
1735 K Street
Washington DC, 2006
301-590-6500
www.finra.org

U.S. Securities and Exchange Commission
100 F Street, NE
Washington, DC 20549
www.sec.gov

Micah Issitt/Editor

Quantitative Analyst

Snapshot

Career Cluster(s): Financial Services, Mathematics, Economics
Interests: Financial planning, research, data analysis, mathematics, statistics
Earnings (Yearly Average): $81,760
Employment & Outlook: Faster Than Average Growth Expected

OVERVIEW

Sphere of Work

A quantitative analyst, sometimes called a "quant," is a type of financial analyst who typically works for investment companies or other asset trading companies and uses detailed mathematical analyses to help companies make informed investment and financial decisions. As stock and asset traders increasingly rely on algorithms for electronic trading, the demand for skills analysts has increased in the twenty-first century. Quantitative analysts engineer and utilize software programs and algorithms to analyze stock trends and economic patterns and use the resulting financial data to

help traders make informed decisions. Quantitative analysts may also help banks and financial institutions to value their assets, or may help to estimate the risk of new projects. Though quantitative analysts are financial industry professionals, professionals in the field tend to have backgrounds in statistics, mathematics, or computer science.

Work Environment

Quantitative analysts typically work indoors in office environments and generally work full time. Digital tools and personal computers are essential in analytical finance and quants spend much of their time working with computers to analyze, create, and utilize financial algorithms. Quantitative analysts may conduct much of their work independently, but meet regularly with traders, financial advisors and managers, and other finance industry professionals. In addition, quantitative analysts may work with other types of financial analysts or with other mathematicians, programmers, or statisticians.

Profile

Working Conditions: Work Indoors
Physical Strength: Light Work
Education Needs: Bachelor's Degree, Master's Degree
Licensure/Certification: Required for some positions
Opportunities For Experience: Part-time work
Holland Interest Score*: CIE

* See Appendix A

Occupation Interest

Quantitative analysts need a strong background and interest in mathematics and statistics as much of their job involves creating and using algorithms to analyze financial data. In addition, quantitative analysts should have an interest in investigation and analysis and should enjoy problem solving. Though much of a quantitative analyst's work can be done independently, quantitative analysts should also have good communication skills as they often are required to explain complex statistical patterns to their clients or to finance managers and other financial experts. Individuals who are more interested in mathematics might work as quantitative analysts in the mathematical finance field, while those more interested in computing might work in software or algorithm development.

A Day in the Life—Duties and Responsibilities

A typical day for a quantitative analyst depends on the analyst's specific subspecialty in the field. In general, quantitative analysts spend much of their time analyzing data derived from software programs and using this data to help guide company investments and other financial decisions. Some quantitative analysts specialize in software development and so may spend much of their time writing computer code to create new analysis algorithms. Quantitative analysts who work in risk management or mitigation may spend part of a typical day meeting with financial professionals to discuss potential future financial transactions and then will spend time analyzing data to help their clients compare the risk and reward of various strategies. Some quantitative analysts work for universities or other academic institutions studying mathematic finance and so may spend much of their time conducting research and experiments and writing research reports on various quantitative experiments. In some cases, a quantitative analyst may work independently, both analyzing algorithms and preparing reports for their clients, while in other cases quantitative analysts work with other mathematicians, programmers, computer scientists, physicists, and statisticians and so may limit their work to a certain facet of a project. Quantitative analysts must also conduct research regularly to understand local and global economic trends and to stay ahead of developments in their field, which may include new algorithms or software programs developed by statisticians and researchers.

Duties and Responsibilities

- **Performing complex mathematical analysis and computations**
- **Programming and utilizing analytical software and algorithms**
- **Meeting with financial professionals to discuss potential transactions and investments**
- **Examining accounts and assets to assess value**
- **Helping professionals to manage risk**
- **Creating an testing mathematical models**
- **Researching new developments in the field**

OCCUPATION SPECIALTIES

Algorithmic Trading Quantitative Analyst

Algorithmic Trading Quants (ATQs), utilize statistical analysis to make stock trades based on algorithms. The ATQ specialty is among the most lucrative subfield of quantitative analysis as ATQs are typically more intimately involved in making trades and so profit from the success of investments made on behalf of a company or client.

Risk Manager

Risk managers are analysts who specialize in helping investors or companies weigh and manage the risk of financial transactions. Risk managers use specialize algorithms and models to test various financial strategies and help financial institutions to avoid investing in ways that create unnecessary risk for the company and its clients/investors.

Front Office Quantitative Analyst

Front office quants work in financial institutions and help to identify profitable trades for the company. Increasingly, the role of front office quants has been blended with algorithmic trading analysts and other trading positions that were once independent.

Model Validation Specialist

Model validation (MV) is the process of testing quantitative models developed by analysts, statisticians, and mathematicians to determine whether or not the models will function in real-world financial environments. Model validation specialists may have a background in computer science as well as mathematics and statistics. Model validation can also be an entrance level position for analysts who later transition to front office or algorithmic trading.

WORK ENVIRONMENT

Relevant Skills and Abilities

Communication Skills
- Writing detailed reports on analyses

Interpersonal/Social Skills
- Being able to work with a team
- Working independently

Organization & Management Skills
- Maintaining detailed records and storing data
- Performing rapid analyses to meet deadlines

Research & Planning Skills
- Researching economic trends
- Researching investment opportunities
- Researching new algorithms and statistical research

Technical Skills
- Performing complex calculations
- Utilizing specialized programs and mathematic processes
- Creating or using statistical models
- Using digital software and other tools

Physical Environment

Quantitative analysts work in office environments. Much of a quantitative analyst's work involves using computers and other digital tools to collect and analyze data and to create or utilize algorithms that can help make financial decisions or analyze the impact of investments, trades, purchases, or other changes to an institution's financial position. In some cases, quantitative analysts may work in private offices or computer-lab environments, while others may work in collaborative office environments with other mathematicians and financial professionals.

Human Environment

Quantitative analysis is a complex filed that may involve input from accountants, investment sales agents, mathematicians, statisticians, computer scientists, and physicists and quantitative analysts may spend time in meetings with other professionals when working on a specific project. Quantitative analysts who work for financial institutions or for clients may also meet with clients to discuss financial needs and goals and to strategize about future plans based on the analyst's data.

Technological Environment

Quantitative analysts need to have expert knowledge of computer science and mathematics and must be fluent in a number of software systems and programs. While some quantitative analysts may use spreadsheet and accounting software in their work, others use computers to create new programs using computer languages like C++, Python, or Java. There are a variety of analytical software programs available for completing complex statistical analysis, such as MathWorks MATLAB and StataCorp, that may be used by quantitative analysts working with algorithmic trading or testing statistical models. Quantitative analysts might also use other financial analysis programs like Oracle E-Business Suite Financials or Wolfram Research Mathematica, to analyze financial data. Because quantitative analysts blend computer science and statistics with real world financial transactions, professionals in the field should be fluent in software systems for both financial and more general mathematical applications.

EDUCATION, TRAINING, AND ADVANCEMENT

High School/Secondary

Only individuals with strong interest and skill in mathematics should consider attempting to pursue a career in quantitative analysis and high school students pursuing a career in the field should focus on mathematics, statistics, and computer science with the goal of obtaining at least a Bachelor's Degree after graduation. In addition, basic knowledge of composition, English, and other branches of communication will be helpful for professionals in the field. Students interested in becoming analysts should also take advantage of opportunities to take college preparatory classes as well as classes in critical thinking and research.

Suggested High School Subjects

- Algebra
- Applied Math
- College Preparatory
- Computer Science
- English
- Business
- Economics
- Law
- Public Speaking
- Calculus
- Accounting

Famous First

France is world famous for quantitative analysis, with France hosting seven of the top fifteen institutions in the world for finance education. One of the nation's most famous quantitative analysts is Nicole El Karoui, a professor at the *Ecole Polytechnique*, who created the first university program in the world to teach complex-derivative pricing, a common and influential technique in quantitative analysis. Though the quantitative analysis field is largely male dominated, with only around 7 percent of the world's quants being women, El Karoui has become one of the most influential figures in analytical finance.

College/Postsecondary

While some entry-level quantitative analysis positions may require only a Bachelor's Degree in a related field, increasing competition in the field gives an advantage to candidates who obtain advanced degrees and have specialized knowledge in computer programming or statistics. As quantitative analysts have a variety of options in terms of their role, with some working directly in trading for financial institutions while others work behind the scenes in research and analysis, students preparing for careers in the field have a variety of options in terms of academic training. In general, most quantitative analysts have degrees in mathematics, statistics, or related subfields, while others may approach the field from computer science or engineering. Top positions in the field might require a PhD or equivalent in mathematics, statistics, or computer science.

Related College Majors

- Economic Analysis
- Mathematics, General
- Statistics
- Mathematical Finance
- Statistical Analysis

Adult Job Seekers

Individuals with a Bachelor's Degree in mathematics, computer science, statistics, or a related field can apply for entry-level positions. In some financial institutions, beginning analysts may spend a year or more training with senior analysts and, in some cases, new hires may work in a field like model validation or as research assistants before transitioning to a role in algorithmic trading, risk management, or front office quantitative analysis.

Professional Certification and Licensure

There are no specific licenses or certificates needed for individuals seeking to become quantitative analysts, but analysts who purchase and sell assets may need to be licensed through the Financial Industry Regulatory Authority (FINRA). In general, financial industry licenses are tied to specific positions and may require sponsorship by a company or financial organization and so analysts will typically only be asked to pass licensing exams after obtaining a position. Individuals who have obtained a Bachelor's Degree in a related field may choose to advance their career by pursuing a Chartered Financial Analyst (CFA) certification, in which students learn about aspects of finance, economics, and accounting and sit for a series of tests to measure their knowledge in the field.

Additional Requirements

While all financial analysts must be skilled in mathematics, quantitative analysts are math specialists who spend much of their time working with complex mathematical or statistical models. Prospective analysts should be detail oriented and should have a strong interest in problem solving and research. While quantitative analysts earn higher than average salaries, professionals in the field report that long hours and overtime work are common and prospective analysts should therefore have a strong work ethic. Front office analysts and specialists in algorithmic trading must be able to cope with high pressure environments as traders compete to analyze and trade as fast as possible and the ability to cope with pressure and to meet tight deadlines is therefore essential for some positions in the field.

Fun Fact

Quants, as they're called, get together each year for the MoMath Masters competition. A sample question: Let *m* be the smallest positive integer such that $m^2+7m+89$ is divisible by 77. What is *m*? The answer is 18. Go figure.

Source: https://blogs.wsj.com/moneybeat

EARNINGS AND ADVANCEMENT

The Bureau of Labor Statistics (BLS) estimates the median salary for all financial analysts as approximately $81,760 in May of 2016, with those at the higher end of the spectrum earning more than $160,000, while those at the lowest end of the spectrum earned salaries less than $50,000. Individuals working in the securities and financial investments fields have the highest level of earning potential with an average salary of over $96,000. Advancing in the quantitative analysis field might involve working up within a company from a low level or research position to a higher level position. Alternately, individuals with experience can attempt to advance by applying for more lucrative or more advanced positions in high level investment firms or other financial institutions.

Metropolitan Areas with the Highest Employment Level in this Occupation

Metropolitan area	Employment	Employment per thousand jobs	Hourly mean wage
New York-Jersey City-White Plains, NY-NJ Metropolitan Division	47,190	7.17	$64.00
Chicago-Naperville-Arlington Heights, IL Metropolitan Division	10,610	2.92	$45.45
Boston-Cambridge-Newton, MA NECTA Division	9,990	5.54	$47.90
Washington-Arlington-Alexandria, DC-VA-MD-WV Metropolitan Division	9,390	3.77	$46.58
Houston-The Woodlands-Sugar Land, TX	8,040	2.74	$46.68
Los Angeles-Long Beach-Glendale, CA Metropolitan Division	8,010	1.90	$47.05
San Francisco-Redwood City-South San Francisco, CA Metropolitan Division	7,300	6.84	$68.19
Dallas-Plano-Irving, TX Metropolitan Division	7,000	2.88	$45.66
Atlanta-Sandy Springs-Roswell, GA	5,800	2.27	$39.12
Minneapolis-St. Paul-Bloomington, MN-WI	5,790	3.03	$43.06

Source: Bureau of Labor Statistics

EMPLOYMENT AND OUTLOOK

In 2016, there were 281,610 professional financial analysts in the United States and the field was growing by an estimated 12-16 percent per year, marking faster than average growth when compared to the 6-7 percent growth recorded for all occupations in the United States. Growth in the quantitative analysis field, specifically, has been driven by the increasing popularity of algorithm-based investment and trading and the increasing integration of computer science and digital technology into the financial field. As this trend continues, there is likely to be increased opportunities for quantitative analysts and especially for those who have advanced knowledge of computer science and experience with emerging algorithms or analytical models.

Related Occupations

- Budget Analysts
- Financial Managers
- Personal Financial Advisors
- Securities, Commodities, And Financial Services Sales Agents
- Accountants
- Financial Analysts

Related Military Occupations

- Military Investment Manager

Conversation With . . .
PEG DiORIO

Senior Vice President, Quantitative Equity
Voya Investment Management, New York
Quantitative Analyst, 24 years

1. What was your individual career path in terms of education/training, entry-level job, or other significant opportunity?

I took something of a circuitous path. I went to community college in upstate New York, then went to the State University of New York (SUNY) at Stony Brook. I drifted through a few majors—engineering, computer science—and graduated with a degree in Applied Math and Statistics, but wasn't sure what I wanted to do. I always liked teaching and decided to get a teaching certificate in math. I was teaching high school math and realized I needed a master's in order to get permanently certified. I went to New York University and was paying for it myself and wanted to get the most bang for my buck, so I got a master's in math, versus education. It's now called Mathematical Finance, and at the time was a new joint program between the Stern School of Business and the Courant math school at NYU. One of the guys in my study group worked at a financial group called Sanford Bernstein and suggested that I think about working there, but I didn't know much about finance. He said, "It's not a big deal, it's just math. You'll figure it out." So I figured I'd give it a try. I learned a huge amount there. I worked in their private client group for about three years and started doing quantitative projects with other groups. I had worked with the head of the quant research group for a long time and saw an empty cube and said, "Hey, are you thinking about hiring somebody?" I jumped to that team and was there for about 13 years. I joined Voya five years ago as a quant analyst and now lead a team of quants with Assets Under Management (AUM) totaling about $19 billion.

Some of the key things that happened in my career were making the leap into finance —it wasn't something I had thought about doing my whole life—and then moving into the quant group. It's often said that women can be hesitant to jump in or believe they're qualified to do things they haven't tried, but I fell into it and really like it.

2. **What are the most important skills and/or qualities for someone in your profession?**

   Math and problem solving are really key, as are being inquisitive and having the drive to keep learning and trying out new things, new technologies, new research methods to help predict stock performance. Humility is really important, coupled with enjoying collaboration and not being discouraged by failure. We're always thinking up complex new ideas and hypotheses and reading papers, vetting other people's research, sharing with each other. We are investing other people's money here on the buy side. So, you have to consider: what are the pitfalls? What have I not thought of? Also, when you're in research, you will come up with a lot of ideas that just don't work. You can't get frustrated and discouraged by that.

3. **What do you wish you had known going into this profession?**

   There's often a perception that quants and other mathematical or programming professionals are thrown into a little dark corner and don't get to talk to anybody. That is not definitely not the case. We're always collaborating, getting together and talking about the ideas.

   Also, while it's important to know a lot of methods, you have to be able to explain your ideas in terms that different audiences can understand.

4. **Are there many job opportunities in your profession? In what specific areas?**

   Quantitative finance has grown enormously. Data analytics is also huge and growing and certainly not limited to finance. It's growing in so many industries. There are jobs not just doing the research, but also as the liaison between people who are doing the research and various audiences inside and outside the firm.

5. **How do you see your profession changing in the next five years? What role will technology play in those changes, and what skills will be required?**

   There's really just so much more data. One of the biggest challenges is figuring out what is good and what's the noise, what's the junk. You need to keep on top of new programming languages, software, tools, methods and analytics to do that.

6. **What do you enjoy most about your job? What do you enjoy least about your job?**

   The best thing is really the collaborative process that we have. And that the work is so varied. There are always new problems to solve, new twists on things, new investment ideas. The heated, excited debate is really fun.

   The data is a double-edged sword. You can get a lot of great insights from it and it's fun to work with, but it's very messy and can have mistakes in it, so it takes a lot of work to check the data before you're ready to actually use it or test it.

7. Can you suggest a valuable "try this" for students considering a career in your profession?

You definitely have to have an analytical and kind of scientific way of thinking and to really enjoy problem solving and puzzles and figuring how to tackle a problem. A classic example is this: If you are out in the rain and you don't have an umbrella, how would you get less wet—should you run or should you walk and why is that? If you would enjoy puzzling through that and not get annoyed by it, quantitative analysis could be a good fit for you.

SELECTED SCHOOLS

Many colleges and universities, especially those with business schools, offer programs in finance and business administration. The student can also gain initial training through enrollment at a technical or community college. For advanced positions, a master's of business administration (MBA) with a concentration in finance is usually expected. Below are listed some of the more prominent institutions in this field.

Carnegie Mellon University
Tepper School of Business
500 Forbes Avenue
Pittsburgh, PA 15213
412.268.2268
tepper.cmu.edu

Indiana University, Bloomington
Kelley School of Business
1309 E. 10th Street
Bloomington, IN 47405
812.855.8100
kelley.iu.edu

Massachusetts Institute of Technology
Sloan School of Management
50 Memorial Drive
Cambridge, MA 02142
617.253.2659
mitsloan.mit.edu

New York University
Stern School of Business
665 Broadway, 11th Floor
New York, NY 10012
212.998.4500
www.stern.nyu.edu

University of California, Berkeley
Haas School of Business
S450 Student Services Building #1900
Berkeley, CA 94720
510.642.1421
haas.berkeley.edu

University of Michigan, Ann Arbor
Ross School of Business
701 Tappan Avenue
Ann Arbor, MI 48109
734.763.5796
michiganross.umich.edu

University of North Carolina, Chapel Hill
Kenan-Flagler Business School
Campus Box 3490, McColl Building
Chapel Hill, NC 27599
919.962.3235
www.kenan-flagler.unc.edu

University of Pennsylvania
The Wharton School
1 College Hall
Philadelphia, PA 19104
215.898.6376
www.wharton.upenn.edu

MORE INFORMATION

Society of Quantitative Analysts
230 Washington Ave, Suite 101
Albany, NY 12203
518-694-3157
www.sqa-us.org

CFA Institute
Charlottesville, VA
434-951-5499
www.cfainstitute.org

International Association for Quantitative Finance (IAQF)
www.iaqf.org

Financial Industry Regulatory Authority (FINRA)
1735 K Street
Washington DC, 2006
301-590-6500
www.finra.org

U.S. Securities and Exchange Commission
100 F Street, NE
Washington, DC 20549
www.sec.gov

Micah Issitt/Editor

Real Estate Appraiser

Snapshot

Career Cluster(s): Financial Services, Real Estate
Interests: Practical work, real estate, research, data analysis
Earnings (Yearly Average): $51,850
Employment & Outlook: Average Growth Expected

OVERVIEW

Sphere of Work

Real estate appraisers estimate the value of property, including both land and any buildings or other construction located on a parcel of land. Appraisers typically specialize in either commercial or residential property and typically work in government offices, for real estate developers, or independently. Real estate appraisers estimate the value of property when property is going to be sold, insured, developed, or mortgaged, and therefore provide a service to both the real estate sale and development industry and to consumers looking to purchase or develop property for personal or professional reasons.

Work Environment

Real estate appraisers spend much of their time traveling within a certain region and might spend at least part of any day either traveling between locations or visiting properties to conduct an appraisal. When not actively traveling or conducting an appraisal, real estate appraisers typically work in office environments using computers and other digital tools to communicate with clients, to prepare documentation, and to manage and plan current and upcoming appraisals. Real estate appraisers work alongside other professionals in the real estate field, such as property developers, real estate agents and sellers, and banking professionals who insure and provide mortgages for property projects.

Profile

Working Conditions: Work Indoors and outdoors
Physical Strength: Light Work
Education Needs: Bachelor's Degree
Licensure/Certification: License or certification required
Opportunities For Experience: Part-time work, On-the-job training
Holland Interest Score*: ECR

* See Appendix A

Occupation Interest

Real estate appraisal is a practical, conventional career that may appeal to individuals interested in construction and architecture and/or in city planning and urban/suburban development. Appraisers should also have an interest in economics as much of their work involves conducting research on property and economic trends and developments. In addition, real estate appraisers need skill in accounting and professionals in the field will benefit from a strong interest in mathematics.

A Day in the Life—Duties and Responsibilities

A typical day for a real estate appraiser might involve speaking to clients about new projects or researching properties and the local property market to prepare for appraisals. Before conducting an appraisal, a real estate appraiser might have meetings with property owners, developers, potential buyers, real estate sales associates, or government representatives. Real estate appraisers must maintain a detailed knowledge of property values in their area and so spend time researching real estate sales, improvements, and changing property values in various areas. Appraisers are also responsible for verifying descriptions of real estate that appear in advertisements and other records to ensure that property sellers are ethically advertising or documenting properties in the area.

An appraiser may conduct several appraisals in a day and may therefore spend much of his or her time traveling within their region and visiting different properties. Estimating the value of a property often depends on comparing the property in question to similar properties in the same area, known as "comparables," and an appraiser might also spend time researching and estimating the value of comparable properties before finishing an appraisal. When visiting a parcel of land or property for an appraisal, the appraiser must conduct a detailed inspection and many follow a checklist when examining various key factors that contribute to the value of a parcel of land or a specific property, such as the nature of the surrounding area, nearby amenities, and the specific features of a building, such as size, number of rooms, general condition, and other features that contribute to the value of a property. After conducting a physical inspection, the appraiser spends time in an office compiling data and preparing an official appraisal that will be delivered to their client.

Duties and Responsibilities

- **Visiting properties and documenting interior and exterior characteristics**
- **Researching real estate and economic trends**
- **Meeting with clients, developers, sales agents, and other real estate professionals**
- **Preparing written reports on property values**
- **Inspecting new and existing properties**
- **Verifying descriptions of real estate appearing in advertisements or records**
- **Traveling to sites for appraisals and meetings**

OCCUPATION SPECIALTIES

Commercial Real Estate Appraiser

A commercial real estate specialist appraises properties and land that will be used for commercial purposes. Appraisers in the commercial field must have knowledge of how to appraise a variety of commercial property types, such as office buildings, hotels and motels, and commercial storefront properties.

Residential Real Estate Appraiser

Residential appraisers specialize in estimating the value of properties and land used for residential purposes. Appraisers specializing in residential property need to be familiar with characteristics common to homes of various sizes and rental properties.

Independent Fee Appraiser

Independent fee appraisers are independent real estate appraisers who earn income based on the value of the properties they evaluate and the number of clients that the appraiser works with. Independent appraisers may work with real estate companies or other developers or may work primarily with private clients.

WORK ENVIRONMENT

Physical Environment

Real estate appraisers spend part of their time working outdoors, traveling and visiting properties to document internal and external characteristics, and part of their time working in office environments, where they meet with clients, conduct research, compile and evaluate data, and prepare reports. Real estate appraisers travel regularly and so might spend much of their time either using a car or public transportation to travel between properties. Time spent traveling or visiting properties depends on the appraiser's specialty, as residential appraisers tend to spend more time traveling and visiting properties than commercial appraisers, who perform more of their work in offices where they analyze data.

Relevant Skills and Abilities

Communication Skills
- Preparing clear reports and letters to clients
- Explaining complex information to clients

Interpersonal/Social Skills
- Being able to work with a team
- Working independently

Organization & Management Skills
- Managing and training junior appraisers
- Creating and maintaining detailed records

Research & Planning Skills
- Researching property values
- Maintaining records of comparable properties

Technical Skills
- Performing calculations
- Using digital software and other tools

Human Environment

About one quarter of all real estate appraisers in the United States work independently and may offer their services to various companies and consumers. Whether working independently or as part of a firm or company, appraisers may work alongside a number of other professionals, including property developers, sales agents, banking officials, and consumers.

Technological Environment

Appraisers regularly use word processing tools to create documents and reports and may also use spreadsheets and other organizational tools for keeping records. There are a variety of software systems that can be used directly in the appraisal process, such as CPR Visual Estimator, Real Estate Center Caparate Calculator, and the RealData Comparative Lease Analysis program. In general, appraisers will learn to use industry specific software during job training. In some cases, real estate appraisers might also need to be familiar with mapping and design software for preparing diagrams and maps to be included in their reports.

EDUCATION, TRAINING, AND ADVANCEMENT

High School/Secondary

Requirements for real estate appraisal are based on state standards, but most states require appraisers to have at least a Bachelor's Degree and high school students seeking to become appraisers should therefore concentrate on fulfilling the requirements to pursue a higher education degree. High school students will benefit from experience with mathematics, drafting, composition, English, and basic computer science as well. Depending on an appraiser's intended region of specialization, appraisers might also benefit from training in a second language.

Suggested High School Subjects

- Algebra
- College Preparatory
- Computer Science
- English
- Geometry
- Graphic Arts
- Industrial Arts
- Business
- Public Speaking
- Technical Writing
- Languages

Famous First

The first professional organization for real estate appraisal in the United States was the American Institute of Real Estate Appraisers (AIREA), which formed in Cincinnati, Ohio, in 1932, through a collaboration among 120 real estate appraisers from across the nation. That same year, the newly formed organization started one of the world's first appraisal publications, *The Journal of the Appraisal Institute.* In 1991, AIREA joined with the Society of Real Estate Appraisers, which formed in 1935 to promote standardized training in the field, to form a new national organization, the Appraisal Institute, which publishes research and promoted education and standards for the industry.

College/Postsecondary

In general, appraisers are required to have at least a bachelor's degree, though requirements vary by state. A professional's choice of subject for his or her bachelor's degree can help to prepare the appraiser for various facets of the industry. Degrees in mathematics, finance, business, or economics provides a future appraiser with experience in related skills. Training in architecture, building science, industrial design, and urban planning will also provide information useful for professional appraisers. For those interested in an advanced degree, training in real estate law or property management will introduce skills relevant to property appraisal and may help professionals to advance within an appraisal company.

Related College Majors

- Architecture
- Engineering, General
- Building Science
- Urban Planning
- Industrial Design
- Business Accounting
- Finance, General
- Business, General
- Economics, General
- Mathematics
- Real Estate Law

Adult Job Seekers

Individuals with required levels of education for their state can apply for open positions as real estate appraisers. In general, appraisers may be required, after being hired, to take classes in real estate appraisal offered by independent appraisal firms, colleges, or private institutes. Real estate appraisers need to be licensed and beginning appraisers may spend months or years training under an experienced appraiser before they qualify for state-mandated licensing and/or certification exams.

Professional Certification and Licensure

Federal law requires all real estate appraisers who work on properties insured or supported by federal funds, to be licensed according to state guidelines. The federal government currently recognizes two official appraiser licenses, one for trainees and one for working professionals working with residential property, as well as two professional certifications, one for residential appraisal professionals and one for general professionals that will allow the professional to specialize in commercial property. Individuals seeking a trainee's license, generally need to have completed at least 15 hours of instruction on appraisal and to pass an exam before receiving their license. Those seeking a residential real estate appraiser license must adhere to state guidelines, but will generally need to have completed at least 30 credit hours of college education and to have more than 2000 hours of experience over at least one year of training. Certification programs are more advanced than licensing programs, and generally require an additional 1000+ hours of time spent on the job and a Bachelor's Degree on higher. State real estate boards provide information on local requirements for both licensing and certification and can help to direct prospective professionals towards appropriate resources.

Additional Requirements

Real estate appraisers need to be competent in math, as much of their job involves analyzing information and making calculations to create estimates. Appraisers also need excellent analytical and organizational skills as the job requires precise and careful planning. In addition, real estate appraisers should have at least moderate customer-service and interpersonal communication skills as appraisers regularly meet with clients and other real estate professionals and need to be able to communicate effectively, sometimes across cultural or linguistic barriers.

Fun Fact

Why do we call it real estate? "Real" is an archaic term for actual or physical things, and real estate means land and buildings fixed to the land, as opposed to moveable property like clothes or tools.

Source: https://english.stackexchange.com/questions/

EARNINGS AND ADVANCEMENT

According to the Bureau of Labor Statistics (BLS), real estate appraisers and assessors earn a median salary of approximately $51,850, as of May 2016. Those at the lower end of the pay spectrum in the field, which includes trainees and individuals working in lower-income areas, earned less than $27,000, while individuals at the upper end of the spectrum earned more than $97,000. Independent appraisers may earn income based on the estimated value of properties that they are asked to evaluate and so may have widely varying income from year to year or month to month depending on the financial outlook in their region, fluctuations in the property market, average income, and the number of clients that the appraiser works with each month or year.. Advancing in the field may involve preparing and completing the requirements for higher level certification and licensing or, for independent appraisers, gaining new clients.

Metropolitan Areas with the Highest Employment Level in this Occupation

Metropolitan area	Employment	Employment per thousand jobs	Hourly mean wage
Atlanta-Sandy Springs-Roswell, GA	1,780	0.70	$25.70
New York-Jersey City-White Plains, NY-NJ Metropolitan Division	1,750	0.27	$29.62
Minneapolis-St. Paul-Bloomington, MN-WI	1,620	0.85	$35.15
Dallas-Plano-Irving, TX Metropolitan Division	1,410	0.58	$34.36
Chicago-Naperville-Arlington Heights, IL Metropolitan Division	1,300	0.36	$27.76
Houston-The Woodlands-Sugar Land, TX	1,180	0.40	$30.69
Los Angeles-Long Beach-Glendale, CA Metropolitan Division	1,060	0.25	$40.53
Miami-Miami Beach-Kendall, FL Metropolitan Division	850	0.75	$22.62
St. Louis, MO-IL	830	0.62	$28.87
Denver-Aurora-Lakewood, CO	810	0.57	$35.18

Source: Bureau of Labor Statistics

EMPLOYMENT AND OUTLOOK

In 2014, the BLS estimated that there were approximately 85,800 professional real estate appraisers and assessors in the U.S., with the number expected to increase to 92,500 by 2024. In general, the BLS estimates that the appraisal field will grow by 8 percent annually, which is about average when compared to the 6-8 percent growth estimated for all U.S. occupations. The increasing use of digital tools for communication and to prepared reports and complete appraisals has made it possible for individual appraisers to spend less time on a specific appraisal and has therefore limited growth in terms of demand for new appraisers. Appraisers with higher levels of work experience, training, and potentially with the ability to appraise properties in different facets of the market, are expected to have access to better jobs as the market becomes more competitive.

Related Occupations

- Accountants
- Budget Specialists
- Financial Managers
- Real Estate Brokers and Sales Agents
- Construction and Building Inspectors
- Claims Adjusters, Appraisers, Examiners, and Investigators

Conversation With . . .
GERALD NAGLE

Independent Real Estate Appraiser
Central Massachusetts
Real estate appraisal, 5 years

1. What was your individual career path in terms of education/training, entry-level job, or other significant opportunity?

I started out in Michigan, where I earned an associate degree in electrical engineering technology. I spent 32 years working for a company that produced electrical test and measurement equipment for companies that make electronic products like games, computers, disc drives and televisions. I moved from Michigan to California to Colorado, then Massachusetts, and I held many positions, including board test programmer, customer telephone support, software development and instrumentation, and software diagnostics. It was always challenging and interesting.

At 55, I was furloughed. I spent a year interviewing in a tight job market, then, frustrated, decided to take a new direction. A friend suggested real estate appraising. Like my former career, there's an analytical nature to this work. No two homes are the same, even in the same tract, so it's very analytical in terms of trying to decide how to adjust for the differences.

I also was drawn to the independence of the work.

To become a real estate appraiser, you must find a licensed appraiser to sponsor you and accept responsibility for the work you perform until you complete your education process and obtain a license. The licensing process is rigorous. In Massachusetts, a student has to pass three courses, totaling 75 hours of class time, in order to qualify for a trainee license. An additional four classes (also 75 hours of class time), plus 2,000 hours of experience, are required to prepare for the exam to become a licensed residential appraiser— the lowest of three licensing levels required to practice.

To become a certified residential appraiser, which is the license I hold, an additional 50 hours of class time is required, plus a total of 2,500 hours of documented experience over a period of no less than 2 years.

I'm an independent contractor for a company that gets work from banks and mortgage corporations. My day-to-day assignments are all residential appraisals, including single-family homes, condos, and multi-family properties of up to four units.

2. What are the most important skills and/or qualities for someone in your profession?

You must be self-motivated; most real estate appraisers are independent and there's no time to goof off. It helps to have an analytical mind and a skill for problem solving.

3. What do you wish you had known going into this profession?

How challenging it is to find time for the classes, gain experience, and ultimately prepare for the license examination.

4. Are there many job opportunities in your profession? In what specific areas?

The average age of real estate appraisers is 60 years old. This is bad and good news. The bad is that you have to find a sponsor. The good is that there will likely be a large number of appraisers dropping out of the market, creating opportunities for new appraisers to connect with the major banks and lending institutions—which increases the percentage of the fee that ends up in the appraiser's wallet. If you work for an appraisal company, they take a percentage of the fee, which means an appraiser has to do more assignments in order to earn a living.

5. How do you see your profession changing in the next five years, what role will technology play in those changes, and what skills will be required?

Lenders are looking for ways to eliminate the human performing the appraisal. The good news is that the accuracy of the data still requires a human to interpret it. Real estate appraisers are looking for "comparables" – similar homes in a specific market to help set a home's selling price. In most cases, humans are still needed to qualify a competitive comparable.

6. What do you enjoy most about your job? What do you enjoy least about your job?

I like the freedom to set my own schedule, and to work as much as I choose for the income I want to achieve.

I least enjoy clients who pressure me for a quick turnaround. The quicker the turnaround, the more difficult it is to do more than one inspection a day—and that impacts my income.

7. Can you suggest a valuable "try this" for students considering a career in your profession?

The Multiple Listing Service, or MLS, is the most informative tool for gathering information about a property. Realtors pay for access to it, and might be willing to allow access to a curious student.

In addition, communities provide property records, often online. Or, find an appraiser willing to take you along for an inspection. Real estate agents often have the names and phone numbers for local appraisers.

SELECTED SCHOOLS

Many colleges and universities, especially those with business schools, offer programs in business and finance. The student can also gain initial training at a technical or community college. For some of the more prominent institutions in this field, see the list of selected schools in the "Accountant" and "Finance Manager" chapters of this volume.

MORE INFORMATION

Appraisal Institute
200 W. Madison, Suite 1500
Chicago, IL 60606
888-756-4624
www.appraisalinstitute.org

American Society of Appraisers
11107 Sunset Hills Rd, Ste 310
Reston, VA 20190
800.272-8258
www.appraisers.org

National Association of Real Estate Appraisers
Palm Springs, CA
877-743-6806
www.narea-assoc.org

Appraisers Association
212 West 35th Street, 11th Floor South
New York, NY 10001
212-889-5404
www.appraisersassociation.org

National Association of Independent Fee Appraisers
330 North Wabash Ave, Suite 2000
Chicago, IL 60611
312-321-6830
www.naifa.com

Micah Issitt/Editor

Regulatory Compliance Officer

Snapshot

Career Cluster(s): Financial Services, Management
Interests: Financial regulation, management, governmental oversight, law
Earnings (Yearly Average): $66,540
Employment & Outlook: Slower than average growth expected

OVERVIEW

Sphere of Work

Regulatory compliance officers are responsible for making sure that companies adhere to financial laws and regulations and that company employees and managers adhere to ethical guidelines for their industry. Compliance officers work in a number of industries under different titles, such as environmental compliance inspector or licensing examiner, though the duties for all compliance positions are similar. In the financial industry, compliance officers are responsible for ensuring that the company, or its employees, don't violate federal regulations on financial transactions and trades. Towards this goal, compliance officers are

required to learn about any changes in relevant regulations and to make sure that company employees understand the legal and ethical guidelines of their industry. In industries with stringent and changing regulations, like the finance industry, compliance officers protect companies from potentially disastrous legal issues and help managers to determine the regulatory risks of investments and other corporate activities.

Work Environment

Regulatory compliance officers tend to work indoors, in office environments, and typically work full time. In some cases, compliance officers might be asked to travel within or between companies to conduct inspections. In some cases, compliance officers may oversee other employees, in a management capacity, while, in other companies, the compliance officer may work largely independently.

Profile

Working Conditions: Work Indoors
Physical Strength: Light Work
Education Needs: Bachelor's Degree
Licensure/Certification: Required for some positions
Opportunities For Experience: Part-time work, Military service
Holland Interest Score*: CE

* See Appendix A

Occupation Interest

Regulatory positions may appeal to individuals who have a strong appreciation for ethical guidelines and want to help ensure that companies and individuals follow ethical principles. In addition, compliance officers should be comfortable interacting with others regularly as much of the job includes meeting with professionals within a company and conducting interviews. Compliance officers are also responsible for making sure that employees adhere to internal company policies and so act as managers who are often required to determine when employees are guilty of violating corporate or regulatory rules. As such, potential compliance officers should be interested in taking on a management role and comfortable enforcing rules when applicable.

A Day in the Life—Duties and Responsibilities

When beginning a career in compliance, a professional must first conduct research to obtain a detailed understanding of regulations and laws governing his or her industry. In the financial industry, and many other sectors employing compliance officers, regulations may change at the local, state, or federal level and compliance officers must ensure that they have learned about any changes in relevant regulations.

Compliance officers spend much of their time in meetings and conducting inspections. Compliance officers also spend time creating and updating documentation on corporate compliance or regarding the results of inspections and interviews with employees. It is common for compliance officers to conduct regular training sessions with company employees to inform them of changes to policies or regulations. When an infraction is suspected, compliance officers may conduct detailed interviews with employees and managers and may be responsible for determining any punitive actions necessary to address the situation and to avoid regulatory issues. In a research capacity, compliance officers might also consult with corporate managers to discuss potential changes in policies or the ethnical/regulatory risks that may result from upcoming corporate projects.

Duties and Responsibilities

- **Referring to laws and company policies**
- **Conducting inspections, interviews, and investigations**
- **Developing and leading training sessions for staff**
- **Consulting with managers and executives**
- **Researching and interpreting changes in regulations**
- **Creating and maintaining detailed regulatory documentation**
- **Conducting employee evaluations and orientations**

OCCUPATION SPECIALTIES

Bank Compliance Officer

Bank compliance officers work in banking institutions and oversee accounting, investment, and lending activities to ensure that employees follow relevant laws and adhere to internal company policies.

Environmental Compliance Officer

An environmental compliance specialist helps to ensure that companies are aware of and adhere to environmental regulations at the federal, state, and local levels. Environmental compliance officers help to inspect potential sources of pollution and examine permits and licenses for companies engaged in activities with potential environmental impact.

Equal Opportunity Compliance Officer

Equal opportunity compliance specialists oversee hiring and human resources activities within a company or institution to ensure that the company/institution or its staff does not violate any local or federal laws regarding equal opportunity. Equal opportunity specialists also meet with employees to handle allegations of misconduct or discrimination.

License Inspector

A license inspector is responsible for ensuring that companies or institutions obtain the correct licenses or permits for any activities and also that institutions adhere to the terms of a license or permit once granted by the appropriate regulatory agency.

Medical Compliance Officer

Medical compliance officers work in the medical industry, helping to ensure that hospitals and other medical institutions adhere to federal and state regulations regarding the treatment of patients and their families. Medical compliance officers help to ensure patient privacy and confidentiality and help to keep an institution's staff informed about changes in relevant policies.

WORK ENVIRONMENT

Relevant Skills and Abilities

Communication Skills
- Speaking directly with employees
- Conducting interviews and evaluations
- Explaining complex topics

Interpersonal/Social Skills
- Being able to work with a team
- Working independently

Organization & Management Skills
- Managing employees
- Creating and maintaining detailed records

Research & Planning Skills
- Researching new regulations and changes to relevant laws

Technical Skills
- Using digital software and personal computers
- Maintaining detailed knowledge of company policy
- Maintaining knowledge of relevant regulations and laws

Physical Environment

Compliance officers typically work in office environments and most work full time. In the case that a compliance officer suspects or has discovered evidence of major regulatory violations, overtime work may be necessary. Compliance officers working in large companies, or companies with branches, may be asked to travel to conduct training sessions, inspections, or investigations.

Human Environment

Depending on the size and other specifics of a company's operation, a compliance officer may either work independently or may be part of a team that manages compliance and regulatory issues. Much of a compliance officer's work involves meeting with company representatives and employees and compliance officers need to be comfortable communicating with a wide variety of people. Compliance officers are typically considered managers and, in some companies, may be responsible for penalizing employees who have violated company policies. In other cases, compliance officers conduct interviews and investigations and recommend potential penalties to human resources officials or regulatory agencies. Some compliance officers may be responsible for managing a team of regulatory specialists within an institution.

Technological Environment

Compliance officers regularly use computers and other digital tools to create documentation, presentations, and to keep records and to communicate with other employees or managers. Compliance officers may use spreadsheets, word processing programs, and other data collection/management software in their jobs and may also need to utilize management software to schedule appointments and to conduct investigations. Presentation software may be used to create training programs to introduce regulations and policies to employees. In some cases, financial industry compliance officers need to have familiarity with accounting software in order to complex calculations needed for inspections or investigations.

EDUCATION, TRAINING, AND ADVANCEMENT

High School/Secondary

High school students interested in a career in regulatory compliance should prepare for higher education as most jobs in the field require at least a Bachelor's Degree in a related field. Those interested in working in financial regulation should take any available classes that will help orient them towards the financial industry, such as business, economics, accounting, and mathematics. In addition, basic skills in composition, computer science, public speaking, and technical writing will be helpful for professionals in the field.

Suggested High School Subjects

- Algebra
- Applied Math
- College Preparatory
- Computer Science

- English
- Business
- Calculus
- Accounting
- Introduction to Computers
- Composition
- Public Speaking

Famous First

The modern field of regulatory compliance can be traced to the early twentieth century, when a new public safety movement began in the United States, resulting in the formation of regulatory agencies like the Food and Drug Administration, which was created in 1906. The emergence of regulatory agencies resulted from the increasing realization that, left to their own devices, companies would do little to ensure public safety or welfare. Legislators therefore determined that the best way to protect the public from corporate malpractice, manipulation, and exploitation was to create centralized agencies responsible for creating and enforcing regulations. Gradually, corporations began employing internal officials responsible for ensuring that employees adhered to regulatory guidelines.

College/Postsecondary

In general, compliance officer positions require a bachelor's degree in a related field. In the financial industry, compliance officers typically have degrees in business, finance, or accounting. In some cases, companies may require compliance officers or compliance managers to have legal training and experience in regulatory law. Some companies might also require a master's degree, such as a Masters of Business Administration (MBA) or higher level degree for some advanced regulatory positions. In general, those interested in careers in compliance should focus on studying aspects of their chosen industry as well as law and management.

Related College Majors

- Business Accounting
- Finance, General

- Business, General
- Financial Management
- Regulatory Law
- Law, General
- Masters of Business Administration
- Economics

Adult Job Seekers

Individuals with a bachelor's degree and sufficient experience can apply for open positions in the field. Many companies offer on-the-job training to help orient employees to company culture and policies. Individuals might be asked to demonstrate detailed knowledge of relevant laws and regulations when seeking employment in the field.

Professional Certification and Licensure

While there are no required certifications or licenses for compliance officers, there are a variety of organizations and institutions that offer training specific to the field and obtaining voluntary certification in regulatory compliance can increase employment opportunities. For instance, the Financial Industry Regulatory Authority (FINRA), offers certification in compliance and ethnics aimed specifically at individuals involved in banks, investment firms, and other financial industry occupations that involve investments. The Society of Corporate Compliance and Ethics (SCCE) offers a Certified Compliance and Ethics Professional Program (CCEP) that provides training in ethical and regulatory principles for students with a bachelor's degree who are seeking employment in the compliance field. Another organization offering formal certification is the National Regulatory Services Office (NRS), which offers an Investment Adviser Certified Compliance Professional program aimed at providing direct training for compliance professionals involved in financial or investment companies.

Additional Requirements

Compliance officers are often employed by banks, investment companies, or other corporations, but are also responsible, ethnically and professionally, for ensuring compliance to applicable laws and regulations, even when compliance is a detriment to a company's business practices or earnings. Compliance officers therefore have to be able to manage dual allegiance as company employees who police behavior within their own companies. As compliance officers may need to make difficult decisions that can affect the livelihoods of others, professionals in the field need to be confident and dedicated to their role and should be comfortable making difficult decisions. Compliance officers are also often responsible for ensuring that a company's staff is aware of regulations and policies and so needs to have at least moderate ability to teach and good communication skills.

Fun Fact

Back in 2011, a competition for "America's Funniest Compliance Officer" was held at New York's Comic Strip comedy club. It's not a joke, but it's funny.

Source: https://www.wsj.com/articles/

EARNINGS AND ADVANCEMENT

According to the Bureau of Labor Statistics (BLS), the median wage for professionals in the compliance industry was $66,540 in May of 2016. However, salaries in the field range widely depending on a person's specialization, experience, and employer, with a range of less than $35,000 to more than $100,000. Compliance officers with advanced degrees and/or professional certification are more likely to qualify for higher pay positions or to work in compliance management in larger companies. Advancing in the field typically involves accruing sufficient work experience to qualify for higher-pay or more prestigious positions in the field. Professionals already working in compliance might also advance by seeking further education through a professional certification or training program.

Metropolitan Areas with the Highest Employment Level in this Occupation

Metropolitan area	Employment	Employment per thousand jobs	Hourly mean wage
New York-Jersey City-White Plains, NY-NJ Metropolitan Division	14,380	2.18	$40.17
Washington-Arlington-Alexandria, DC-VA-MD-WV Metropolitan Division	8,890	3.57	$41.76
Los Angeles-Long Beach-Glendale, CA Metropolitan Division	8,650	2.05	$36.95
Houston-The Woodlands-Sugar Land, TX	6,020	2.05	$38.82
Chicago-Naperville-Arlington Heights, IL Metropolitan Division	5,570	1.53	$36.28
Atlanta-Sandy Springs-Roswell, GA	5,080	1.99	$29.93
Dallas-Plano-Irving, TX Metropolitan Division	4,880	2.01	$37.20
Seattle-Bellevue-Everett, WA Metropolitan Division	4,600	2.89	$45.25
Boston-Cambridge-Newton, MA NECTA Division	4,460	2.47	$42.28
San Diego-Carlsbad, CA	4,320	3.11	$37.81

Source: Bureau of Labor Statistics

EMPLOYMENT AND OUTLOOK

As of 2016, the BLS estimated an average of 2-3 percent annual growth in the compliance field, which is much slower than the 6-7 percent average for all U.S. occupations. A relative lack of available jobs, with an estimated 273,910 professionals employed in 2014, means that competition for available positions is likely to be high. Individuals with advanced degrees, higher levels of work experience, and complimentary experience in law and other related fields, will likely have an advantage in finding employment.

Related Occupations

- Accountants
- Financial Analysts
- Budget Specialists
- Financial Managers
- Appraisers, Examiners, and Investigators
- Environmental Compliance Officers

Related Military Occupations

- Military Compliance Analyst

Conversation With . . .
CHARLES V. SENATORE

Head of Risk Oversight
Devonshire Investors, Fidelity Investments
Boston, Massachusetts
Compliance professional, 23 years

1. What was your individual career path in terms of education/training, entry-level job, or other significant opportunity?

My plan all along was to be a courtroom and appellate litigator, and I expected that to be my path. I graduated from law school and worked as a litigation associate in law firms in Miami. After that, I went into government service and became an Assistant U.S. Attorney in the Southern District of Florida, becoming chief of the public corruption section before leaving to become a litigation partner in a major national law firm.

Within a few years of leaving the U.S. Attorney's office, I had the opportunity to join the Securities and Exchange Commission (SEC) in a senior role, so I left private practice to became Regional Director for the SEC's then Southeast Region, headquartered in Miami. This exposed me to the workings, operations and policy nuances pertaining to the SEC, and was a significant turning point in my career.

When it was time to leave the SEC, I considered career opportunities in the financial services industry, and chose that path as opposed to returning to a law firm partnership. I joined Merrill Lynch's Regulatory Affairs group and ultimately was asked to lead that group.

I was approached by Merrill Lynch leadership to take over the compliance program for its retail private client brokerage business. This was another unanticipated development in my career path, which ultimately led me to co-lead global compliance for the firm. After five years, I was recruited by Fidelity Investments to lead its global compliance and ethics program, which I did for approximately eleven years before transitioning into my current role.

As a compliance and ethics officer, I've been active in the Ethics and Compliance Initiative (ECI) and particularly its predecessor—the Ethics Resource Center. It was useful as a resource for thought leadership and the chance to exchange ideas with other industry leaders.

2. What are the most important skills and/or qualities for someone in your profession?

A successful chief compliance officer needs a basket of skills. In addition to subject matter expertise in law and regulation, one needs to understand the underlying business, have the skills to lead a complex organization, and have a sense of managing and operations, and business processes. One must have strong communication skills and the ability to influence, both to create support for your program and to drive behaviors. Most importantly, this profession requires a strong sense of ethics, a degree of personal courage, and emotional intelligence with respect to dealing with others. A consultant once told me that the chief compliance officer skill set correlates highly with the skill set needed to be a successful CEO.

3. What do you wish you had known going into this profession?

Actually, I went in with eyes wide open. What I didn't anticipate was the degree of importance the profession would ultimately have. When I started, I was several layers down in the organization. Eventually, the role changed to the point where I was working with the highest levels of the firm.

4. Are there many job opportunities in your profession? In what specific areas?

Compliance is a hot area. As the regulatory environment becomes more complex and global, and as the risks that companies face continue to grow, the need for skilled compliance officers will be increasing for the foreseeable future.

5. How do you see your profession changing in the next five years? What role will technology play in those changes, and what skills will be required?

The biggest changes will be in the technology space, as business processes will increasingly rely on—and in many cases, be performed by—technology. The compliance officer of the future will need to be familiar with the language and principles of how systems are constructed, run, and tested.

6. What do you enjoy most about your job? What do you enjoy least about your job?

The wide scope of challenges, the breadth of matters I am asked to address, and my integration with the leadership of the firm make the job unique and terrific.

What I enjoy least is "not knowing what I don't know." What I mean by this is that organizations are so vast and complex that it's difficult to know what is going on in every corner of the business, and something significant possibly could be missed. The only way to address this is to have assessed the risks as best as you can, and hope you prioritize the right areas for your attention.

7. Can you suggest a valuable "try this" for students considering a career in your profession?

Try to do an internship or volunteer with a government agency to get a sense of what they expect of those they regulate, or perhaps get a job at a regulated company such as financial services or health care. It might not be necessary to actually work in the compliance area, because other positions can give students a chance to observe how they address their compliance issues.

SELECTED SCHOOLS

Many colleges and universities, especially those with business schools, offer programs in business and finance. The student can also gain initial training at a technical or community college. For some of the more prominent institutions in this field, see the list of selected schools in the "Accountant" and "Finance Manager" chapters of this volume.

MORE INFORMATION

Financial Industry Regulatory Authority (FINRA)
1735 K Street
Washington DC, 2006
301-590-6500
www.finra.org

National Regulatory Services
29 Brook Street
PO Box 71
Lakeville, CT 06039
860-435-0200
www.nrs-inc.com

U.S. Securities and Exchange Commission
100 F Street, NE
Washington, DC 20549
www.sec.gov

Ethics & Compliance Initiative
2345 Crystal Drive, Suite 201
Arlington, VA 22202
703-647-2185
www.ecoaconnects.theecoa.org

Compliance Certification Board
6500 Barrie Rd, Ste 250
Minneapolis, MN 55435
888-580-8373
www.compliancecertification.org

Micah Issitt/Editor

Securities, Commodities & Financial Services Sales Agents

Snapshot

Career Cluster(s): Financial Services, Accounting, Sales
Interests: Working with people, customer services, economics, finance, sales
Earnings (Yearly Average): $67,310
Employment & Outlook: Faster Than Average Growth Expected

OVERVIEW

Sphere of Work

Securities, commodities, and financial services sales agents purchase and sell interest in stocks, commodities, and financial services, like insurance or banking services. This field includes professionals such as brokers, stock traders, investment bankers, and insurance/banking sales associates, and professionals in the field

generally need detailed knowledge of finance and economics as well as excellent customer service and sales skills. In general, sales agents earn commission when they organize a sale or purchase, in addition to a minimum salary.

Work Environment

Sales agents work in office environments and spend most of their time communicating with customers or clients either in person or through telephone or digital communication. Many financial sales agencies offer 24-hour customer service, which means that sales agents may work irregular hours, including nights and weekends. In most industries, sales agents work full time, though overtime is common in the field. Sales agents known as "floor brokers" work directly on trading room floors, large open rooms in a securities or commodities exchange, where hundreds of traders gather to buy and sell stocks and other assets. In general, financial sales is a collaborative field and sales agents work alongside other financial professionals as well as with clients and customers.

Profile

Working Conditions: Work Indoors
Physical Strength: Light Work
Education Needs: Bachelor's Degree
Licensure/Certification: Licensing required, Certification optional
Opportunities For Experience: Part-time work, On-the-job training
Holland Interest Score*: EC

* See Appendix A

Occupation Interest

Individuals seeking to become financial sales agents should have a strong interest in finance and mathematics. Though knowledge of the financial industry is important, sales agents are primarily customer service professionals and should also have a strong interest in communication and working with people.

A Day in the Life—Duties and Responsibilities

A typical day for a sales agent depends on the agent's specific role or field. Brokers, for instance, sell securities and commodities to customers directly, and so spend much of their time communicating with clients, either via email, telephone, or in person, to advise clients on purchasing opportunities. Investment bankers, on the other hand, help corporations to obtain funding for projects and facilitate meetings between companies and investors. Most sales agents spend at least part of a typical day meeting with clients or other professionals. An important part of the job involves finding new clients and building a client portfolio, and sales agents may therefore need to spend time each day on marketing, advertising, and contacting new potential clients to discuss their services. In some cases, this might involve cold calling clients, while, in other cases, agents will contact clients who have reached out to their firm or agency for information.

When not actively buying or selling securities, like bonds or stocks, or commodities, which include physical goods like precious metals and agricultural products, sales agents need to conduct research to keep up with financial trends and to learn about current or future opportunities or problems for their clients. This research often involves tracking the performance of specific securities or commodities, and analyzing companies to determine how the market will likely change in the future.

Duties and Responsibilities

- **Contact new or prospective clients to pitch services**
- **Research and consult clients on opportunities**
- **Buy or sell assets for clients, including securities and commodities**
- **Explaining investments, regulations, and financial processes to clients.**
- **Research financial markets to learn about new opportunities**
- **Working with portfolio managers, financial managers, and other financial professionals**
- **Creating and preparing contracts for clients**

OCCUPATION SPECIALTIES

Investment Banker

Investment bankers work with banks and other companies, helping companies to obtain revenue for projects and connecting companies with investors. Investment banking firms are often involved in the IPO (Initial Public Offering) process in which a formerly private company transitions to public ownership by selling stock. Investment bankers find clients who may want to invest and help to determine the value of the company in preparation for the company's IPO.

Broker

Brokers and floor brokers buy and sell securities and commodities directly to clients, which may be individual customers or corporations. Some brokers work independently, and must develop a list of clients to earn revenues, while others work as part of an investment team for a financial institution or financial firm.

Financial Services Sales Agent

A financial services sales agent sells financial services to customers. Financial services is a broad field that can include buying and selling securities or commodities, but also may involve a variety of other services including insurance and banking services. Sales agents specializing in selling insurance typically need financial expertise as well as experience with the specific type of insurance they sell, which may be personal, retirement, property, medical, or a variety of different insurance types.

WORK ENVIRONMENT

Relevant Skills and Abilities

Communication Skills
- Speaking with clients and other professionals
- Writing clear reports for clients and other professionals

Interpersonal/Social Skills
- Being able to work with a team
- Working independently
- Meeting new clients
- Selling services to customers

Organization & Management Skills
- Maintaining regular contact with clients
- Keeping detailed records and accounts

Research & Planning Skills
- Researching industry trends
- Researching changes in financial markets
- Finding new clients

Technical Skills
- Keeping detailed accounts
- Using financial analysis and organizational software

Physical Environment

Financial sales agents typically work in office environments or on sales floors. In call centers for customer service and sales, dozens of agents may work in cubicles in a single room while, in other cases, sales agents may work from a private office. Sales agents do not regularly need to travel, though some might be asked to travel between different offices or branches or to travel for meetings with clients.

Human Environment

Securities, commodities, and financial services sales professionals all work closely with customers, who may be individuals or corporations, to determine the needs of each client and to provide recommendations on investments or services. Financial sales is therefore a communicative field in which professionals need to be comfortable speaking with and working with customers and other professionals from a variety of background. Sales agents may be asked to attend daily meetings and often communicate with clients via telephone, email, or other digital communication.

Technological Environment

The online marketplace is changing the securities, commodities, and financial services sales industry as customers and agents are more likely to trade commodities and securities electronically, rather than on the floor of an exchange market. As a result, securities and commodities sales professionals have increasingly transitioned to making electronic trades for their clients. In some companies, sales agents may use a customer management program, such as Salesforce software, to keep track of their customers. In addition, sales agents may need to learn to use financial analysis software, like Bloomberg Professional, or Oracle E-Business, and may use spreadsheets and accounting software to manage customer profiles.

EDUCATION, TRAINING, AND ADVANCEMENT

High School/Secondary

High school students interested in careers in financial sales should prepare for higher education as most financial services and sales firms require a bachelor's degree for entry-level positions. Students will also benefit from taking any available classes in mathematics, economics, finance, business, composition, English, public speaking, and law. Classes in basic computer science will also help to prepare students for working with digital sales, management, and analysis software.

Suggested High School Subjects

- Algebra
- Applied Math
- College Preparatory
- Computer Science
- English
- Business
- Economics
- Law

- Public Speaking
- Accounting

Famous First

Ohio born Victoria Woodhull was a pioneering women's suffrage activist and entrepreneur who, in 1870, along with her sister Victoria Claflin, opened the first female-owned brokerage firm on Wall Street. Woodhull's firm, Woodhull, Claflin & Company, was highly successful, and both Woodhull and her sister became wealthy from their efforts. Two years later, Woodhull became the first woman in history to run for the presidency of the United States. Though Woodhull was constitutionally ineligible, as she was not yet 35 years old at the time, and was incarcerated on obscenity charges on election day, her controversial candidacy was intended to spark controversy and became one of many controversial statements that Woodhull made in a lifelong campaign against the marginalization of women.

College/Postsecondary

While many securities, commodities, and financial services agents may begin working after completing a bachelor's degree, when applying for entry-level positions, those with advanced degrees in business, accounting, financial management, or a related field, will have an advantage on the job market. It is common for sales agents to obtain a Masters of Business Administration (MBA) degree to advance in their careers. While many sales agents study business, education in finance, economic, accounting, or law can also provide a background for a career in financial sales.

Related College Majors

- Financial Management
- Accounting, General
- Business Accounting
- Finance, General
- Business, General
- Law, General
- Corporate Law

- Financial Law
- Masters of Business Administration

Adult Job Seekers

Individuals with a bachelor's degree or higher in a related field can apply for entry level jobs in financial sales. Large, prestigious firms may offer internships to promising students prior to the student finishing his or her bachelor's program. After being hired, sales agents will typically participate in an extended training period, working under one or more experienced sales agents. During this training period, depending on the company, beginning sales agents learn about company policies and procedures and participate in sales meetings and calls. As the trainee advances, he or she will begin to develop a list of clients. In some companies, trainees may be provided with a broader education on the finance industry before they begin working independently.

Professional Certification and Licensure

Any professional individual who purchases securities and must be licensed by the state, with different licenses for various types of financial products. Depending on their position, a sales agent may need to obtain licenses for selling commodities, securities, financial services, insurance, or other licenses covering a variety of financial products. Many financial agencies provide training or assistance for employees before taking licensing exams. Brokers and other investment professionals will need to register with the Financial Industry Regulatory Authority (FINRA) before they can legally begin working.

Some financial sales agents choose to pursue professional certification as a Chartered Financial Analyst (CFA) or a Certified Financial Planner (CFP), or a Certified Public Accountant (CPA). Students who wish to participate in certification programs typically need to have completed a bachelor's degree and/or to have worked in the field for more than a year. While not required to work as a professional sales agent, professional certification can provide an advantage in the job market or can help qualify a sales professional for advancement within a firm.

Additional Requirements

Financial sales agents must have excellent sales and communication skills as much of the job involves meeting and forming relationships with new clients. Many sales agents are responsible for creating their own client base by calling or emailing potential clients and so professional sales associates need to be confident and comfortable with sales and interpersonal communication. In addition, sales agents must be goal and detail oriented, as precise accounting and communication is required in the field. Basic skill with mathematics is also key for successful agents. In addition, agents need to have excellent analytical skills, allowing them to discover investment opportunities or to estimate changes in the financial market.

Fun Fact

Here's how long your money lasts: a $1 bill lasts less than six years (on average), while a $5 or $10 will go a little more than four years. If you've got a $100 bill, however, it ought to last about 15 years.

Source: https://www.usatoday.com

EARNINGS AND ADVANCEMENT

The Bureau of Labor Statistics estimates the median annual wage for securities, commodities, and financial services sales agents at approximately $67,310 in May of 2016. Salaries in the field range widely from a lower level of less than $33,340 to well over $100,000 per year, depending on experience and the overall success of a sales agent's company. Agents who attract and maintain relationships with lucrative clients are more likely to advance to senior positions. Sales agents can also decide to become portfolio managers, who are agents who may purchase securities and commodities for clients, but also manage client investment portfolios. In some cases, sales agents can transition to other, higher paid financial services fields, such as by becoming a personal financial adviser or by transitioning to management.

Metropolitan Areas with the Highest Employment Level in this Occupation

Metropolitan area	Employment	Employment per thousand jobs	Hourly mean wage
New York-Jersey City-White Plains, NY-NJ Metropolitan Division	54,730	8.31	N/A
Chicago-Naperville-Arlington Heights, IL Metropolitan Division	15,630	4.30	$47.43
Los Angeles-Long Beach-Glendale, CA Metropolitan Division	13,040	3.09	$40.77
Houston-The Woodlands-Sugar Land, TX	10,150	3.46	$41.23
Dallas-Plano-Irving, TX Metropolitan Division	9,780	4.03	$51.16
Boston-Cambridge-Newton, MA NECTA Division	8,020	4.45	$61.03
Denver-Aurora-Lakewood, CO	7,760	5.48	$40.03
Anaheim-Santa Ana-Irvine, CA Metropolitan Division	6,760	4.33	$40.47
Atlanta-Sandy Springs-Roswell, GA	5,800	2.27	$48.78
Minneapolis-St. Paul-Bloomington, MN-WI	5,790	3.03	$49.48

Source: Bureau of Labor Statistics

EMPLOYMENT AND OUTLOOK

As of 2014, the BLS estimated that there were 341,500 professional financial sales agents in the United States, with a projected growth of 10 annual growth, which is faster than average compared to the 6-7 percent predicted for all U.S. occupations. Economic growth creates demand for sales agents, while periods of economic stability can reduce opportunities as investment companies reduced staff while they wait for the economy to improve. There is some evidence that automated trading, which occurs in large companies and in the NASDAQ stock exchange, has reduced opportunities for sales agents.

Related Occupations

- Insurance Sales Agents
- Financial Managers
- Personal Financial Advisors
- Accountants
- Financial Analysts
- Real Estate Brokers and Sales Agents

Related Military Occupations

- Military Insurance Sales Agent
- Army Retirement Planning Specialist

Conversation With . . .
PATRICK K. HOLT

Macro Strategy Analyst, LPL Financial Research
Charlotte, North Carolina
Financial field, 4 years

1. What was your individual career path in terms of education/training, entry-level job, or other significant opportunity?

I wasn't really exposed to the financial world growing up. I majored in English at North Carolina State University and after graduation did door-to-door sales for AT&T, which sharpened my sales skills extremely quickly. A cousin told me Vanguard was hiring in their call center, so I put in an application. I did a mock phone call during the job interview and tried to sell Vanguard funds. They said they thought I'd be great for a different position in the call center and moved me up to the business development group's sales.

I loved it. I read everything I could about financial markets, listened to podcasts, and learned as much as I could. I started studying for my Series 7 and 63 licensing exams, which are required to become a securities broker. The licenses keep you accountable in this heavily-regulated industry.

I did consultative, soft sales, as opposed to hard sales. Say you have a retirement account managed by John Smith, it's underperforming, you've heard good things about Vanguard, and you call. I would ask you open-ended questions, you tell me about your situation, your goals, and what you want. I used that information to suggest a product that is appropriate for your goals and needs.

I was promoted to high net worth sales, investors with more than $1 million. I used my sales skills and my English degree and writing to empathize with people and establish a rapport over the phone. Because I was able to understand people, rather than just knowing numbers, I advanced quickly.

Vanguard sells low-fee index fees, which have been outperforming expensive actively managed funds. Vanguard, which is the second largest money manager in the world, runs at-cost. So, basically, I was able to sell that story because it's a great story. What I love is stories.

I left to make more money, plus I was getting bored. Once you get a taste of corporate advancement, it becomes a game. It's rewarding.

A friend had gone to LPL's Research department and I told him to let me know if they had any openings. A month later, he called to tell me about an opening. I'm not doing sales, but I'm around very smart people and learning about the market. Basically, financial advisers call and ask me questions about the market. Also, I wanted to be writing. I recently wrote my first post for the LPL research blog, about Bitcoin. I also was recently promoted to market strategy analyst.

I also have to say: as far back as I can remember, my parents have told me to be nice to everyone. It sounds less profound than it truly is. Every opportunity I've had is because I took my parents' advice to heart. In addition, my dad always said to keep learning, and I have. He said that he knew one day I would be using my English degree and writing, and while I never really believed him, I adopted that confidence and used it as a way to provide myself with career direction.

2. What are the most important skills and/or qualities for someone in your profession?

Active listening; really understanding your clients on a personal and on a financial level and making them feel comfortable with the solution you are offering.

3. What do you wish you had known going into this profession?

More about the markets, such as what factors influence prices.

4. Are there many job opportunities in your profession? In what specific areas?

Yes. Definitely. There are not as many opportunities as in programming, but a salesperson in finance will always have an opportunity.

5. How do you see your profession changing in the next five years, what role will technology play in those changes, and what skills will be required?

In the next five years, not a whole lot. In the next 10 years, all portfolios will be automated. Everything will be done by a robot. The human will be the go-between to inform clients. So, active listening and being able to connect is going to be more important.

6. What do you enjoy most about your job? What do you enjoy least about your job?

Connecting with clients and the amazing feeling of really helping someone. I really liked the times I had a two-hour conversation with someone and I'd see the light bulb go off and know I was helping them prepare for retirement and doing the right thing.

I didn't like working in a call center. It is, by nature, repetitive. I wanted to learn new things.

7. Can you suggest a valuable "try this" for students considering a career in your profession?

Shadow a local adviser, especially an up-and-comer who is talking with clients. See how they impact people's lives.

SELECTED SCHOOLS

Many colleges and universities, especially those with business schools, offer programs in business and finance. The student can also gain initial training at a technical or community college. For some of the more prominent institutions in this field, see the list of selected schools in the "Accountant" and "Finance Manager" chapters of this volume.

MORE INFORMATION

National Association of Active Investment Managers
6732 W. Coal Mine Ave. #446
Littleton, CO 80123
888-261-0787
www.naaim.org

Academy of Certified Portfolio Managers
PO Box 1322
New York, New York 10025
212-854-8404
www.academyofcpm.org

CFA Institute
Charlottesville, VA
434-951-5499
www.cfainstitute.org

Financial Industry Regulatory Authority (FINRA)
1735 K Street
Washington DC, 2006
301-590-6500
www.finra.org

U.S. Securities and Exchange Commission
100 F Street, NE
Washington, DC 20549
www.sec.gov

Micah Issitt/Editor

Tax & Revenue Agent

Snapshot

Career Cluster(s): Financial Services, Accounting, Government
Interests: Enforcing regulations, accounting, analysis, investigation, customer service
Earnings (Yearly Average): $52,060
Employment & Outlook: Decline expected

OVERVIEW

Sphere of Work

Tax and revenue agents are responsible for making sure that citizens and corporations pay appropriate taxes to federal, state, and local governments. Agents conduct financial investigations, known as audits, identify citizens and corporations that owe taxes, and attempt to collect tax payments.

Tax and revenue officials need detailed, accurate, and current knowledge of tax laws and regulations and must be capable of creating and maintaining detailed records of audits and other activities. Examiners and revenue agents are typically responsible for evaluating tax information, filed by individuals and/ or corporations, while collectors are responsible for collecting owed taxes from citizens or companies if and when the company or citizen has failed to respond to notification of owed taxes delivered by an examiner.

Work Environment

Tax and revenue agents work in office environments and spend much of their time using computers and other digital tools to analyze financial data and to prepare reports and documentation. As tax and revenue agents work in governmental positions, they typically work alongside other revenue or tax agents or collectors in either private offices or in shared office spaces working alongside a number of other examiners or collectors. Tax audits are often conducted on-site and tax officials may travel to homes or businesses to examine financial records. Most tax officials work full time schedules, though overtime work may be required during and after tax season.

Profile

Working Conditions: Work Indoors
Physical Strength: Light Work
Education Needs: Bachelor's Degree
Licensure/Certification: Not required
Opportunities For Experience: On-the-job training
Holland Interest Score*: CE

* See Appendix A

Occupation Interest

Tax collecting and examination are conventional fields that might appeal to individuals who enjoy routine and careful, analytical work. Professionals in the field should have an interest in detailed work, investigation, and in working independently. As examiners and collectors are often forced to deal with confrontational situations, those seeking work in the field should be comfortable communicating with individuals form a variety of background and should be able to deal with tense, stressful situations.

A Day in the Life—Duties and Responsibilities

A typical day for a tax examiner, collector, or revenue agent depends on the professional's specific field and area of expertise. Before conducting an investigation or audit, examiners must first conduct research, looking over financial records and other data to determine when and if an audit is warranted. Examiners must also spend time composing formal letters and other documents to be delivered to individuals or businesses notifying them of a potential audit. During an examination, a tax or revenue agent might travel to an off-site location to examine financial records, while some investigations can be conducted electronically. During an audit, the examiner will also interview the individual or corporate representatives involved.

Some tax agents may spend much or all of their time calling or emailing individuals or corporations that owe revenues or might be targeted for a tax audit. Call centers that contact customers for tax reasons may have dozens or hundreds of employees working to communicate with taxpayers or companies and to collect owed taxes. During and after an investigation, or while attempting to collect taxes from another party, tax and revenue agents must create and maintain detailed records to ensure that the examination and interactions with taxpayers and companies adhere to legal standards. Because accurate documentation and accounting are required, tax agents must either be skilled in accounting practices or must work alongside accountants to accurately evaluate financial data.

Duties and Responsibilities

- **Obtain and analyze financial data and tax returns**
- **Create and maintain documentation of communication and accounting**
- **Contact taxpayers or corporations to address problems and request information**
- **Learn about changes to tax laws at the federal, state, and local level**
- **Collect overdue payments from companies or individuals**
- **Conduct field audits for individuals and/or corporations**
- **Work alongside other tax/revenue agents or accountants**

OCCUPATION SPECIALTIES

Tax Examiner

Tax examiners are responsible for investigating issues that occur with basic tax returns and generally involve individual taxpayers and small businesses. Tax examiners spend much of their time evaluating tax returns and conducting data entry, but may also contact taxpayers or businesses to resolve tax issues.

Revenue Agent

Revenue agents are employed by the federal government and work for the U.S. Internal Revenue Service (IRS). In contrast to tax examiners at the federal, state, and local level, revenue agents are typically responsible for investigating tax discrepancies involving large corporations or complicated business conglomerates. There are many subspecialties within the field, and revenue agents may specialize in a specific industry, developing detailed knowledge of accounting within a certain field.

Tax Collector

Tax collectors specialize in obtaining payment from individuals or businesses after an examination. Tax collectors contact and prepare documentation for individuals and businesses and are empowered to make payment arrangements in an effort to collect owed revenue. Collectors also investigate cases in which individuals or businesses cannot pay owed taxes and determine when it is necessary for the IRS or local tax agencies to pursue punitive measures or to collect owed revenues by placing a lien on property or other assets.

WORK ENVIRONMENT

Relevant Skills and Abilities

Communication Skills
- Speaking with clients and other professionals
- Creating business and official documents

Interpersonal/Social Skills
- Working with other tax specialists
- Working independently
- Contacting individuals/businesses about tax issues
- Negotiating with individuals or business representatives

Organization & Management Skills
- Creating and maintaining detailed records
- Managing staff and other financial professionals

Research & Planning Skills
- Researching changes in tax codes
- Investigating accounts and records

Technical Skills
- Using financial analysis and organizational software
- Using computers and digital communication technology

Physical Environment

Tax agents and collectors work in office environments that may range from large, shared office spaces and call centers to individual, private offices, depending on the specific field, level of experience, and seniority. Examiners and revenue agents are more likely to travel to conduct field audits after a tax issue has been identified, while collectors can conduct most of their work from a single location without traveling.

Human Environment

Tax and revenue agents work alongside accountants, managers, and other agents to complete their work. For instance, examiners and collectors work closely to handle a single account, with the examiner or agent determining when an individual or company owes tax revenues, and the collector attempting to obtain payment from the same individual or company. In addition, tax and revenue officials may work with legal officials and may utilize assistance from clerical and data entry professionals. Depending on the agent's role, communicating with individuals and business representatives is a major part of the job and examiners and collectors often face confrontational situations when collecting debts or informing individuals about tax issues.

Technological Environment

Tax specialists use computers, servers, and the Internet to collect data, to conduct analyses, and to compose and deliver official documents to individuals, businesses, and other tax/revenue officials. Tax specialists frequently use accounting software like Intuit QuickBooks and automated tax documentation systems and may also use a variety of spreadsheet and word processing programs to create and maintain documentation and to prepare letters and other official documents. When communicating with individuals and businesses, tax agents use email and telephone systems and often record or keep detailed records of all communications for legal purposes.

EDUCATION, TRAINING, AND ADVANCEMENT

High School/Secondary

Most tax examiner positions require applicants to have at least a bachelor's degree, as well as experiencing in accounting or a related field and high school students seeking work as tax or revenue agents should therefore focus on preparing for higher education. Tax collection positions may not require a bachelor's degree, but typically require some college experience with accounting or finance and work experience. High school students should take classes in mathematics, composition, English, language, business, and accounting, as well as any other college preparatory classes needed to prepare for a bachelor's or associate's degree program.

Suggested High School Subjects

- Algebra
- Mathematics
- Accounting
- College Preparatory
- Computer Science
- English

- Business
- Economics
- Law

Famous First

Tax collection is an extremely old field and there are many tax collectors described in ancient texts. In ancient Rome, tax collectors were known as "telones" who were agents of wealth landowners, known as "Publicans" who contracted with the state to collect taxes. At the time, telones and Publicans were widely despised, in part because the privatization of tax colleting led to corruption, with tax collectors collecting more from citizens than was owed to increase their profit. During the reign of Roman Emperor Caesar Augustus, it was decided that tax collecting needed to be regulated and the government created a rudimentary central authority in charge of taxation.

College/Postsecondary

While many positions in the field require a bachelor's degree, applicants have some flexibility in terms of academic focus. For those seeking work with the Internal Revenue Service, a bachelor's degree is typically a minimum requirement for examiners, agents, and tax collectors. Relevant academic programs that will help to prepare for careers in tax examination or collection include business administration, accounting, mathematics, and finance. Other classes that will be helpful for future tax agents include economics, composition, technical writing, corporate and financial law, and financial management. Individuals with higher level degrees, or certification in accounting, may have an advantage when seeking higher level positions in the field.

Related College Majors

- Financial Management
- Accounting, General
- Bookkeeping
- Financial Analysis
- Business Accounting

- Finance, General
- Business, General
- Law, General
- Corporate Law
- Financial Law
- Masters of Business Administration

Adult Job Seekers

Individuals with a bachelor's degree, or appropriate level of work experience in the tax field, or a related financial field, can apply for open positions with local, state, or federal tax agencies. Typically, both examiners and collectors will need to undergo a training period that can last anywhere from under a month to more than a year before beginning to work independently. Individuals who conduct field audits will typically spend time conducting audits alongside experienced professionals before handling their own audits or investigations.

Professional Certification and Licensure

There are no specific licenses or professional certificates needed to work as a tax or revenue agents. Individuals with professional certification in financial fields may have an advantage when seeking employment or to advance within their organization. Chartered Financial Analyst (CFA) and Certified Public Accountant (CPA) programs typically require applicants to have a bachelor's degree and between 1 and 4 years of work experience and provide training in a variety of financial industry techniques and fields. While such certification programs are not necessary for those looking to become tax agents, certified professionals may have greater flexibility in terms of career path and opportunities for management and advancement.

Additional Requirements

Tax and revenue agents need to be comfortable communicating with individuals and business representatives, often in confrontational situations and should be able to manage stress and have excellent interpersonal communication skills. In addition, tax and revenue agents need to be fluent with computers, software, and digital tools and should have excellent analytical skill. Tax examination is a detail oriented position that requires precise calculations and careful, detailed documentation and individuals should therefore also have skill with technical writing and mathematics or accounting.

Fun Fact

Tax Collector is one of the oldest jobs known to mankind. In ancient China, the tax man collected pressed tea, while Amazonian tribesmen paid in shrunken heads.

Source: http://www.economist.com/node/276962

EARNINGS AND ADVANCEMENT

According to the Bureau of Labor Statistics (BLS), the media annual wage for tax examiners, collectors, and revenue agents was $52,060 in May of 2016. Those working for the federal government have higher annual wages on average, and salaries in the field range from a low level of less than $31,000 to over $97,000 at the higher end of the spectrum. Advancement in the field can involve transitioning from trainee or entry level positions to senior examiner or collector roles, or into management. In addition, individuals who begin as tax examiners or collectors can seek to become revenue agents, who typically earn higher annual wages. Advanced degrees, work experience, and professional training can create opportunities for advancement.

Metropolitan Areas with the Highest Employment Level in this Occupation

Metropolitan area	Employment	Employment per thousand jobs	Hourly mean wage
Sacramento--Roseville--Arden-Arcade, CA	3,220	3.53	$26.25
Austin-Round Rock, TX	2,130	2.21	$21.48
New York-Jersey City-White Plains, NY-NJ Metropolitan Division	1,900	0.29	$39.62
Ogden-Clearfield, UT	1,760	7.22	$23.02
Cincinnati, OH-KY-IN	1,610	1.55	$26.12
Philadelphia, PA Metropolitan Division	1,610	1.81	$25.85
Kansas City, MO-KS	1,610	1.54	$21.05
Albany-Schenectady-Troy, NY	1,600	3.62	$27.57
Atlanta-Sandy Springs-Roswell, GA	1,440	0.56	$25.93
Nassau County-Suffolk County, NY Metropolitan Division	1,320	1.03	$28.96

Source: Bureau of Labor Statistics

EMPLOYMENT AND OUTLOOK

In 2014, the Bureau of Labor Statistics estimated that employment opportunities in the field would decline by approximately 6 percent between 2014 and 2024, due to financial instability and broad reductions in state, local, and federal budgets. The IRS experienced significant budget reductions in the 2010s, with an overall 19 percent reduction in federal job opportunities. Therefore, opportunities for work as tax examiners or collectors are expected to be greater at the state and local level and should increase at pace with hiring patterns for other state and local government positions. With few new positions opening in the field, competition for remaining positions will intensify, thus providing greater advantages to candidates with higher levels of work experience in related fields and education.

Related Occupations

- Accountants and Auditors
- Budget Analysts
- Cost Estimators
- Bookkeeping, Accounting, and Auditing Clerks
- Financial Analysts
- Financial Managers
- Loan Officers
- Personal Financial Advisors
- Real Estate Brokers and Sales Agents

Conversation With . . .
DEBBI ROBERTS-McGINNIS

Collector of Revenue
Polk County, Missouri
Tax collection, 23 years

1. **What was your individual career path in terms of education/training, entry-level job, or other significant opportunity?**

   I have a bachelor's degree is in agricultural economics from Missouri State University. That opened the door into banking, then auditing for the State of Missouri, and finally into an elected position as the Tax Collector for my county. However, a college degree is not mandatory for this position. Having experience in accounting, record-keeping or banking are assets that prove to be beneficial in many areas.

2. **What are the most important skills and/or qualities for someone in your profession?**

   I believe the most important asset is the ability to educate people about taxes. Taxation is difficult. It's difficult to understand and difficult to afford. The goal is to erase the confusion about where the money ends up and what services it provides, and how the amount of a tax bill is determined and why it may be different from your neighbor's bill or friend's bill.

3. **What do you wish you had known going into this profession?**

   If you don't have thick skin, you are going to end up highly stressed and crying in the bathroom. I was astonished at the tone and attitude of some taxpayers toward my staff and myself regarding their taxes. That's where education comes in. They didn't understand how their property was assessed, how the tax amount was determined or why it was a reoccurring annual tax. Many times, it was people who had moved to the state and were unfamiliar with our laws and procedures.

4. **Are there many job opportunities in your profession? In what specific areas?**

   There are 3,066 counties in the United States. Every government in existence must have a funding source and taxes are the most common. That means someone must collect those taxes and that person is either elected or appointed by the governmental body they serve. In some states, this is done at the city and town level, rather than the county level. With elected positions, the term of office is usually every four years, which translates to the opportunity of a new tax collector. While the field of tax collectors nationwide is small, the experience garnered can open doors in other tax fields, banking, accounting and auditing, both in public service and in the private sector. And many tax offices have several employees.

5. How do you see your profession changing in the next five years? What role will technology play in those changes, and what skills will be required?

This profession is vastly influenced by technology. The laws by which we must abide change slowly, usually not more than once a year since it is governed by state statute. The skill to implement those changes, the need for speed and efficiency and the vast amount of reporting and transparency require increased use of technology to keep your head above water. People working in tax and revenue collection must be very comfortable using computers. You have to be a quick learner when being trained for a certain task, but it's also highly valuable to understand the overall goal and have the ability to make alterations and revisions that improve the process. Spreadsheets and data processing are not going to fade away. New, faster, more interactive technology will continue to be developed and implemented in tax collection. Recognizing the growth of an online presence for the tax office is imperative. People don't pay taxes in person in this era like they did 20 years ago. The ability to adapt will prove indispensable.

6. What do you enjoy most about your job? What do you enjoy least about your job?

I love the "rush" of tax season. There's fulfillment in knowing you are doing your job well and helping people even when the pace can be chaotic. And I celebrate monthly when the reports balance to the penny on the first attempt. The only day I dread coming to work is the day I sell tax liens for delinquent real estate. It's a part of the job that I must complete, but it's not one I take joy in.

7. Can you suggest a valuable "try this" for students considering a career in your profession?

I would suggest job shadowing in the tax collector's office of your municipality. The daily interaction between customers and staff will give you a good perspective of what a typical day entails, plus you get the benefit and seeing the joy and disappointments of dealing with the public without having to solve the problem!

SELECTED SCHOOLS

Many colleges and universities, especially those with business schools, offer programs in business and finance. The student can also gain initial training at a technical or community college. For some of the more prominent institutions in this field, see the list of selected schools in the "Accountant" and "Finance Manager" chapters of this volume.

MORE INFORMATION

U.S. Internal Revenue Service (IRS)
1111 Constitution Ave, NW
Washington, DC 20224
www.irs.gov

Office of Personnel Management
1900 E Street, NW
Washington, DC 20415-1000
202-606-1800
www.opm.gov

CFA Institute
Charlottesville, VA
434-951-5499
www.cfainstitute.org

Micah Issitt/Editor

Treasurer & Controller

Snapshot

Career Cluster(s): Financial Services, Accounting, Finance, Management
Interests: Financial planning, accounting, business, research
Earnings (Yearly Average): $121,750 (financial managers)
Employment & Outlook: Average growth expected

OVERVIEW

Sphere of Work

Treasurers and controllers are financial managers; executives responsible for overseeing the financial activities of an organization or corporation. Treasurers, also known as finance officers, work with organizational budgets and oversee investments, while controllers are specialist financial managers who are typically in charge of preparing analyses and reports on an organization's financial status. With the advent of digital tools capable of facilitating accounting and automatically producing financial report, financial

managers are spending less time preparing reports and more time completing big picture analyses and recommending strategies to company management. Financial managers must be experts in accounting, economics, and/or finance and must also be experts in their chosen field. For instance, oil industry financial managers must have detailed knowledge about the petroleum exploration and sales industry in order to help their company maximize profit and avoid losses.

Work Environment

Treasurers and controllers work in office environments, and, as both are typically considered upper management, are often provided with a private office. Much of a treasurer or controller's work is done on a computer using spreadsheet and financial analysis software, as well as word processing or presentation software to prepare and deliver reports based on their analyses. The specific Work Environment for a treasurer or controller depends on the size and nature of the company with some treasurers or controllers working independently most of the time while others, especially in larger companies, may manage a staff of financial professionals. In some cases, treasurers or controllers might work under the supervision of a company's Chief Financial Officer (CFO), who is an upper level executive in charge of managing all of a company's financial staff.

Profile

Working Conditions: Work Indoors
Physical Strength: Light Work
Education Needs: Bachelor's Degree, Master's Degree
Licensure/Certification: Not required
Opportunities For Experience: Part-time work
Holland Interest Score*: CE

* See Appendix A

Occupation Interest

Those interested in becoming treasurers or controllers should have strong interest in mathematics, accounting, and analysis. Becoming a treasurer or controller generally involves spending years working in a field, as a lower level financial professional, before transitioning to management and candidates therefore need to be both ambitious and enterprising in their approach to career advancement. Because treasurers and controllers are often asked to manage other employees, applicants should also have an interest in communication, problem solving, and project management.

A Day in the Life—Duties and Responsibilities

While treasurers and controllers are both financial managers, professionals in the two jobs focus on different roles within a company or organization. Treasurers, in general, focus on the company's future, determining how to spend a company's budget and working with banking officials to obtain funding for company projects. A treasurer might therefore spend time in meetings with accountants, bank managers, loan officers, and potential investors in an effort to obtain capital for his or her organization. Treasurers are also responsible for meeting with shareholders to discuss a company's financial plans and for managing a company's current and future loans and credit. Treasurers also often make investments on behalf of a company or organization to secure the organization's financial future.

By contrast, controllers focus on a company/organization's history, compliance with regulations and laws, and on internal financial transactions. Depending on the size of a company, a controller might be the head financial executive in a company, or might report to a higher level controller or a chief financial officer, and a controller might spend part of a typical day meeting with other executives or financial professionals. Controllers analyze a company's financial transactions, typically from the previous year, and prepare and deliver reports to both managers and to government or regulatory agencies responsible for overseeing the industry. Each year, controllers also spend time overseeing the company's tax payments and functions as the lead accountant for the organization. A controller might also spend time creating budgets for the upcoming fiscal year.

Duties and Responsibilities

- **Preparing financial forecasts, statements, and reports**
- **Overseeing staff and manage accounting, budget management, and investments**
- **Analyzing financial markets to find opportunities for expansion or investment**
- **Advise executives on budgetary and financial decisions**
- **Report to regulatory or governmental agencies**
- **Conducting post-merger/acquisition analyses**
- **Analyzing and managing financial risk**

OCCUPATION SPECIALTIES

Certified Treasury Professional (CTP)

Certified Treasury Professionals are treasurers who have completed a CTP professional certification program, which involved researching business and financial systems. Some treasurers may seek CTP certification to advance in their careers.

Non-Profit Controller

A non-profit controller, or comptroller, is a budget and accounting specialist who works for non-profit organizations or is employed by the government. Comptrollers have the same roles as controllers in for-profit corporations, but must be experts in non-profit or government finance management.

Chief Financial Officer (CFO)

A chief financial officer is a company or organization's executive officer in charge of managing financial issues. CFOs may begin as controllers or treasurers before advancing to upper level management and CFOs typically oversee a staff of lower level financial officers and professionals. CFOs typically need advanced education or significant work experience in their field before qualifying for a CFO position.

WORK ENVIRONMENT

Relevant Skills and Abilities

Communication Skills
- Participating in meetings and negotiations
- Creating and presenting financial analyses to managers and regulatory agents

Interpersonal/Social Skills
- Being able to work with a team
- Giving presentations and speeches

Organization & Management Skills
- Managing employees
- Preparing and maintaining detailed records
- Meeting deadlines for financial reporting

Research & Planning Skills
- Researching market trends
- Planning for future financial activities

Technical Skills
- Performing detailed financial analyses
- Managing accounting procedures
- Using financial analysis software
- Using budget management and accounting software

Physical Environment

Treasurers and controllers work in offices, and most work full time, though the Bureau of Labor Statistics estimates that one third of financial managers may work overtime in their positions. Most financial manager jobs are found in the finance and insurance market, while other financial managers work in private companies, for scientific organizations, in manufacturing, or in local, state, or federal government positions.

Human Environment

While controllers and treasurers in small organizations or companies might work independently most or all of the time, controllers and treasurers are typically managers and may oversee a staff of other financial professionals, such as accountants, financial analysists, and budget specialists. Even when working independently, controllers and managers are responsible for meeting with other managers to advise on financial decisions. In addition, controllers and treasurers frequently interact with banking and investments professionals. Most financial managers spend much of their time in meetings or giving presentations as well as meeting with investors, stockholders, or regulatory officials. Because treasurers and controllers work closely with other professionals, good interpersonal skills and management skills are essential to professionals in the field.

Technological Environment

Treasurers and controllers utilize computers daily and typically need to be fluent in a number of software programs used for financial analysis, budget management, personnel management, and creating presentations and reports. When handling company accounting, treasurers and controllers may use programs like Sage 50 Accounting or Intuit QuickBooks, while other more specialized programs, like Oracle Hyperion Planning or Oracle E-Business Suite Financials, may be used for budget or financial analyses. In addition, treasurers and controllers regularly use word processing software and spreadsheet/ presentation software, when preparing reports for managers and regulatory agencies. A communication is key to the job, controllers and treasurers also regularly use digital tools, like smartphones and tablets, to communicate with employees, managers, and other professionals.

EDUCATION, TRAINING, AND ADVANCEMENT

High School/Secondary

High school students seeking to become financial managers should prepare for higher education, as most finance executives have at least a bachelor's degree, while postgraduate degrees are common among high-level managers. While in high school, students can prepare for a career in financial management by studying mathematics, business, accounting, public speaking, economics, and technical writing. As finance is increasingly dependent on digital tools and software, introductory courses in basic computing and computer science will be helpful for future financial professionals.

Suggested High School Subjects

- Applied Math
- Algebra
- Calculus
- Statistics
- College Preparatory
- Computer Science
- English
- Business
- Calculus
- Accounting
- Public Speaking
- Economics
- History

Famous First

Elouise Pepion Cobell, also known as Yellow Bird Woman, was a tribal leader for the Blackfoot Confederacy and an activist for Native American rights, who, in 1987, founded the first national bank on a Native American reservation, becoming the first Native American woman to work as a bank treasurer. In 1997, Cobell won a MacArthur Genius Award for her joint work on establishing a Native American-owned bank and work on combating illiteracy and later engaged in a class action suit against the federal government for mismanagement of trust funds and leasing fees.

College/Postsecondary

Those seeking to become treasurers or controllers will need at least a bachelor's degree in a related field, such as business administration, finance, accounting, economics, financial law, marketing, or financial management. For those seeking upper management or high level treasurer/controller positions, post graduate degrees may be necessary and will provide advantages on the job market. While many chief executives obtain Masters of Business

Administration (MBA) degrees, financial executives are more likely to enter the field by way of training in accounting or finance.

Related College Majors

- Business Accounting
- Finance, General
- Business, General
- Financial Management
- Financial Law
- Business Management
- Marketing
- Masters of Business Administration
- Economics
- Financial Analysis

Adult Job Seekers

Individuals with at least a bachelor's degree, and between one and five years of experience in their fields may be eligible for a job as a controller or treasurer. In addition to education and experience in finance, it is helpful for those seeking to work as treasurers or controllers, to have specific experience in their chosen field. For instance, those applying for positions as comptrollers or treasurers for government or non-profit organizations, will benefit from previous work experience in government or non-profit finance or management. Most controllers or treasurers will spend time working in other financial positions, such as financial analysis, financial sales, or accounting, before transitioning to financial management.

Professional Certification and Licensure

While there are no specific licensing or certification requirements to become a controller or treasurer, professionals in the field might seek to advance by completing a professional certification program. Among programs that apply to treasurer or controller positions are Chartered Financial Analyst (CFA) programs and Certified Treasury Professional (CTP) programs. Both CFA and CTP programs typically require that applicants have completed a bachelor's degree in a related field as well as work experience. CFA programs typically require applicants to have completed four years of work experience and require that the applicant passes three separate exams before receiving certification. CTP programs typically involve only a single exam and require applicants to have at least two years of experience in their field.

Additional Requirements

Financial management is a detail oriented field that requires precision and accuracy. Those seeking to become financial managers should have excellent analytical skills and should be proficient in mathematics, statistics, and accounting. In addition, financial managers need to be highly organized and to keep detailed records of accounting and other activities to make informed financial decisions and avoid regulatory or legal problems. As controllers and treasurers are managers, professionals in the field also need excellent communication and personnel management skills.

Fun Fact

Immediately after President Lincoln's assassination, the U.S. Treasury Dept. building served as President Andrew Johnson's temporary White House.

Source: https://www.treasury.gov

EARNINGS AND ADVANCEMENT

The Bureau of Labor Statistics (BLS) estimates a median salary for financial managers of approximately $121,750 in May of 2016, with those at the lower level earning less than $65,000, while higher payed positions can have annual salaries of over $200,000. In general, individuals working in professional and technical organizations earned the highest salaries, while government employees tend to earn lower average salaries. Advancement in the field generally involves accruing experience within a company or participating in additional educational programs that can help qualify a professional for higher level executive roles. Controllers and treasurers can also seek a postgraduate degree or can complete a professional certification course in an effort to advance in their career.

Metropolitan Areas with the Highest Employment Level in this Occupation

Metropolitan area	Employment	Employment per thousand jobs	Hourly mean wage
New York-Jersey City-White Plains, NY-NJ Metropolitan Division	38,310	5.82	$96.50
Chicago-Naperville-Arlington Heights, IL Metropolitan Division	24,060	6.61	$65.05
Boston-Cambridge-Newton, MA NECTA Division	19,970	11.07	$71.90
Los Angeles-Long Beach-Glendale, CA Metropolitan Division	18,060	4.28	$75.69
Washington-Arlington-Alexandria, DC-VA-MD-WV Metropolitan Division	15,660	6.29	$77.20
Atlanta-Sandy Springs-Roswell, GA	12,730	4.99	$71.48
Minneapolis-St. Paul-Bloomington, MN-WI	11,790	6.17	$69.94
Houston-The Woodlands-Sugar Land, TX	8,780	2.99	$78.50
Phoenix-Mesa-Scottsdale, AZ	8,730	4.51	$56.13
Anaheim-Santa Ana-Irvine, CA Metropolitan Division	8,490	5.43	$68.93

Source: Bureau of Labor Statistics

EMPLOYMENT AND OUTLOOK

The Bureau of Labor Statistics recorded approximately 555,900 professional financial managers working in 2014, with an average growth of 7 percent per year, marking average growth compared to the 6-7 percent expected for all careers in the United States. While demand for financial management is expected to remain steady over the subsequent decade, competition for positions will be high due to a large number of potential candidates for each available position. Individuals with postgraduate degrees and/or professional certification will therefore have an advantage in seeking jobs. There may be more limited opportunities for financial managers in government due to budget cuts at the state and federal levels, leading to an overall decline in federal and state-government hiring.

Related Occupations

- Accountants and Auditors
- Budget Analysts
- Financial Managers
- Corporate Lawyers
- Insurance Underwriters
- Personal Financial Advisors
- Loan Officers
- Executive Managers

Conversation With . . .
DAVID H. LILLARD, JR.

Tennessee State Treasurer
Treasurer, 8 years

1. **What was your individual career path in terms of education/training, entry-level job, or other significant opportunity?**

   Growing up I revered my father. He was raised on a farm in western Kentucky, became a pharmacist, and built a small, successful chain of local drugstores. Watching his growth in the business world inspired me to pursue a career in finance.

   As I began to map out my education, I focused on a combination of degrees that would help me comprehensively understand the business world. After earning my undergraduate degree, I continued on to law school at the University of Memphis, then earned a master's of Laws in Taxation from the University of Florida. Diversifying my education helped me to understand the financial world in a more complete way.

   Throughout school I sought practical experience to give me the opportunity to apply lessons from the classroom in a real life context. While still an undergraduate, I started working on the finances at my father's companies, eventually becoming the Chief Financial Officer. The lessons I learned confirmed my interest in finance and showed me the time, dedication, and effort necessary to succeed.

   After graduating, I moved on to practice business law for 25 years in the private sector, focusing on finance, securities, and tax law. I also served various roles in local government and eventually was elected by the Tennessee General Assembly to the position of State Treasurer. My team of 260 individuals and I internally direct multiple state programs and manage investments valued at approximately $50 billion.

2. **What are the most important skills and/or qualities for someone in your profession?**

   A leader in the financial world needs excellent decision-making skills; your job is to make the tough calls. You have to evaluate all options and decide what policies and products your organization will offer to the public. Every day I use critical-thinking strategies to determine what opportunities will better the financial lives of individuals in the state of Tennessee. Strong decision making and critical thinking skills make for the most effective financial leaders.

3. **What do you wish you had known going into this profession?**

I wish I had even more training. You really can't get enough education in specialty areas. I think you should treat life as a continual learning process. Even if you are no longer in a formal or academic educational setting, growth and learning can continue by being open to new ideas and learning new concepts as you proceed through life.

4. **Are there many job opportunities in your profession? In what specific areas?**

Job opportunities within public treasury management are many and they are broad. Positions range from service counselors who help individuals with retirement and college savings processes to investment professionals who manage portfolios reaching into the billions. While degrees in accounting, finance, and other investment-related fields lend themselves naturally, there are other important underlying functions of treasury as well, including risk management and communications.

5. **How do you see your profession changing in the next five years, what role will technology play in those changes, and what skills will be required?**

As influences like technology and automation shape the finance industry, it is important that all individuals, regardless of function, gain a better understanding of information technology. Whether working specifically in an IT department or not, learning about these subject matters is vital because it will allow you to harness the power of technology to more effectively do your job. The domination of technology in treasury functions will continue to grow.

6. **What do you enjoy most about your job? What do you enjoy least about your job?**

One of the greatest joys in serving as State Treasurer is that the products and services we provide help Tennesseans achieve their life-long goals, such as a college education, retirement, financial stability, and many others. The ability to help individuals reach a milestone and better their lives is my favorite part of my job.

One of the more difficult aspects of being a leader, regardless of the industry, is making personnel decisions. Ultimately, it is your responsibility to hire and retain the best employees, the ones who can have the most significant positive impact on your organization, and for me, the ones who can create the best programs for the people of Tennessee.

7. Can you suggest a valuable "try this" for students considering a career in your profession?

Follow the stock market closely for a period of time, investigate how to build a portfolio, examine treasury programs and functions across the country, or play an online stock exchange game that allows you to hypothetically invest. As you continue your education, think about opportunities for practical experience. Internships are a fantastic way to apply academic concepts to the real world. The Tennessee Treasury Department, along with many others nationwide, brings in students each year to serve in a variety of roles, giving them real life work experience in the financial field.

SELECTED SCHOOLS

Many colleges and universities, especially those with business schools, offer programs in finance and business administration. The student can also gain initial training through enrollment at a technical or community college. For advanced positions, a master's of business administration (MBA) with a concentration in finance is usually expected. Below are listed some of the more prominent institutions in this field.

Carnegie Mellon University
Tepper School of Business
500 Forbes Avenue
Pittsburgh, PA 15213
412.268.2268
tepper.cmu.edu

Indiana University, Bloomington
Kelley School of Business
1309 E. 10th Street
Bloomington, IN 47405
812.855.8100
kelley.iu.edu

Massachusetts Institute of Technology
Sloan School of Management
50 Memorial Drive
Cambridge, MA 02142
617.253.2659
mitsloan.mit.edu

New York University
Stern School of Business
665 Broadway, 11th Floor
New York, NY 10012
212.998.4500
www.stern.nyu.edu

University of California, Berkeley
Haas School of Business
S450 Student Services Building #1900
Berkeley, CA 94720
510.642.1421
haas.berkeley.edu

University of Michigan, Ann Arbor
Ross School of Business
701 Tappan Avenue
Ann Arbor, MI 48109
734.763.5796
michiganross.umich.edu

University of North Carolina, Chapel Hill
Kenan-Flagler Business School
Campus Box 3490, McColl Building
Chapel Hill, NC 27599
919.962.3235
www.kenan-flagler.unc.edu

University of Pennsylvania
The Wharton School
1 College Hall
Philadelphia, PA 19104
215.898.6376
www.wharton.upenn.edu

MORE INFORMATION

CFA Institute
Charlottesville, VA
434-951-5499
www.cfainstitute.org

Association for Financial Professionals (AFP)
4520 East-West Highway, Suite 800
Bethesda, MD 20814
301-907-2862
www.afponline.org

Financial Management Association International
University of South Florida
College of Business Adminsitration
813-974-2084
www.fma.org

Financial Industry Regulatory Authority (FINRA)
1735 K Street
Washington DC, 2006
301-590-6500
www.finra.org

Micah Issitt/Editor

Venture Capital Professional

Snapshot

Career Cluster(s): Investing, financial analysis, financial services, finance, economics
Interests: Financial planning, accounting, investments
Earnings (Yearly Average): $81,760
Employment & Outlook: Faster Than Average Growth Expected

OVERVIEW

Sphere of Work

A venture capital professional is an investment expert who specializes in investing in high risk startup businesses or corporate expansion projects that traditional lending institutions are more likely to avoid. In return for their investment, venture capital firms typically take an active role in managing the company in an effort to protect their investment. By investing in unproven companies, venture capitalists take a significant risk, but with the potential for more lucrative rewards. For instance, venture capital firms funded some

of the Internet companies, like Facebook, Twitter, and Google, that went on to produce massive rewards for initial investors. To balance risk and potential reward, venture capital investors need to conduct thorough research and so perform many of the same activities as other types of financial analysts.

Work Environment

Venture capital professionals work in office environments using digital tools to analyze emerging companies and industries. In some cases, venture investors might travel to visit new companies or to meet with entrepreneurs managing potential new investment opportunities. In venture capital firms, investment experts work alongside financial advisors, financial managers, accountants, and other investment, budget, and finance experts.

Profile

Working Conditions: Work Indoors
Physical Strength: Light Work
Education Needs: Bachelor's Degree
Licensure/Certification: Required for some positions
Opportunities For Experience: Part-time work
Holland Interest Score*: CIE

* See Appendix A

Occupation Interest

Venture capital investment is a complex activity that requires intense research and analysis and involves significant financial risk for the investor. Individuals looking to enter the field should have a strong interest in finance, economics, and research and should be comfortable working in highly competitive, high pressure situations. Venture capitalists should also have a strong interest in management, business, and working with others as venture capital specialists typically spend time working with managers and finance experts in the companies they invest in and benefit from strong interpersonal communication skills.

A Day in the Life—Duties and Responsibilities

The basic tasks for a venture capital professional can be divided into two broad activities. The first is to identify and analyze new potential investment opportunities. When working on sourcing new investments, capitalists may spend time calling and speaking with company representatives, visiting new businesses, and researching industry trends. Once the professional has identified a potential investment, he or she will typically set up meetings with company representatives to explain the investment process and pitch a new partnership with the company. If the company is interested in making a deal, representatives of the two companies work together to perform due diligence analysis and to determine the details of a final agreement.

When not working on setting up new deals, venture capital professionals spend time working with companies involved in past deals. In some cases, venture capital firms participate in managing the companies that they invest in and so a professional representing a capital firm may spend time meeting with managers and financial officials in companies that the firm has invested in. As the company develops, venture capital professionals may help to guide the company in financial decisions and may adjust the terms of their investment contract as needed based on how the company develops. In firms, venture capital associates might also spend time creating and maintaining detailed financial documentation of the deals they have worked on and giving presentations and reports to senior managers.

Duties and Responsibilities

- **Researching and locating new investment opportunities**
- **Calling or emailing managers at companies**
- **Explaining investments to clients**
- **Advising on financial and management decisions**
- **Preparing reports and financial analyses**
- **Preparing contracts for partnerships**

OCCUPATION SPECIALTIES

Venture Capital Associate

A venture capital associate is an entry level venture capital professional and are typically charged with analytical and industry research. Some venture capital firms have both junior and senior associates who may handle different activities for the firm.

Venture Capital Principal

Principals are mid-level professionals in a venture capital firm, who are typically responsible for overseeing the operations of the firm itself and looking for problems with the firm's investments. Principals are often responsible for finding new investment opportunities and for finalizing deals based on research conducted by associates.

Venture Capital Partner

Venture capital partners are ownership-level executives in a venture capital firm and typically handle big-picture matters for the company, including identifying fields or industries that might hold fruitful investments and on approving deals created by principals and associates.

WORK ENVIRONMENT

Physical Environment

Venture capital professionals typically work in office environments and most work full time, though overtime work is common, especially during the later stages of finalizing new deals. Depending on seniority, professionals in a venture capital firm may have private offices or may share office space with other professionals in the firm. In some cases, associates and principals in a firm may need to travel to conduct in-person meetings with representatives of companies targeted for potential investment. As venture capital firms can invest on a national or international scale, professionals may be asked to travel to distant locations when working on a specific deal.

Relevant Skills and Abilities

Communication Skills
- Speaking with clients and other professionals
- Writing reports, letters, and emails

Interpersonal/Social Skills
- Being able to work with a team
- Meeting with new potential clients
- Working independently

Organization & Management Skills
- Arranging meetings and keeping appointments
- Managing junior associates and employees
- Maintaining legal and regulatory records

Research & Planning Skills
- Researching economic trends
- Learning about new industries
- Researching investment opportunities

Technical Skills
- Performing complex calculations
- Using digital software and other tools
- Creating contracts and technical documents

Human Environment

Venture capital firms typically employ a number of financial and business experts to handle various aspects of the company's activities. Associates and principals work directly on deals, under the supervision of the firm's partners, but are also assisted by clerks, accountants, financial analysts, and other employees. Venture capital associates and principals spend considerable time in meetings or speaking with other professionals via telephone or digital channels both when trying to set up new deals and when working on the details of an investment in progress.

Technological Environment

Venture capital professionals need to be familiar with a variety of specialized and more general digital tools and software systems. Specialized financial planning software, such as the Wealth Tec Foundations suite, Oracle E-Business Suite Financials, or Ibbotson Portfolio Strategist, helpful for professionals working on managing the company's assets, while word processing software, spreadsheet creation tools, and presentation tools are also commonly used by professionals in the field. In addition, venture capital professionals use mobile technology and computers to share information with their clients and to communicate with clients and other professionals.

EDUCATION, TRAINING, AND ADVANCEMENT

High School/Secondary

While there are no specific education requirements to become a venture capital associate, many firms hire only individuals who have at least a bachelor's degree. High school students interested in a career in venture capital investments should therefore focus on preparing for higher education and should take any available classes that will introduce them to mathematics, accounting, and management. In addition, classes that provide basic information about using computers and technical writing will be helpful for those seeking to work in all financial careers.

Suggested High School Subjects

- Algebra
- Calculus
- Statistics
- Applied Math
- College Preparatory
- Computer Science
- English
- Composition
- Business
- Economics
- Law
- Public Speaking

Famous First

In 1983, African American entrepreneur Reginald Lewis started a venture capital firm, TLC Group L.P., which became one of the first African American-owned and operated venture capital firms in the nation. Lewis went on to invest in Beatrice Foods, which he successfully built into the largest African American-owned business in the nation and the first to earn over $1 billion in profits. During the 1980s, Lewis was the richest African American in the United States.

College/Postsecondary

Most venture capital firms prefer applicants with bachelor degrees for entry level, associate positions, and may look for candidates with postgraduate degrees for higher level positions. A masters of business administration (MBA) degree is common in all financial fields and many upper level financial analysts and venture capital executives pursue business administration degrees. In addition, individuals looking to get involved in venture capital investment can choose to study accounting, finance, or financial law.

Related College Majors

- Financial Management
- Accounting, General
- Economics, General
- Economic Analysis
- Business Accounting
- Finance, General
- Business, General
- Mathematics, General
- Law, General
- Corporate Law
- Financial Law

Adult Job Seekers

Job seekers with a bachelor's degree, or equivalent work experience, can apply for open positions at venture capital firms. Individuals with limited prior experience will most likely qualify for associate or junior associate positions and will spend time working under more experienced analysts and professionals before being eligible to move up within a company or to apply for higher level positions at other companies. On-the-job training can last for one to several years, and junior associates continue learning from senior associates before advancing to senior positions.

Professional Certification and Licensure

There are specific licenses for individuals who purchase and sell various types of investments and individuals in venture capital investment might need licenses with the state if they plan on purchasing securities or commodities directly. In addition, venture capitalists who work with the public must be registered with the federal Securities and Exchange Commission, the branch of the federal government responsible for regulating the financial industry. While professional certification is not required, some financial analysts/advisors choose to pursue certification as a Chartered Financial Analyst (CFA), a Certified Financial Planner (CFP), or a Certified Public Accountant (CPA). CFO, CFA, and CPA applicants typically need to have completed a Bachelor's Degree and to have spent time working in the field before applying for acceptance to a professional certification program.

Additional Requirements

Venture capital investment is a high risk field and successful professionals in the field must be comfortable taking risks in hopes of finding a lucrative investment. Venture capital professionals also need excellent analytical and decision-making skills, as they must often seize new opportunities before a competing firm beats them to a profitable investment. Because venture capital is an analytical, statistical, financial field, those hoping to work in the industry should have a good grasp of mathematics and accounting. Those with more advanced education or experience in high level finance will be more likely to succeed as venture capital associates.

Fun Fact

A whopping $58.8 billion in venture capital was invested in U.S. startups in 2015, with the software industry getting the biggest share of the pie, followed by biotechnology.

Source: http://nvca.org/pressreleases/

EARNINGS AND ADVANCEMENT

The Bureau of Labor Statistics (BLS) estimates the average annual salary for financial analysts at $81,760 in 2016, and a range of between $50,000 and over $160,000. Venture capital is one of the most lucrative branches of finance as venture firms tend to invest large sums in new or growing companies and therefore, if an investment succeeds, can earn higher dividends than other types of investors. While the BLS places the average salary for financial analysts at just over $80,000, salaries in venture capital tend to be higher, with associates earning between $80,000 to over $100,000, and higher level positions often bringing in salaries of over $200,000. High salaries in the field are supported, in part, by bonuses based on earnings from investments. Associates and principals who forge lucrative deals, therefore, earn higher wages. However, because venture capital is a high risk field, poor investments or financial instability can drastically reduce a firm's annual earnings. Advancing in venture capital investment typically involves working up through a company from associate to principal and, for qualified and successful candidates, earning partnership with a successful firm.

Metropolitan Areas with the Highest Employment Level in this Occupation

Metropolitan area	Employment	Employment per thousand jobs	Hourly mean wage
New York-Jersey City-White Plains, NY-NJ Metropolitan Division	47,190	7.17	$64.00
Chicago-Naperville-Arlington Heights, IL Metropolitan Division	10,610	2.92	$45.45
Boston-Cambridge-Newton, MA NECTA Division	9,990	5.54	$47.90
Washington-Arlington-Alexandria, DC-VA-MD-WV Metropolitan Division	9,390	3.77	$46.58
Houston-The Woodlands-Sugar Land, TX	8,040	2.74	$46.68
Los Angeles-Long Beach-Glendale, CA Metropolitan Division	8,010	1.90	$47.05
San Francisco-Redwood City-South San Francisco, CA Metropolitan Division	7,300	6.84	$68.19
Dallas-Plano-Irving, TX Metropolitan Division	7,000	2.88	$45.66
Atlanta-Sandy Springs-Roswell, GA	5,800	2.27	$39.12
Minneapolis-St. Paul-Bloomington, MN-WI	5,790	3.03	$43.06

Source: Bureau of Labor Statistics

EMPLOYMENT AND OUTLOOK

The BLS does not currently compile estimates of the venture capital field specifically, but BLS data from 2014 suggests that there were 281,610 professional financial analysts in the United States and that the field is growing by an average of 12 percent per year, marking higher than average growth in comparison to the 6-7 percent annual growth for all occupations. Venture capital investments grew rapidly in the dot com era with companies investing in a wide variety of new online business ventures, but the "dot com bust" of the 2000s saw a massive reduction in new online businesses, with a subsequent reduction in venture capital firms as well. Venture capital investment thrives when the economy is strong, like many financial fields, and shrinks during times of economic turmoil. While job growth in the financial industry is strong overall, because venture capital investment is a high pay field, competition for available positions is high and candidates with advanced degrees, high levels of work experience, and/or professional certification will have an advantage when seeking employment.

Related Occupations

- Budget Analysts
- Financial Managers
- Personal Financial Advisors
- Securities, Commodities, And Financial Services Sales Agents
- Accountants
- Financial Analysts

Related Military Occupations

- Military Investment Manager

SELECTED SCHOOLS

Many colleges and universities, especially those with business schools, offer programs in finance and business administration. The student can also gain initial training through enrollment at a technical or community college. For advanced positions, a master's of business administration (MBA) with a concentration in finance is usually expected. Below are listed some of the more prominent institutions in this field.

Carnegie Mellon University
Tepper School of Business
500 Forbes Avenue
Pittsburgh, PA 15213
412.268.2268
tepper.cmu.edu

Indiana University, Bloomington
Kelley School of Business
1309 E. 10th Street
Bloomington, IN 47405
812.855.8100
kelley.iu.edu

Massachusetts Institute of Technology
Sloan School of Management
50 Memorial Drive
Cambridge, MA 02142
617.253.2659
mitsloan.mit.edu

New York University
Stern School of Business
665 Broadway, 11th Floor
New York, NY 10012
212.998.4500
www.stern.nyu.edu

University of California, Berkeley
Haas School of Business
S450 Student Services Building #1900
Berkeley, CA 94720
510.642.1421
haas.berkeley.edu

University of Michigan, Ann Arbor
Ross School of Business
701 Tappan Avenue
Ann Arbor, MI 48109
734.763.5796
michiganross.umich.edu

University of North Carolina, Chapel Hill
Kenan-Flagler Business School
Campus Box 3490, McColl Building
Chapel Hill, NC 27599
919.962.3235
www.kenan-flagler.unc.edu

University of Pennsylvania
The Wharton School
1 College Hall
Philadelphia, PA 19104
215.898.6376
www.wharton.upenn.edu

MORE INFORMATION

National Association of Active Investment Managers
6732 W. Coal Mine Ave. #446
Littleton, CO 80123
888-261-0787
www.naaim.org

Academy of Certified Portfolio Managers
PO Box 1322
New York, New York 10025
212-854-8404
www.academyofcpm.org

CFA Institute
Charlottesville, VA
434-951-5499
www.cfainstitute.org

Financial Industry Regulatory Authority (FINRA)
1735 K Street
Washington DC, 2006
301-590-6500
www.finra.org

U.S. Securities and Exchange Commission
100 F Street, NE
Washington, DC 20549
www.sec.gov

Micah Issitt/Editor

What Are Your Career Interests?

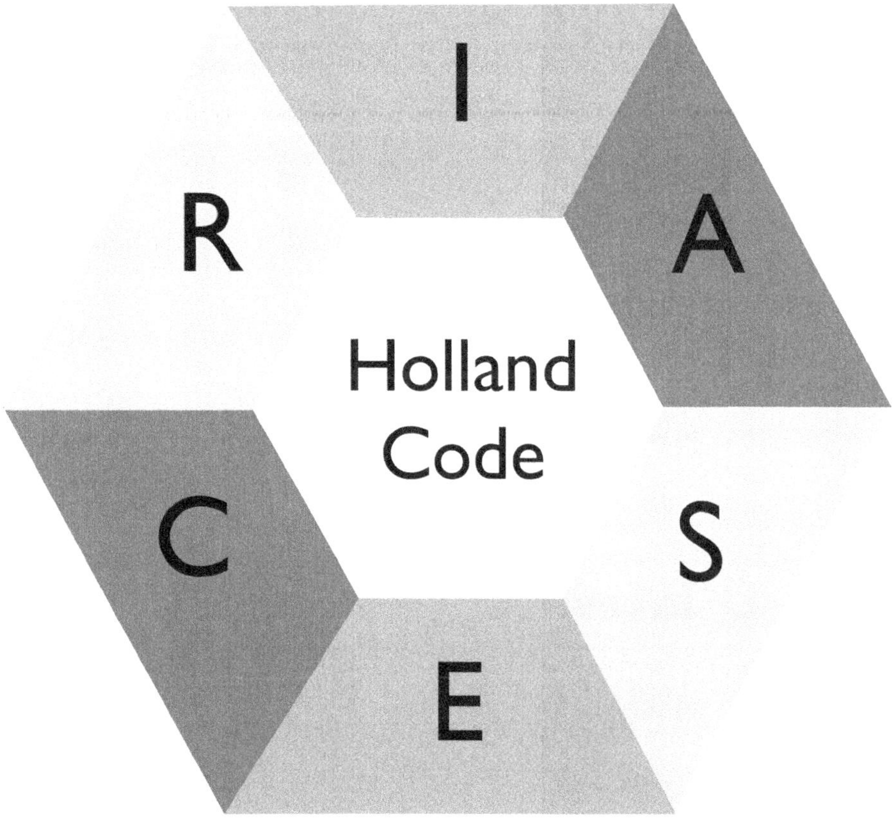

This is based on Dr. John Holland's theory that people and work environments can be loosely classified into six different groups. Each of the letters above corresponds to one of the six groups described in the following pages.

Different people's personalities may find different environments more to their liking. While you may have some interests in and similarities to several of the six groups, you may be attracted primarily to two or three of the areas. These two or three letters are your "Holland Code." For example, with a code of "RES" you would most resemble the Realistic type, somewhat less resemble the Enterprising type, and resemble the Social type even less. The types that are not in your code are the types you resemble least of all.

Most people, and most jobs, are best represented by some combination of two or three of the Holland interest areas. In addition, most people are most satisfied if there is some degree of fit between their personality and their work environment.

The rest of the pages in this booklet further explain each type and provide some examples of career possibilities, areas of study at MU, and co-curricular activities for each code. To take a more in-depth look at your Holland Code, take a self-assessment such as the SDS, Discover, or a card sort at the MU Career Center with a Career Specialist.

Realistic *(Doers)*

People who have athletic ability, prefer to work with objects, machines, tools, plants or animals, or to be outdoors.

Are you?
practical
straightforward/frank
mechanically inclined
stable
concrete
reserved
self-controlled
independent
ambitious
systematic

Can you?
fix electrical things
solve electrical problems
pitch a tent
play a sport
read a blueprint
plant a garden
operate tools and machine

Like to?
tinker with machines/vehicles
work outdoors
be physically active
use your hands
build things
tend/train animals
work on electronic equipment

Career Possibilities (Holland Code):

Air Traffic Controller (SER)
Archaeologist (IRE)
Athletic Trainer (SRE)
Cartographer (IRE)
Commercial Airline Pilot (RIE)
Commercial Drafter (IRE)
Corrections Officer (SER)
Dental Technician (REI)
Farm Manager (ESR)
Fish and Game Warden (RES)
Floral Designer (RAE)
Forester (RIS)
Geodetic Surveyor (IRE)
Industrial Arts Teacher (IER)
Laboratory Technician (RIE)
Landscape Architect (AIR)
Mechanical Engineer (RIS)
Optician (REI)
Petroleum Geologist (RIE)
Police Officer (SER)
Practical Nurse (SER)
Property Manager (ESR)
Recreation Manager (SER)
Service Manager (ERS)
Software Technician (RCI)
Ultrasound Technologist (RSI)
Vocational Rehabilitation Consultant (ESR)

Investigative *(Thinkers)*

People who like to observe, learn, investigate, analyze, evaluate, or solve problems.

Are you?
inquisitive
analytical
scientific
observant/precise
scholarly
cautious
intellectually self-confident
Independent
logical
complex
Curious

Can you?
think abstractly
solve math problems
understand scientific theories
do complex calculations
use a microscope or computer
interpret formulas

Like to?
explore a variety of ideas
work independently
perform lab experiments
deal with abstractions
do research
be challenged

Career Possibilities (Holland Code):

Actuary (ISE)
Agronomist (IRS)
Anesthesiologist (IRS)
Anthropologist (IRE)
Archaeologist (IRE)
Biochemist (IRS)
Biologist (ISR)
Chemical Engineer (IRE)
Chemist (IRE)
Computer Systems Analyst (IER)
Dentist (ISR)
Ecologist (IRE)
Economist (IAS)
Electrical Engineer (IRE)
Geologist (IRE)
Horticulturist (IRS)
Mathematician (IER)
Medical Technologist (ISA)
Meteorologist (IRS)
Nurse Practitioner (ISA)
Pharmacist (IES)
Physician, General Practice (ISE)
Psychologist (IES)
Research Analyst (IRC)
Statistician (IRE)
Surgeon (IRA)
Technical Writer (IRS)
Veterinarian (IRS)

Artistic *(Creators)*

People who have artistic, innovating, or intuitional abilities and like to work in unstructured situations using their imagination and creativity.

Are you?
creative
imaginative
innovative
unconventional
emotional
independent
Expressive
original
introspective
impulsive
sensitive
courageous
complicated
idealistic
nonconforming

Can you?
sketch, draw, paint
play a musical instrument
write stories, poetry, music
sing, act, dance
design fashions or interiors

Like to?
attend concerts, theatre, art exhibits
read fiction, plays, and poetry
work on crafts
take photography
express yourself creatively
deal with ambiguous ideas

Career Possibilities (Holland Code):

Actor (AES)
Advertising Art Director (AES)
Advertising Manager (ASE)
Architect (AIR)
Art Teacher (ASE)
Artist (ASI)
Copy Writer (ASI)
Dance Instructor (AER)
Drama Coach (ASE)
English Teacher (ASE)
Entertainer/Performer (AES)
Fashion Illustrator (ASR)
Interior Designer (AES)
Intelligence Research Specialist (AEI)
Journalist/Reporter (ASE)
Landscape Architect (AIR)
Librarian (SAI)
Medical Illustrator (AIE)
Museum Curator (AES)
Music Teacher (ASI)
Photographer (AES)
Writer (ASI)
Graphic Designer (AES)

Social *(Helpers)*

People who like to work with people to enlighten, inform, help, train, or cure them, or are skilled with words.

Are you?
friendly
helpful
idealistic
insightful
outgoing
understanding
cooperative
generous
responsible
forgiving
patient
kind

Can you?
teach/train others
express yourself clearly
lead a group discussion
mediate disputes
plan and supervise an activity
cooperate well with others

Like to?
work in groups
help people with problems
do volunteer work
work with young people
serve others

Career Possibilities (Holland Code):

City Manager (SEC)
Clinical Dietitian (SIE)
College/University Faculty (SEI)
Community Org. Director (SEA)
Consumer Affairs Director (SER)Counselor/Therapist (SAE)
Historian (SEI)
Hospital Administrator (SER)
Psychologist (SEI)
Insurance Claims Examiner (SIE)
Librarian (SAI)
Medical Assistant (SCR)
Minister/Priest/Rabbi (SAI)
Paralegal (SCE)
Park Naturalist (SEI)
Physical Therapist (SIE)
Police Officer (SER)
Probation and Parole Officer (SEC)
Real Estate Appraiser (SCE)
Recreation Director (SER)
Registered Nurse (SIA)
Teacher (SAE)
Social Worker (SEA)
Speech Pathologist (SAI)
Vocational-Rehab. Counselor (SEC)
Volunteer Services Director (SEC)

Enterprising *(Persuaders)*

People who like to work with people, influencing, persuading, leading or managing for organizational goals or economic gain.

Are you?
self-confident
assertive
persuasive
energetic
adventurous
popular
ambitious
agreeable
talkative
extroverted
spontaneous
optimistic

Can you?
initiate projects
convince people to do things your way
sell things
give talks or speeches
organize activities
lead a group
persuade others

Like to?
make decisions
be elected to office
start your own business
campaign politically
meet important people
have power or status

Career Possibilities (Holland Code):

Advertising Executive (ESA)
Advertising Sales Rep (ESR)
Banker/Financial Planner (ESR)
Branch Manager (ESA)
Business Manager (ESC)
Buyer (ESA)
Chamber of Commerce Exec (ESA)
Credit Analyst (EAS)
Customer Service Manager (ESA)
Education & Training Manager (EIS)
Emergency Medical Technician (ESI)
Entrepreneur (ESA)
Foreign Service Officer (ESA)
Funeral Director (ESR)
Insurance Manager (ESC)
Interpreter (ESA)
Lawyer/Attorney (ESA)
Lobbyist (ESA)
Office Manager (ESR)
Personnel Recruiter (ESR)
Politician (ESA)
Public Relations Rep (EAS)
Retail Store Manager (ESR)
Sales Manager (ESA)
Sales Representative (ERS)
Social Service Director (ESA)
Stockbroker (ESI)
Tax Accountant (ECS)

Conventional *(Organizers)*

People who like to work with data, have clerical or numerical ability, carry out tasks in detail, or follow through on others' instructions.

Are you?
well-organized
accurate
numerically inclined
methodical
conscientious
efficient
conforming
practical
thrifty
systematic
structured
polite
ambitious
obedient
persistent

Can you?
work well within a system
do a lot of paper work in a short time
keep accurate records
use a computer terminal
write effective business letters

Like to?
follow clearly defined procedures
use data processing equipment
work with numbers
type or take shorthand
be responsible for details
collect or organize things

Career Possibilities (Holland Code):

Abstractor (CSI)
Accountant (CSE)
Administrative Assistant (ESC)
Budget Analyst (CER)
Business Manager (ESC)
Business Programmer (CRI)
Business Teacher (CSE)
Catalog Librarian (CSE)
Claims Adjuster (SEC)
Computer Operator (CSR)
Congressional-District Aide (CES)
Cost Accountant (CES)
Court Reporter (CSE)
Credit Manager (ESC)
Customs Inspector (CEI)
Editorial Assistant (CSI)
Elementary School Teacher (SEC)
Financial Analyst (CSI)
Insurance Manager (ESC)
Insurance Underwriter (CSE)
Internal Auditor (ICR)
Kindergarten Teacher (ESC)
Medical Records Technician (CSE)
Museum Registrar (CSE)
Paralegal (SCE)
Safety Inspector (RCS)
Tax Accountant (ECS)
Tax Consultant (CES)
Travel Agent (ECS)

BIBLIOGRAPHY

Works Used

"Business and Financial Occupations." *Bureau of Labor Statistics*. Office of Occupational Statistics and Employment Projections. Dec 17, 2015. Web. 7 Jun 2017.

Fisher, Ronald C. *State and Local Public Finance*. New York: Routledge, 2015.

Jones, Charles P. and Gerald R. Jensen. *Investments: Analysis and Management*. Thirteenth Ed. Hoboken, NJ: Wiley Press, 2016.

Melicher, Ronald W. and Norton, Edgar A, eds. *Introduction to Finance: Markets, Investments, and Financial Management*. Sixteenth Edition. Hoboken, NJ: Wiley Publishers, 2016.

Ross, Stephen A., Westerfield, Randolph W., and Bradford D. Jordan. *Essentials of Corporate Finance*. Ninth Edition. New York: McGraw-Hill Education, 2017.

Singh, Nitish and Thomas J. Bussen. *Compliance Management*. Santa Barbara, CA: Praeger Press, 2015.

Websites

Bureau of Labor Statistics
www.bls.org
The Bureau of Labor Statistics, established in 1884, is a U.S. governmental organization and branch of the Department of Labor, responsible for collecting, analyzing, and maintaining facts about American industry and the state of the labor force. The BLS provides a searchable database that allows visitors to view career profiles, research economic and growth information on various occupations, and to read articles about the U.S. labor market.

O*NET Resource Center
www.onetcenter.org
O*NET is a collaborative projects sponsored by the US Department of Labor and the North Carolina Department of Commerce that provides a variety of online tools for exploring career options and providing analysis on various US occupations. O*NET also provides web-based tools that visitors can use to evaluate their interests, education, and skills, and learn about potential career paths.

Investopedia
www.investopedia.com
Investopedia is a free, web-based encyclopedia that provides information about investing and the financial industry. Investopedia provides a good resource for students learning about possible career paths and has articles written by professionals in the field and a dictionary of financial terminology.

Vault

www.vault.com

Vault is an informational website, started in 1997 by entrepreneur Mark Oldman, that provides analysis of the U.S. job market, with a focus on leading companies in finance, and also provides annual rankings of companies and career fields. Vault's career guides are typically written by professionals in the field and the website invites employees in various fields to contribute to the website's content and to review their places of work for ranking purposes.

CNN Money

www.money.cnn.com

CNN Money is a website created in 2001 through a project htat involved editors from the popular financial magazines *Money* and *Fortune* and since managed by CNN, a division of Time Warner Cable. CNN Money provides articles on financial tops and contains a database of financial information.

American Finance Association

www.afajof.org

The American Finance Association is an academic organization dedicated to the study of finance and economics. The organization was formed in 1939 and, since 1946, has published the influential journal *Finance*, which covers a variety of financial and economic topics. The AFA provides networking links for professionals, funds and supports studies in finance, and provides information on financial careers.

INDEX

A

B

C

D

E

F

Q

R

S

T

U

V

W